Social History of Africa

INSIDERS AND OUTSIDERS

Social History of Africa
Series Editors:
Allen Isaacman and Jean Hay

INSIDERS
AND
OUTSIDERS

The Indian Working Class
of Durban, 1910-1990

Bill Freund

HEINEMANN
Portsmouth, NH

UNIVERSITY OF NATAL PRESS
Pietermaritzburg

JAMES CURREY
London

Heinemann
A division of Reed Elsevier Inc.
361 Hanover Street
Portsmouth, NH 03801–3912

James Currey Ltd
54b Thornhill Square, Islington
London N1 1BE

University of Natal Press
Private Bag X01, Scottsville 3209
Pietermaritzburg, South Africa

ISBN 0–435–08959–5 (Heinemann cloth)
ISBN 0–435–08961–7 (Heinemann paper)
ISBN 0–85255–666–7 (James Currey cloth)
ISBN 0–85255–616–0 (James Currey paper)
ISBN 0–86980–912–1 (University of Natal Press cloth)
ISBN 0–86980–908–3 (University of Natal Press paper)

First published 1995.
Credits for reprinted material are on p. xii.

Library of Congress Cataloging-in-Publication Data
Freund, Bill.
    Insiders and outsiders: the Indian working class of Durban,
1910–1990 / Bill Freund.
        p.   cm.   (Social history of Africa)
    Includes bibliographical references and index.
    ISBN 0–435–08959–5 (cloth).   ISBN 0–435–08961–7 (pbk.)
    1. East Indians—Employment—South Africa—Durban—History.
2. Durban (South Africa)—Social conditions. 3. Durban (South
Africa)—History.   I. Title.   II. Series.
HD8801.Z8D8725 1994
331.6'2154068455—dc20   94–35201
                                                               CIP

British Library Cataloguing in Publication Data
Freund, Bill
    Insiders and Outsiders: Indian Working Class
    of Durban, 1910–90.   (Social history of Africa).
    I. Title II. Series
    305.5620968455

Cartography by Jenny McDowell.
Cover design by Jenny Greenleaf.
Text design by G&H Soho Ltd.
Printed in the Republic of South Africa.
95 96 97 98 99 9 8 7 6 5 4 3 2 1

CONTENTS

ILLUSTRATIONS

TABLES

CREDITS

The author and publishers are grateful to the following individuals and institutions for permission to reproduce photographs:

Iain Edwards, Department of Economic History, University of Natal, Durban.
Institute for Black Research, University of Natal, Durban.
Local History Museum, Durban.

Photographs from University of Natal, Department of Economics, *Studies in Indian Employment*, Cape Town: Oxford University Press, 1961, reproduced by permission of the publishers.

Cover photograph courtesy of the Institute for Black Research, University of Natal, Durban.

PREFACE

This book originated in my desire to attempt a study of economic history "from below," to look at economic development and economic institutions in terms of the interplay of social forces and the initiatives of particular classes and particular cultural formations at grassroots level. How and why did Durban become the city that it is? My view is that it was not simply the result of the choices of either state or capital — entrepreneurs or city officials. Nor can popular forces simply be encapsulated as *resisting* initiatives from above; for better and worse, they are also always creating.

I quickly realised that the Indian working class presented a particular analytical challenge in coming to grips with this question. Suffering from discrimination and a history of poverty, it nonetheless contrasted with the African working class by having, after the end of the indenture system in 1911, no barriers to free movement of labour, at least within Natal province, such as the bearing of passes, and no restriction on combining into trade unions. It apparently faced the market as a "free" labour force under capitalism. Until the 1940s, relatively few Africans settled permanently in Durban so that the Indian working class was extremely important and indeed, has remained relatively important since that time. The Indian population of South Africa numbers almost 1 000 000 (956 000 estimated in 1990) and, of that number, the majority live in and around Durban. The majority of those in turn can still readily be described as working class and a large majority are the descendants of those brought to South Africa under the indenture system before Union.

I became aware that Indians were inclined not to see their own history in South Africa as very important or interesting compared to that of whites or Africans, apart from a political history of resistance to apartheid or a recollection of the heroic days of Congress under the leadership of M.K. Gandhi. Indians, as I have come to realise, have a perspective on South African society that is different from that of either whites or Africans, which illuminates our knowledge of the whole. As research proceeded, I became increasingly interested in the cultural and social history of Durban Indians and this book is intended at least as a first introduction to some of the themes in that history. However, what I offer is hardly more than an introduction. It remained my decision to produce a short book that continued to focus on large structural concerns rather than devote myself to a study of great depth that might be pursued over many years. I hope others, though, will be taking another road.

There are also certain other things which this book is not. It is not, first of all, a history of "the Indian community." I deliberately ignore the better-known scions of the merchant class, who came to South Africa as part of the great diaspora of Indian commercial strata, except where they touch on working-class history. At the same time, while ethnicity is sometimes part of my analysis, this book is not essentially about defining ethnicity and what makes the Indians of South Africa Indian. Nor is it a study of their political history. While I touch on politics often and inevitably in dealing with themes such as militancy and incorporation, it is subordinate to other issues in this volume which interest me more.

By contrast, a number of questions crossed my mind which have become crucial to several of the chapters that follow. Why did the Indian peasantry rise and decline like the African peasantry, but with a different chronology, and with what policy implications for the present? This was the subject of an article published in the *Journal of Peasant Studies* and largely reproduced here as Chapter Two, by permission of the journal. What was the economic logic of the Indian family and to what extent do new interests in the politics and economics of gender help us to understand that logic? On this theme I wrote a capsule history of the family and Indian working-class women for a path-breaking Durban conference on gender in South Africa. This was afterwards published in the *Journal of Southern African Studies*; material from it appears throughout the book. Why did Indian workers become intensely militant and why did this militancy subside? The basis of Chapter Four is a paper on this subject which I have presented at the African Studies Centre at the University of Cape Town, for the · School of Oriental and African Studies in London and elsewhere.

Above all, what can this history tell us about the changing nature of South African capitalism in the twentieth century? This concern underlies the whole book and cannot be confronted without a concept of class. For employers, the workforce is a totality to be differentiated and the wage bill is a totality to be met. In that sense, the working class is a real structural entity and workers confront real structural economic constraints and challenges. With Michael Storper and Richard Walker, I "recognise that class structuring is inextricably bound up with the development of capitalism as a system of production, circulation and exploitation."[1] Understanding that system is my greatest concern. Moreover, there is certainly an urban South African culture, and specifically a working-class culture, identifiable in terms of predilections, idioms and amusements, that over the past century has penetrated and connected the lives of Durban people of all colours. In Chapter Two, these cultural currents cross with others which defined an Indian world to create what I call a room with several doors and windows.

Intent on capturing both economic and cultural dimensions, this study could not meaningfully unfold through the chronological perusal of official records; it depends on a disparate and wide range of sources, including oral material. This is the first project that I have undertaken in which interview material has been important. I have come to realise why good interviewers become virtually overwhelmed by the wisdom, experiential richness and conviction of the people to whom they speak, and can understand the desire to give the floor to them as much as possible. No analytical study really does justice to the interview experience. I have only used a fraction of the material made available to me by a number of people to whom I have spoken, selected, if that is the right word, for their willing availability and variety. I can only hope that my interviewees, to whom I am deeply grateful for allowing a short intrusion in their lives, have had a large if sometimes intangible influence in the writing of this book as a whole, far more than can be traced through the footnotes.

Nonetheless, this study does not pretend to be one in which people simply speak "for themselves;" nor do I see myself as merely the convenient provider of a tape recorder. The sense people make of their own lives, the very essence of autobiography, is not sufficient or satisfactory for me in the work I set for myself. I attempt in this book to unite an interest in people, in agency, with my conviction about the importance of structures — structures which do limit the circumstances in which men and women pursue their destiny. What interests me is how the two intertwine and connect. In justifying, musing over, defining their lives, people will use patterns of thought containing blatant contradictions. They will create a logic which serves their own self-esteem. Their words contain important presences, but also hide equally important absences. The absences interest me as much as the articulated concerns.

In the fourth chapter, when I consider the history of Indian labour militancy, I pay rather little attention to my informants' voices. Some informants remembered the activity, remembered the militancy, but they did not connect it to some aspects of what actually happened politically, especially to the parting of the ways between underground, virtually illegal non-racial unionism and a legal, more moderate unionism which nonetheless secured advances for its numerous Indian members. The desire to connect historic militancy unproblematically to the latter road was great. Nor, despite as much prompting as I dared, was there much interest in remembering the role of African workers, or the inter-relationship between Africans and Indians. Yet this inter-relationship existed and was of great importance to political actors at the time. Simply to let the ordinary person "speak" would have suppressed the questions that seemed, and still seem, pressing to me. Other sections of this volume are far closer to the voices that I heard, but that reflection is not more honest: it too is part of a selection process that I made and for which I must take responsibility. I am especially uncomfortable with those writers who hide their own agenda while apparently foregrounding the hidden voices of "ordinary" people; the logic of this book acknowledges the integrative and controlling voice of an analytically minded author constructing a text.

During the course of researching and writing this study, it became increasingly obvious to me that my approach will be very unsatisfying to many who, during the 1970s and 1980s, considered class as a key operative factor in historical understanding of society but now wish to abandon it (or, under the flag of "post-modernism," the search for any kind of material or objective truth). Perhaps primarily mirroring political changes in recent years, their focus has shifted instead to concentrating on identity: the self-identification of the subject, the struggle of the subject against an oppressive and self-defined "power," overrrides any outside construction based on economic history or material reality. Realising identity, not class, is the liberatory project. Often gender and ethnicity become the self-"invention" which must be unpacked and studied. For some, there is no reality beyond such inventions. This quest may lead to something new and revelatory; more frequently, the hidden "discourse" turns out to be merely the obvious or familiar dressed up with some elegant terminology.

It is undoubtedly true that class is rarely by itself the factor which unifies and structures people's actions; action is structured by identity. As E.P. Thompson famously noted, class is a relationship, not a "thing." To think that the working class has a bounded and strictly definable objective reality, and will then inevitably act according to a given appropriate consciousness, is nonsense. Indeed, the objective situation of people always is mediated by many other factors which promote crisis and change and create (and alter) identity in the kaleidoscopic making of real history, whether global or microscopic.

It is the *intersections* of structure and agency, the interplay between economic and social history and how they impact on one another, rather than the quest for identity, that engages me. This study does not abandon the quest for unveiling structure as well as motive or agency and it is premised on the central role of an author and the interpretative net that he is casting. Thus it is a project which may frustrate those who find one dimension or another irrelevant to their own intellectual (and other) project. I hope it might yet represent a new departure for historians and social scientists in a period where the questions that have most vexed writers on South Africa in the last generation or two are rapidly seeming less relevant.

This book breaks down into the following chapters. The first looks at the Indian working class during the phase of unfreedom, when it was indentured to white Natal employers. Indenture removed internal class differences to a large extent and was a powerful common experience. The material included here is a synthesis of existing historical information and serves as a prelude to the main story. The second chapter considers the conditions under which the ex-indentured workers could stay on the land, particularly as small-scale farmers. The first indentured workers arrived in Natal in 1860, and most chose to stay on in the colony as free workers. Thus, while indenture expanded, the free Indian workforce was growing simultaneously. For most, one can talk about a peasant experience that reached its apogee in the late nineteenth and early twentieth centuries, although a handful became successful agrarian landowners and others were essentially proletarianised.

The peasant road for Natal Indians was a road which led to the edge of the town, especially Durban, and which led out of agriculture entirely. In 1911 the indenture system was abolished. The third chapter looks at the phase of post-indenture settlement generally, considering aspects of the material and cultural circumstances of the emerging Indian working class as it tried to find footholds in the urban economy. The conditions under which that class lived and worked were fluid by contrast with an industrial working class, and relatively unregulated by the state during the period when Natal remained a colony and even after Union in 1910. Petty bourgeois interests existed interspersed with proletarian activities; some social mobility into the bourgeoisie took place from an early date. The relationship of Indian workers to other Durban workers as well as to other Indians is considered.

Discrimination and exclusion in an era when the South African state actively sought the repatriation of the Indian community, now rigidly defined as one of four South African "races," were hallmarks of the inter-war period. Despite this, the commitment of the Indian population to industrial work increased very substantially. The fourth chapter and the fifth are really crucial in terms of the central events in working-class history in Durban. They cover the phase of worker militancy, which is inseparable from the racially segmented labour market and its stresses, and then look at the restructuring of the city on class and race terms in the context of the Group Areas Act of 1950. The recovery from the Depression of the urban economy after 1933, the era of the long boom, saw the Indian working class led by a coterie of militant Communist Party members who saw the salvation of Indian workers in struggles against residential segregation, and in attempts to take over Indian communal organisations and establish alliances with Africans.

In these chapters, an effort is made to re-examine these activities by exploring their relationship to the interplay of class and ethnic identities and struggles. The implacable hostility of white Durban to any effort at deracialisation, the rise of the National Party to power in 1948, the 1949 "race riots" which underscored the difficulty of forging unity between Africans and Indians, led to the decline of this militancy in time. The Group Areas Act of 1950, culminating a long thrust on the part of the state to create neighbourhoods segregated by race (but also by class), helped to restructure many aspects of identity and activity on the part of the Indian working class. The economic prosperity of the high apartheid years (especially the 1960s) as well as growing educational qualification on the part of Indians went together with a growing desire on the part of the state to embrace Indians as junior partners rather than hated Oriental intriguers and rivals. While Chapter Five explains how Group Areas proceeded, the last chapter in the volume considers some economic and social themes in the history of Indian working-class life as it was reconstituted in the new state-built urban townships in the final third of the twentieth century.

✳ ✳ ✳

Apart from those interviewed, I should also thank the Natal Indian Cane Growers' Assocation, Stanger, for letting me inspect their past annual reports and the Documentation Centre at the University of Durban-Westville where I located much interesting material (and especially to Mr K. Chetty for his assistance). While I was on sabbatical leave and working with material there, I felt that I had a pleasant academic holiday home at the Institute for Social and Economic Research on that campus, thanks to Professor John Butler-Adam (its Director at the time) and my other Westville friends. The Killie Campbell Africana Library of the University of Natal provided some interesting files and material. So did the records available in the Natal Archives in Pietermaritzburg. An enjoyable and useful part of the production end of this project has been working with an editor available "down the road," our former student Dr Jenny Edley, at the University of Natal Press and with Mrs Gail Longano, our departmental secretary in Durban.

In addition, I would like to thank the following people for their particular help with research assistance, their critical insights and their encouragement: Jo Beall, Gina Buijs, Iain Edwards, Shireen Hassim, Alan Mabin, Jeff McCarthy, Rajend Mesthrie, Mike Morris, Rob Morrell, Rooksana Omar, Tim Quinlan, Steve Schmidt, and Anne Vaughan. A particularly important person in the production of this book has been my friend and former graduate student, Vishnu Padayachee. He has often pointed me back on the right track, he has made available to me his own interesting collection of photocopies and documents which have saved me much time and effort and above all, he has made me feel that the project was worthwhile and that my outsider's perspective contained advantages. Therefore I would like to dedicate this book to him.

1

A Passage from India: Indentured Immigrants Come to Natal, 1860–1911

Inseparable from the onset and extension of European colonial systems was the "labour question." How could the authorities organise a labour force to extract the minerals, to grow the plantation crops, to transport the raw materials and to work the docks in a way that would make such systems profitable and self-sustaining? Indigenous people were difficult to conquer and put to labour satisfactorily without instituting coercion too heavy to allow for a stable system of exploitation. Moreover, they often retained a capacity for resistance, or flight into the interior, that reduced the bargaining position of the new authorities. Colonial settlers saw the new-found lands as zones of opportunity and were equally difficult to subject to a labour regime that they had left Europe in order to escape. Their co-operation was moreover crucial in maintaining law and order overseas.

The most notorious answer to the question lay in the revival of the moribund institution of chattel slavery which succeeded in underpinning the economic development of plantation economies in tropical and semi-tropical regions from the seventeenth century onwards. In the Cape of Good Hope, for instance, the Dutch East India Company organised the transport of slaves from elsewhere in Africa and Asia, and these formed the basis of the colonial labour system until the early nineteenth century. Although the slaves never formed an overall majority of the colonial population, they outnumbered the settler community, and the slave system pervaded the life and thought of the colony for generations.[1]

In the nineteenth century, however, first the slave trade and then legalised slavery was abolished despite their continued economic efficacy in at least some contexts. A large, sophisticated and distinguished literature has debated and continues to debate why abolition did take place. This is not an appropriate place to enter the fray, but it needs to be said at least that amongst the most convincing explanations have been the economic competition between different slave colonies; the fear of slave revolts,

1

especially after the Haitian Revolution; and the desire to see labour retained in Africa, the source of almost all slaves, for the advance of capitalist development on the African continent.[2] Yet the intelligence that directed the whole anti-slavery movement concentrated above all on the growing conviction of the moral and practical superiority of a wage labour system over the shackles and whips of slavery.

At the Cape, the slave trade ended in 1807 and the slaves were emancipated in 1834. The colony itself hardly knew an abolitionist movement. Its leading citizens held slaves themselves as valued property and were convinced of the system's economic importance, even if the more far-sighted could see in the abstract that a free labour system might be superior in the interests of colonial development. Unfortunately for the abolitionist movement, moreover, the abolition of slavery could not immediately evoke the advantages of such a system. Instead, dislocation and economic decline were foreseeable should ex-slaves succeed in evading controls to work on their own account.

As a result, in South Africa as elsewhere, post-slavery nineteenth-century colonialism came to rely on alternative systems of unfree labour. In the interior republics, extensive use was made of captive black children — "apprentices."[3] In the Cape, freed slaves — "Prize Negroes" — played their part in addressing the labour question in the first years after the trade was abolished. In early Australia, the massive use of convict labour was crucial to colonial development.[4] The origins of parliamentary democracy at the Cape in 1853 are closely linked to the popular movement which successfully aimed at preventing its becoming a penal settlement. Looking broadly at the Empire, however, no unfree labour system was more important than the use of indentured labour, particularly from the vast British domains in India, in filling the gap that existed after abolition. In fact, before abolition, Indian slaves played a minor but not insignificant part in a few colonies, notably the Cape and Mauritius.[5]

Indenture, like slavery before it, represented the revival of a system in abeyance. The indenture contract allowed for the employment of wage workers, under conditions giving a very high level of control to employers and usually involving transportation, for a fixed term. Masters were virtually entirely free to set the terms of work; they could prevent the workers from leaving their grounds. Indentured workers from England itself had once played an important part in securing dependent labour in the seventeenth century, especially in the Caribbean and the future United States of America, before the real dominance of the slave trade.[6] In Mauritius, a sugar island that had been conquered from the French during the Napoleonic Wars, the indenture system was introduced as early as 1834, almost immediately after the abolition of slavery.

By the time Natal began to import indentured labour from India in 1860, a dozen tropical territories, mainly but not entirely British, were already doing so. It was a well-established system into which Natal could tap.[7] The official view of the Raj was that the export of labour was a partial solution to the great problems of rural overpopulation and poverty; it supported indenture under conditions that looked respectable so long as Indians were themselves poorly represented in the colonial system. The already vast rural population of India not only suffered from the vagaries of the climate, but was imbedded in a complex and in some respects very exploitative and oppressive social system. Cultivators were enmeshed in networks of debt, and men who made their living by procuring labour could utilise these and other social and economic channels to fish deeply in the waters of Indian village life for men.

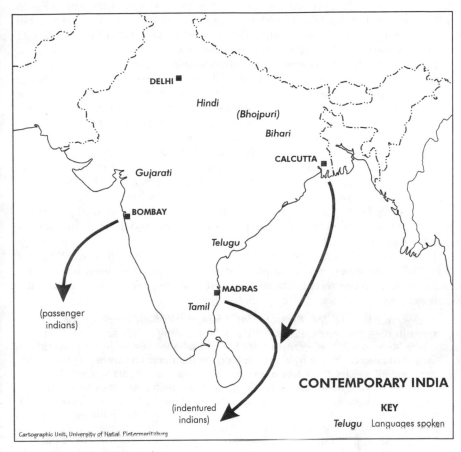

India, main emigration routes

Nonetheless, the indenture system did not affect all parts of India. It was a striking feature that most workers came from one of two regions: the borderlands of the United Provinces (Uttar Pradesh) and Bihar; that is to say, the middle of the Hindi-speaking Gangetic plains of north India, and the districts bordering the south-eastern Indian coast where Tamil and (further north) Telugu were spoken. In Natal over the course of time, it was the south Indian emigration that became predominant while the tendency was for north Indians to come from districts further to the west.

Between 1860, when the first ship arrived off Durban harbour, and the end of the indenture system in 1911, slightly more than 150 000 indentured workers arrived in Natal from India. Until their arrival, Natal, annexed by the British in 1843, was a classic example of a colony which lacked the essential work-force component its would-be capitalists demanded. The small British settler population wanted cheap land, not jobs, and was well able to evade the less attractive forms of wage labour. Africans were numerous and by no means unwilling to work for a wage, or uninterested in the social, economic and cultural possibilities offered by the new colonial regime.[8] Indeed, many flocked south of the Tugela into the colony from the domains of the Zulu king to exploit those possibilities. However, they wanted to work on their own terms, and in their own time, in a way that would either minimise disruption of the household economy, or maximise the acquisition of new rights as colonists.

For many employers, indentured labour, whose importation was both administratively and financially assisted by the colonial government, seemed to offer a better way than dependence on either whites or Africans. In particular, the importation of Indian workers into Natal was to be associated with the development of the sugar plantations of the coastal districts north and south of the port town of Durban. It was increasingly clear during the 1850s that sugar grew well in the rich coastal belt and presented more economic possibilities than any other crop being tried.[9]

The link between Indians and sugar is not an exact one. It is true that some of the early clamourers for indentured labour were not sugar planters and that some sugar planters remained dependent on African labour even at the height of indenture (the Indian percentage of sugar-cane workers in the fields rarely exceeded 80 per cent).[10] However, the association was in fact close and strong; sugar and the indenture system expanded together.

The most important history of the indenture system is entitled *A New System of Slavery*.[11] The harshness of its implementation in Natal has been abundantly demonstrated in more recent scholarship on the subject. To quote, for instance, Maureen Swan:

> A close reading of the Protector of Immigrants' files suggests that in agriculture — and particularly on the labour-intensive sugar plantations where some 60–70 per cent of indentured Indians worked — employers sought to keep costs low by denying workers their contract rights and by a concomitant reliance on labour-coercive techniques. Plantation workers were overworked (as much as a seventeen or eighteen hour day during the overlapping crushing and planting seasons), malnourished and poorly housed. These aspects of their existence gave rise to abnormally high disease and death rates which, an official medical service notwithstanding, remained fairly constant throughout the period under review. In addition, the Natal indentured labour system offered little room for even such basic human comforts as family life. Women, and particularly family women, were so reluctant to emigrate that Natal, like other recruiting colonies, had difficulty in even fulfilling the terms of Government of India legislation which demanded that four women were to be exported for every ten men . . . In short, there is a solid weight of evidence in the Protector's files to suggest that overwork, malnourishment, and squalid living conditions formed the pattern of daily life for most agricultural workers.[12]

In a slightly later contribution, Swan points as well to the abuses of corporal punishment, indebtedness and other forms of indirect control, and general brutality that affected those caught up in the system of indenture.[13]

Jo Beall has demonstrated that under conditions of indenture Indian women experienced particular hardship.[14] The Natal planters resented their presence at first, and were not required to provide adequate rations if they were dependants of an indentured man. Moreover, only Christian marriages were recognised as legal. Independently indentured women suffered from ill-treatment and earned little, while the male to female ratio could result in individual women being vulnerable to sexual and other forms of exploitation by Indian men as well as by the planters.

During the later phases of slavery in the British empire, the state increasingly introduced ameliorative legislation in order to intervene in the slave/master relationship and to prevent the worst abuses. This kind of system was further developed under indenture but, in practice, the Protector's office served the planters' interests and was reluctant to interfere in ways that would anger the employers.[15]

A striking feature of the Colony of Natal was the ambiguous attitude towards the indenture system displayed by whites, who agitated with increasing success for political power in the colony on the basis of a wide but effectively race-defined franchise. As this power increased, the attitude became more critical. Despite the obvious increase in wealth that Natal owed to the arrival of indentured Indians, the indenture system represented a threat. Just as the American small farmers and other producers before the Civil War wanted free soil and free labour and became more and more hostile to slavery, their South African equivalents felt frightened of the competition, not only of unfree labour but also of free labour that might undercut their own position.[16]

Employers who profited from the system were apt to support it, and some of the largest employers of labour were the most enthusiastic.[17] They appreciated the extensive availability of cheap, dependent labour. They also did not object strongly if, at the end of indenture, the worker settled permanently in Natal. This, in fact, is what the majority did in the period before the granting of responsible government to the colony in 1893. Indeed, if small commodity producers made available cheaper food and other consumer items for workers, it was all to the good. The alternative to the settlement of free Indians in Natal was a state-funded passage back to India, which was in fact a requirement under the terms with which the government of India was prepared to authorise the whole system. There was a tendency, throughout the indenture period, for a growing number of indentured workers to be employed outside the sugar fields: growing other tropical crops; working in agriculture in the inland parts of the colony where agriculture was based on grains and pastoral activity; in the coal mines; on the Natal Government Railways system (revenues from which sustained the growth of the colony from the time of the mineral discoveries on the Rand in 1885); and as service and domestic workers. Sugar plantations employed a maximum of 83 per cent of indentured workers at the peak in 1875, but only 54 per cent in 1895, 40 per cent in 1900 and 27 per cent in 1909.[18] This would seem to implicate a much wider range of employers in support of the indenture system.

Yet white populism grew steadily in colonial Natal and felt threatened by the spread of Indian initiative in agriculture and, potentially, in skilled work. Even in 1874, the re-introduction of indenture after several years of suspension was only carried by a single vote in the legislature.[19] The famous mob scene which greeted Gandhi on his return to Durban in 1896 was aimed not at his presence but at the apparent importation into Natal of Indian skilled workers on the indentured system, an importation that threatened to undercut the struggles of white workers for a comfortable living based on labour scarcity.[20] The majority of whites feared the growing numbers of indentured workers being imported. Indians outnumbered whites in the colony by 101 000 to 97 000 in 1904, and pressure to stop immigration grew.

The compromise reached at first was a £3 annual tax imposed on both indentured and ex-indentured workers in 1895 and extended to a tax on their children, even if born in South Africa, in 1903.[21] When applied effectively in the years after the

Anglo-Boer War, it aimed a crippling blow at the prospects of Indian inhabitants of Natal who hoped to strike out on their own after their five-year indenture ended. The alternative, of course, was to return to India and the numbers doing so increased. However, the main impact in fact was dramatically to increase the numbers of workers re-engaging under indenture in the final years of the system.

Indians bitterly resented the tax. As Swan shows, Gandhi was able, through adding tax-payment resistance to his more general passive resistance campaign, to touch a nerve that provoked a militancy never before in evidence. The 1913 passive resistance campaign involved strikes that spread throughout the Indian worker community in Natal, especially amongst the indentured, including sugar-cane workers, with whom Gandhi had previously had little to do.[22] According to Swan,

> the strike had, at one time or another . . . paralyzed the Durban and Pietermaritzburg produce markets, closed down some of the sugar mills, stripped many coastal hotels, restaurants and private residences of their domestics, resulted in some 150 acres of cane being illegally burned, and inconvenienced the coal industry, the Natal Government Railways and other, smaller industries in coastal Natal.[23]

At the time, the strike was viewed in a general sort of way as "political," about the dignity of the Indian in South Africa. The work of Swan and of Beall and North-Coombes makes it much clearer that to an important extent it was a strike against the capitalists of Natal intended to protest against the deteriorating material conditions under which Indians lived and worked. Swan insists, however, that culturally, resistance was expressed in forms reflecting Indian archetypes of great antiquity, which made a long-term connection to labour resistance in twentieth-century South Africa implausible at this stage.[24]

On the eve of World War I, the indenture system was facing major challenges within India. Decrying the abuses of the indenture system had become a major war-cry of the nascent nationalist movement, which saw the continuance of the system as a humiliation for India. It was at the behest of the government of India that it was abolished. However, its future in Natal was dim in any event, given the growing hostility of the white electorate. White society was ever more obsessed with the fear of being outnumbered and ultimately undermined by the "Asiatic menace" — drowned in a sea of cheap labour. The expansion of the sugar industry in the early twentieth century would have required redoubled efforts aimed at massively increasing the scale of indenture if that were to continue as the basis of the sugar industry. This would have been politically impossible in Natal.[25]

According to North-Coombes, ". . . by the first decade of the twentieth century, the sugar industry did not regard its future expansion and development as dependent upon the continuation of indentured Indian immigration."[26] The greatest success of the indenture system had been linked to the financial sustenance of the state, sustenance withdrawn after the granting of responsible government in 1893.[27] According to the Clayton Commission of 1909, only 7 006 of 25 569 indentured workers at the end of the system's existence were working in the canefields.[28] Thus planters thought again about the potential of African workers recruited on a partially coercive basis, both locally from Natal and Zululand and further afield, for instance from Pondoland, now annexed to the eastern Cape. Many employers of indentured labour deplored the continued presence of free Indians in Natal, and some sugar planters had never favoured the indentured system in the first place and were happy to see it go. As is well known, in this period, massive recruitment systems were increasingly successful in getting fragmenting African rural households to shake free migrant male labour for jobs on the mines and elsewhere in very large numbers throughout the region.[29] At first, the end of indenture raised wage rates for Indians and Africans in Natal but it was not a situation that endured for long.[30]

One can in fact talk about two phases of indenture. One lasted from 1860 (with a break for a phase of economic recession between 1867 and 1874) until the institution of the tax of 1895. During this period, indentured immigration expanded and most indentured workers remained in South Africa as free individuals after their five-year term was over. The Wragg Commission found that a quarter-century after the introduction of indenture, only 7 per cent of the workers had returned to India and two-thirds of the resident Indian population was free.[31] After 1895, the tax, coupled in the post-war years with poor economic opportunities, made it difficult to advance to a position of freedom in the same way. Return to India became commoner and re-indenture much commoner. In the final decade of the existence of the indenture system, less than 20 per cent of the workers were able to settle in South Africa as free individuals, where the nineteenth-century figure had been over 50 per cent.[32] After 1911, the whole system was abolished. With the Indian Relief Bill of 1914 that followed the intense struggles up to 1913, the £3 tax was abolished as well.

What we know far too little about is how the system was viewed by the workers themselves. There were several ways in which indenture was different from slavery. Workers did receive wages. They were legally protected, however ineffectively, in certain ways. Above all, however, indenture was not a permanent state. It came to an end after five years. After the era of mineral discoveries had begun and until the £3 tax began to bite, moreover, this meant that the indentured worker was able to look forward to a future in a part of the world with a rapidly, if very unevenly, expanding economy that needed all kinds of workmen and where land was relatively cheap. South Africa, including Natal, was in this regard very different from the sugar islands and enclaves such as Mauritius, Fiji or British Guiana where most indentured workers were sent. In India, according to Hugh Tinker, Natal acquired the reputation of offering indentured workers the highest wages and he suggests that channels of information existed which allowed prospective workers to know which colony might have land available at the end of the indenture period.[33] In 1901, Indians from Natal were "far ahead in order of remittances" compared to indentured workers from all the other colonies to which they had been despatched.[34] This in turn reflected the failure of South African capitalists to discipline and organise free labour in such a way as to lower costs to internationally competitive levels.

For all its harshnesses and abuses, there was an element of voluntary immigration in the passage out of India of the indentured workers. This is captured in a recent memoir by an elderly veteran of the anti-apartheid movement recalling her Tamil father:

> My father came from Mayavurum, a village in Tanjore, and for all his sophistication and business adeptness, Mayavurum clung to him like the well worn dhoti he put on at home to relax in. He had arrived in the country at the age of sixteen, in the late nineteenth century before the colonies and the vanquished Afrikaner Republic [sic] had amalgamated to form the Union of South Africa. Fascinated by the stories of the recruiting agent who had come to his village to indenture workers for the Natal plantation, but not liking the

prospects of binding himself for five years to a plantation owner, he had paid his own passage to the southern African colony and come as a free man.[35]

Others undoubtedly did come under indenture, but knew something of the score and bided their time until they could be free. Tinker argues that returnees to India were largely those who had no resources, the least successful of the indentured workers.[36] Even before indenture ended, the healthier and better-situated pushed themselves to partake in craft activities and establish vegetable gardens to earn an extra income. The Protector of Indians claimed in 1883 that indentured workers would return home at noon to cultivate a private garden and to raise produce or poultry for private sale.[37]

Very little is known about the world the indentured workers made for themselves, apart from the harsh conditions that set limits to their prospects. However, in the nineteenth century, they succeeded in creating a new sort of society, partially through the moulding of a neo-Indian creole identity in South Africa, influenced by interaction with both the indigenous African population and the dominant white colonist element. Probably the most important single element in this new identity was the re-establishment of family life. Children were distinctly unwelcome to the indenturers but it proved so difficult to attract workers, particularly women, to Natal without them that they came to a surprising extent anyway. There was no other way for Natal to attract enough women, 40 for every 100 men, to meet the legal requirements of the Indian government. Once indenture was over, some Indian women must have been able to benefit from the absence of family controls as they existed in rural Indian society (notably of mothers-in-law, few if any of whom were brought along to the new world of Natal) by playing a key role in reconstructing the family as a system of both enterprise and social security. Where families constituted themselves on a successful basis (and, as I shall argue, family labour was virtually essential for that to happen) under freedom, the women were in a crucial position because of their irreplaceable labour role. This reconstitution of the Indian family, however, is a silent and unrecovered part of South African history; there is little research thus far on how it happened, and the problem is underscored by the very negative situation of many or most women under indenture itself.

A second part of the process of reconstitution in South Africa consisted undoubtedly of the advent of organised religion. Only J.B. Brain's work hints at the crucial nature of religious organisations in reconstructing Indian culture in the new world.[38] It is clearer how this could have happened amongst the very small number of Christian and Muslim indentured immigrants as the great majority of their co-religionists were never subjected to this isolating and oppressive labour regime. However, for Hindus where the numerical balance lay the other way, the picture can only be sketched in very vaguely. Construction of shrines and performances of ceremonies associated with folk religion in India began quite early in the indenture period. This was followed by the establishment of temples and the arrival of reform Hindu teachers who aimed at a purer and more philosophical religious practice.[39]

A third element of Indian Hindu society, of course, was the caste system. An important part of what was new in South Africa was that this system was not recreated from Indian precedents. This appears to have been the case in other parts of the world for the new societies created by the ex-indentured workers.[40] A surprising and contradictory point made by Tinker and others is that most indentured lists give relatively middle-caste positions to indentured workers, even though the motivation for indenture, social oppression and desperate poverty, would seem most applicable to those who were considered as pariahs or were at the bottom of the caste totem pole.[41] Perhaps the workers tended to give a better rating to themselves than they would have been recognised as having at home. They certainly did not accept an excluded position for themselves in the new world to which they emigrated. The fading of the caste ties can be related as well to the Hindu prejudice against crossing the ocean, an act with was considered to destroy the social bonds that defined each individual with the system.

In South Africa, caste was never effectively revived. I have found one reference to a traditional village government or *panchayat* in the most thoroughly Indian rural district north of Durban, but in general, caste depended on an intricate web of social relations and occupational inter-dependence which never re-emerged in South Africa.[42] Caste, mostly in connection with intermarriage but occasionally linked to particular styles of worship, has continued to have a meaning for the few descendants of indentured workers who have maintained some sense of themselves as having belonged to a higher caste. Otherwise it is a consciousness that has attenuated and Rajend Mesthrie's study of north-Indian language survival in Natal suggests that the terminology of caste has either fallen into abeyance or is used incorrectly. Caste, Mesthrie argues, exists only as a memory.[43] Instead, the ideology of Indian culture survived in religion and in language practice.

Mesthrie's work enables us to say a little about culture and it must be said first of all that, just as we know little about religious practices, we know equally little about how cuisine, music, the tool-kit, folk art and all sorts of cultural manifestations died, survived or were transmuted in nineteenth-century Natal. Thanks to Mesthrie, we do know a little about language, or rather about the language of the minority of indentured workers and their descendants from the Gangetic plain.

In Mesthrie's view, a process ensued which he calls "koineization", whereby related dialects come together to form a relatively standard speech in a new physical space. He calls the ensuing language for South Africa, Natal Bhojpuri. Standard Bhojpuri is in fact a form of Bihari spoken near to the Hindi-Bihari dividing line in the Ganges valley in north India. In Natal, it was influenced by other forms of Bihari, but also by the speech of those from the Hindi side of that line who became a more important component amongst the indentured immigrants in the later phases of the system.[44] Indians in Natal say that they speak or spoke Hindi, in fact. Natal Bhojpuri, now a dying language (the latest census return estimates that 95 per cent of Indian South Africans speak English as their first language) absorbed words from English and from Zulu and indirectly from Afrikaans via both other languages. Never exactly a polite, written language, Tinker has argued that Natal Bhojpuri gathered strength because it remained the guarded discourse of working people in the very absence of schools that would have offered access to purer use of Indian languages or English.[45]

Even on the ship bringing them across the Indian Ocean, villagers from one corner of India jostled against those from very distant areas, and thereafter in South Africa they continually shared space, rarely forming distinct neighbourhoods. The barriers of language and religion remained, however. Marriages across these barriers were rare until recently.[46] What Mesthrie suggests, and this will be explored in greater depth later, when we move entirely away from indenture, is that a double cultural world gradually unfolded, or more accurately , was created. On the one hand, there was a neo-Indian world of "koineization" which looked very Indian indeed to outsiders. On the other, there was the attraction of the marketplace, the hybrid colonial cultural world outside the home which held great appeal and also had to be entered for practical reasons. Thus, as Mesthrie points out, Bhojpuri-speakers and others also began to communicate in what one could call South African Indian English, "a new variety of English in Natal in a distinctly Indian incarnation" at the same time.[47] English may have been the language of the oppressor, but the incoming group were successful in making it their own in significant ways.

For in South Africa, Hindu villagers became "Indian." They did coalesce in a process, still very shadowily understood, into an ethnic group identified as such despite the internal differences. The South African state tended to lump together Indians, whatever their appearance, as a "race" distinct from other "races." Some, but only some, of this coalescence can be ascribed to structures created by outsiders, particularly the state. Tinker judges that indentured Indians everywhere they went "evolved a style which was certainly 'creolized' but which was still uniquely Indian,"[48] except in those places of settlement, such as the smaller islands of the Antilles, where they were always few in number and creolisation proceeded faster and further.

As with indentured Indian workers elsewhere in the world, and by contrast with the situation that normally prevailed for slaves, a key element here was the presence of what were in South Africa termed "passenger Indians." These were free immigrants, usually involved in commerce either in India or in third countries where they had been living, who were attracted to the business opportunities of the new society. They were interested in the first instance in the custom of the indentured workers, with their distinctive taste in food, clothing and the simplest of luxuries. But this could, of course, serve as a foot in the door opening to other and greater opportunities.[49]

Although most such passenger Indians in South Africa were Muslims from the west coast of India, there was as well a significant Hindu element amongst them. M. K. Gandhi, hired by Indian businessmen as a lawyer and the son of a Hindu official in a small Muslim princely state in Kathiawar, was typical of this element. Although much less noted, there were even some passenger Indians who were from south India, often by way of Mauritius. The Muslim passenger Indians liked to be known as [more-or-less white] "Arabs" in the late nineteenth century, but in practice they established familiar relations of clientage and credit with the Hindu masses. In the lives of indentured workers, utterly wretched as they were at first sight, these Muslim and Hindu fellow-Indian traders were of great importance in opening windows of opportunity facing out on African soil.

For the free Indian workforce, this introductory account has tried to emphasise the inseparable mixture of oppression and opportunity which both existed within the harsh history of indentured labour which brought them to South Africa. For the Natal economy, indenturing Indian immigrants was a decisive step in the effective implantation of profitable capitalist activities, but by the early twentieth century indentured labour could be replaced by the labour of indigenous and contrated Africans on a partially free and partially coercive basis. The economic history of the Indian working class was one that would lead with time into proletarianisation but Natal industry had not developed to a point where a fully fledged proletariat was wanted on a large scale. As the next chapter will show, the possibilities of avoiding or modifying the circumstances of proletarianisation were in fact very considerable for free Indian workers in early twentieth-century Natal.

2

Heaven on Earth in Springfield Flats: The Peasant Option

For immigrants to South African from India, the one positive aspect of indenture was the possibility of a free life in a new country at the end of their servitude. In general, those who returned to India were nearly destitute, and without prospects of making a new life for themselves in Natal. In the last phase of indenture, when the £3 tax made a free life an impossible burden, re-indenture was in fact preferred to a return passage by most workers. Despite hardships, South Africa offered them opportunities. The so-called mineral revolution began, unevenly but quickly, to transform the economy of the southern African region in the last quarter of the nineteenth century. The emergence of massive mining agglomerations, especially on the Witwatersrand after 1886, suddenly created demands for unprecedented supplies of services, commodities and raw materials. Enormous prospects existed for every variety of petty and larger entrepreneur. Workers were in demand and able to command relatively high wages for their services (although living expenses could be equally high).[1]

In Natal, there were no gold or diamond mines. In northern Natal, coal-mining became a major industry, making use of both indentured and non-indentured Indian labour, but it too was essentially an adjunct to the economic activities of the Rand. The coal fuelled the Natal Government Railways, which evacuated gold from and brought supplies to the interior, and the railways provided the revenue which transformed the economic power of the colony of Natal.[2] The possibilities opened to the Natal economy were diverse. Durban grew quickly as a port; skilful dredging finally opened up the safe harbour to ocean-going ships from the 1890s. Consumer-goods manufacturing located there, directly on the sea coast and at a relatively short rail distance to the mining hub in the Transvaal. Having had barely 10 000 inhabitants registered in the census of 1877, Durban by 1910 recorded a population of more than 148 000.[3] The coastal sugar industry found a potential regional market (including a rapidly increasing non-agricultural population) turned into a national one after the Union of 1910, on which basis it could finally expand.

The picture was far from entirely positive, however. Phases of dramatic growth were matched by phases of stagnation when stock exchange speculation led to a collapse in investment and investors felt the squeeze. Economic power became concentrated; organised groups of entrepreneurs and workers competed with each other in the harshest of circumstances.

Before looking at the urban economy and, specifically, the world that Indian workers and their families made for themselves in Durban , this chapter focuses on how they fared within the rural economy. In particular it examines how and why a free peasantry arose amongst the former indentured immigrants from India. During this period, despite intense hostility to what was defined, by a broad section of the white population, as racial competition there were important interests that positively favoured Indian cash-crop production.

The experience of other South African peasantries, including the Xhosa cultivators about whom Colin Bundy and Jack Lewis have written, is very relevant.[4] While Bundy stresses that such a peasantry arose in response to contact with merchant capital, it experienced a relatively early decline and could not long sustain the thirst of the mines for African labour. Lewis qualifies this picture in important ways. He sees cash-crop production as having arisen far more in response to demands for tax and in a form that may have undermined the viability of the extended household and the core of subsistence production. Overall production figures look impressive but are very modest when taken on a per capita or individual household basis; the genuine entrepreneurial success of individuals was significant but exceptional. Finally, he stresses that the efflorescence of eastern-Cape peasant production coincided with the unusually favourable international market prices for raw commodities in the third quarter of the nineteenth century; less favourable prices already presented a significant barrier to the continued development of this kind of production later in the century.

In this chapter, two distinct strata of Indian cultivators are identified and discussed with regard to Natal. The first are more nearly defined as peasants and came to be very largely cultivators of sugar-cane after World War I. The second settled closer to Durban and are essentially market gardeners, combining farming with other pursuits in what proved to be a step in the making of an urban proletariat. As the same initial group of indentured labourers developed in both directions and as agricultural activity needs to be assessed for both groups, they make the subject of an interesting comparison, although the second group (while being more crucial to the structure of this book as having travelled part of the road to working-class formation) is not perhaps best understood as a peasantry.

The fate of commodity-producing peasants in South Africa was bound up with the broader advance of capitalism in agriculture. Applying a famous set of ideas from the work of Lenin to the South African situation, M. L. Morris distinguished between the "American" path to agrarian capitalism, a path in which capitalist smallholders would take a leading role, and the "Prussian" path, where a pre-capitalist landowning stratum would convert to capitalist methods of accumulation and subordinate or drive out potential smallholders. Morris saw South Africa as a good example of a society where the rural question was settled along "Prussian" lines.[5] Critics have pointed out that the analogy does not readily capture the social character of South African farmers, nor does it always help to explain the trajectory of social struggles in the countryside. Nonetheless, Morris certainly captured the basic point that smallholders or peasants might have been, but were not, the main beneficiaries and agents of capitalism in rural South Africa. Instead, a relatively small class of racially defined landlords came to the fore. The bulk of white farmers, of course, were also driven off the land and proletarianised.

In the sugar country of coastal Natal, production came to be dominated in the nineteenth century by a handful of large mills scattered through the countryside. Sugar became more than before the very model of industrial production applied to agriculture, with processing closely linked to growing, transport and credit in a heavily capitalised cycle of operations. A tiny class of millers-cum-planters took command in this economic context.[6] Medium-scale white planters retained some importance in the industry. David Lincoln has successfully captured the economic operations and values of this "sugarocracy" in his doctoral thesis.[7]

The triumph of the "sugarocracy" was not foreordained, however. Another possible way that sugar could have developed would have been through smallholder production, effectively taking much of the risk and dependent on sweated family labour to allow for modest forms of accumulation. Smallholders could have been beholden to the mill. This kind of pattern was in fact the reality in a number of sugar-producing colonies to which indentured labour had been introduced. Looking at those colonies generally, Hugh Tinker has written that from the 1880s ". . . with the trend towards fewer estates, and larger central sugar mills, the Indian shifted from an estate-based population into a rural, smallholder or peasant population."[8] According to North-Coombes, in Mauritius, a smallholder class grew rapidly as indenture went into decline. Politically, this made for a far stabler society where a much broader section of the population believed that they held an interest in existing property relations.[9] Over the past decade, such a class of African smallholders is being encouraged in Natal on an ever larger scale.[10] It may in fact be that this is the future for sugar-growing in the region.

Yet Indian peasants formed a significant section of producers in Natal, particularly between 1890 and 1920. While North-Coombes is correct to contrast their situation with the far greater intrusion of ex-indentured workers into sugar production in Mauritius, the Indian sugar producers were not negligible in numbers or significance in their heyday.[11] Nor were the market gardeners unimportant. Yet neither group was able to expand or develop further from the 1920s onwards. Thereafter it is the stagnation and decline of the Indian peasantry and Indian agricultural activity that needs to be explained. The explanation given below is complex and pertains both to the impact of segregation (the exclusion of Indians through legal discrimation from vital resources and opportunities), and to the inability of the poor generally to compete as South African agriculture became more modernised and land values mounted. Informally and, from the 1940s, formally, Indians were unable to buy "white" land. They were excluded from crucial state assistance, while their own land became too valuable in money terms for what profit could be extracted from it. They were stuck with "poor ground at a high price."[12]

***

In the South African census of 1985, no less than 91 per cent of the Indian population were listed as urban, a higher percentage figure than even the white population exhibited. The popular conception today, and this is held by Indians themselves, also identifies Indians as a commercial, industrial and urban population even though there is a widespread awareness that Indians came to Natal in large part as indentured agricultural workers. As recently as fifty years ago, an Indian source considered that Indians had a "natural aptitude" for sugar-cane growing.[13] By contrast, when the journalist L. E. Neame wrote his polemical study *The Asiatic Danger in the Colonies* in 1907, the heart of his message with regard to Natal was the danger that an industrious Indian peasantry, able to reproduce itself on tiny budgets, was in the process of ousting the white population of rural Natal.[14] Sir John Robinson, journalist and politician, portrayed in his memoirs a typical colonial image of the "frugal and irrepressible 'coolie.'"[15] According to the census of 1904, while "Europeans or whites" largely outnumbered Indians in urban Natal, by three to one in fact, among the female population in rural districts, the Indian advantage was by contrast some two to one, with 38 096 whites and 76 540 Indians.[16] While the white population of Natal was only 39 per cent rural, the Indian population, including indentured workers on the cane fields and in other agricultural operations, was more than 75 per cent rural.[17]

The attitude of white Natal to Indian immigration in the colonial period was deeply ambivalent. On the one hand, whites defined themselves as an exclusive racial community, whose cultural and material interests must always be paramount. Indians were feared as competitors and as bearers of a cheap labour economy that would make impossible the transformation of the entire white population into a community of prosperous property owners and skilled workmen. The introduction and mainte-nance of the indenture system always had many enemies in the settler community and was probably never supported by the majority.

By contrast, large employers of labour not only supported the indenture system and relied on it for their agricultural and other enterprises, but also favoured the dense settlement of free Indians who could offer the colony inexpensive services and supplies. They thus favoured a smallholder or "American" agrarian solution, at least to some extent, from the point of view of the broad economic requirements of colonial growth. In addition, however, this was the means to make the bitter pill of indenture sweeter. Even if it seemed ideal to some that Indian migrants should come to South Africa, work as labourers, and then be packed off when convenient, the lure of such a system for the workers would have been non-existent, given the harsh circumstances of their lives as bondsmen and women.

Indians could and did in fact receive grants of Crown land in the pre-1867 indenture period in lieu of a passage home. In practice, such land grants were very rarely made but ex-indentured workers were well able to secure access to land for agricultural purposes. While some undoubtedly made their way directly into urban employment, it was in fact the route through agriculture that was most utilised by the newly free Indian worker.[18]

Even under indenture, some possibilities for small-scale independent agricul-tural activity existed, as noted in the previous chapter. Already, according to an 1863 report, "while in service many engaged their spare hours in working and trading among themselves the produce of that labour."[19] Such workers looked hungrily at the available land that lay beyond the borders of the planters' property, perhaps land of lesser fertility or on a steep grade, perhaps simply left alone because there were no settlers to take it up. Often, Indian workers came to Natal with an array of rural skills; after all, sugar was also a peasant crop at home. In the first instance, it was often possible for a newly free farmer in Natal to become effectively a tenant-at-will for a short term, clearing bush and gradually building up a property.[20] A biography of one indentured worker family reports with clarity what next happened:

> Across the river in Blackburn to the south, some early settlers had bought a hundred and fifty acres of land and this land had been rented out to free Indians. There were smallholdings of two to five acres and on each plot a settler Indian lived. Most of the houses were built of mud walls thatched with grass (as in an Indian village, in fact). Some were built of flattened out paraffin tins and some of reeds thatched with grass.[21]

The Blackburn Indians were too poor to purchase land, but they were able to rent their patch of ground. They continued, moreover, to work for the planter on a contract basis. Until the iniquitous and much-hated annual £3 tax on free Indians was introduced (for those indentured after 1895), few immigrant Indians renewed their indenture, particularly outside years of severe recession.[22] According to the 1882 divisional report for Umlazi near Durban, they "prefer the independence of a farmer on one acre of land, to employment in European service."[23] In that year, the Protector of Immigrants reported that:

> The facility with which land can be obtained in this Colony, while injurious to the employer of labour, enables any Indian who desires to raise himself in the social scale to do so; with a little industry and moderate good fortune, the man who was yesterday a labourer becomes an employer, competing with his late master.[24]

The re-indenture rate, after the iniquitous tax was introduced but when it was still possible to evade it in various ways, was as low as 20 per cent in 1902 and 13 per cent in 1903 and 1904. The Protector wrote in 1908; "I incline to think that most of them re-indenture from sheer necessity and not from choice or any notion of prospective rights."[25] Moreover, few of these were workers in agriculture.[26]

Any inspection of records that concerns social or economic conditions in Natal in the late nineteenth and early twentieth centuries, quickly reveals numerous references to the expansion of a free Indian peasantry in the sugar-cane country and elsewhere. While early references are mainly to tenant farmers, by the 1890s there is also growing mention of Indian land purchase.[27] The Coolie Commission of 1872 indicated a significant number of Indian-owned farms, growing cane, tobacco, maize and vegetables both around Durban and on the North Coast.[28] Indians owned some 10 000 acres and cultivated another 50 000 as owners and tenants by the first years of the twentieth century.[29]

In the late nineteenth century, Indian farming enterprise was extremely diverse and aimed largely at the domestic market; sugar was not of great significance. In 1898, the *Statistical Yearbook* recorded that Indian farmers grew crops to a value of £90 229, more than half in maize. Second crop in value was beans worth £15 953 and third tobacco, £9 756. The value of the Indian sugar crop was only £2 001.[30] According to the 1904 Natal census, Indians owned 6 052 cattle (compared to 314 000 owned by whites and 343 000 by Africans), 24 039 goats (compared respectively to 176 000 and 797 000) and 148 602 poultry (compared respectively to 463 000 and 613 000).

There are numerous references to Indian maize production. In addition, tobacco was an important early crop. Both could find a large market amongst Africans.[31] Reports also mention the cultivation of rice and there was undoubtedly a general expansion of crops aimed at Indian consumers. In Inanda, the sugar heartland, Indians were the main producers of all crops other than sugar.[32] At the same time, Indians took to the general production of fruit and vegetables largely aimed at the white market. The agricultural commodities that Indians grew became far more abundant than before and also much cheaper, to the delight of the principal figures in the Natal economy. This is why a Natal governor, Sir Henry McCallum, could say with pride that Indian "agriculturists are the keystone of South Coast industries."[33]

McCallum, and those who thought like him in Natal, were not precisely opting for an Indian agrarian base. On the one hand, they had no particular interest in creating a landless Indian proletariat; the sugar industry could expand significantly only by employing contracted African labour and secondary industry was in its infancy. On the other, Indians rented and purchased land just at the time when speculators were unable to find customers who would put it to profitable use.[34] The Natal Land and Colonisation Company , as well as other landowning companies, were quite prepared to sell farms of 40–80 acres to Indians in the early twentieth century.[35] The very success of Indian peasants brought down prices of the commodities they produced, requiring them to survive on margins which would have been intolerable to settler farmers. Early Indian farmers clustered on the edge of the sugar plantations and thus had a dependent relationship to the plantation owners, producing cheap goods for them and their workers, and serving as a transient work-force to supplement the permanent employees.

Indian agrarian producers in Natal in the early twentieth century are best understood as simple commodity producers. In analysing their mode of production, two elements need underscoring. One is the intensity of their market commitment. Undoubtedly, some goods were produced for home consumption as on virtually any farm anywhere. However, what is striking is that the economic basis for Indian owners and tenants lay in production for a market in contrast with the many agrarian producers in South African history who have rather used market involvement to help buttress or sustain a subsistence way of life whose extended reproduction was based on essentially non-market relations. This, according to Lewis, is largely the case for nineteenth-century African market producers of the eastern Cape, and it was also true for the trekboers.[36]

Secondly, unlike most categories of white farmers in South Africa, Indian peasants did not rely primarily on the exploitation of an unfree or even paid labour force. Most of the labour in their system of production was performed within and by the family. Even to the extent that Indian rural producers rented land, they were not exploited significantly as labour tenants or rent-paying tenants on the whole. There was some development of an exploited sugar-producing tenantry in parts of the sugar belt over time, but generally rents were low and the key exploitative element lay in the relationship between peasant cultivators and those who mediated between them and the market, particularly money-lenders and transporters.

The links between poor Indian cultivators and the important class of Indian traders may have been crucial for the survival of an Indian peasantry in Natal, given the overall dominance of the sugar barons.[37] Certainly around Durban, small-scale Indian land purchasers were often the customers of Indian land speculators. The distinct Indian trading class provided credit which was, for instance, unavailable to Africans. It is striking that Indian farming expansion was going on at the same time that the mineral revolution was supposedly committed to smashing African enterprise. Indian success and African failure in this phase, between 1890 and 1914, may be explained by the availability to Indians of credit without recourse to the white banker or farmer.

The characteristic production unit was the extended family. According to an Inanda Division report for 1892/93, the typical Indian smallholding consisted of perhaps five acres, rented for between ten shillings and one pound per acre, and farmed by a partnership of two males.[38] Partnerships typically consisted of fathers and sons and/or brothers but might, often less formally, have embraced a further generation or wider connections. This kind of corporate family structure allowed for a large number of adults to engage in diverse activities and, in particular, for agriculture to be combined with wage labour, and most crucially, for the products of the farm to be marketed without going to an outside party. It is only through the possibility of alternative cash sources, that simple commodity producers can in fact survive through times of adversity and strain.

In addition, as Sir James Liege Hulett quite accurately put it in a speech, "a free Indian made his wife and children work as well as himself."[39] J.S. Done, an Indian writer, wrote in 1906 about Newlands, north of the Umgeni River from Durban, that "all the Indians here, men and women and children, are busily ploughing the hillsides and planting same with mealies, tobacco, beans, etc."[40] Only in desperation did an Indian woman, ensconced within the household, turn to wage labour, but she was customarily intensively involved in agricultural production and marketing as well as domestic labour, ideally within the joint family unit. Thus the Indian smallholding was a family enterprise.

At least in the period before World War I, it was possible within agriculture for some Indians to accumulate to a significant extent. As early as 1871, the will of Cathasamy Chetty of West Street, Durban, a merchant who had branch shops in the countryside, revealed the ownership of a sugar farm at Isipingo, near the site of Louis Botha Airport today, called "Puddles."[41] Others combined agriculture with related business dealings. In Richmond, the son of an indentured worker developed a soap manufactory.[42] Tongaat was the site of Desai's rice mill that came to employ well over a hundred labourers and many skilled workers.[43] Perhaps the first really wealthy Natalian of southern Indian origin, R.B. Chetty, who came as a free immigrant via the Seychelles and Mauritius, grew betel and tobacco on a large scale and used the latter in the manufacture of cigars in the factory he established in Umgeni Road, Durban in 1904.[44] Pungavanam Moodley, an indentured worker, later became a small farmer near Port Shepstone and eventually succeeded in tobacco farming and land speculation on the basis of the 100 acres he initially secured.[45] Also on the South Coast, R.D. Chowtee established a tobacco estate of some 1 200 acres at Sawoti.[46] More modestly, smallholders were sometimes able to establish shops based on the sale of produce from their own ground.[47]

The most spectacular case was that of Babu Bodasing. According to family stories, Bodasing came to Natal as an indentured worker in 1874 from the Agra region. A *kshatriya* (of high caste), he came from a prosperous family who knew about the manufacture of sugar. In South Africa, Bodasing worked in the New Guelderland mill as a sugar maker and/or foreman.[48] Although he at first served a renewed contract, he emerged from indenture with six acres in 1884, farmed with a white partner, growing mealies, tobacco and fresh produce, and owned 100 acres within four years. By the early years of the twentieth century, having married an indentured worker's daughter and procreated a family, he owned shops, stock farms in inland Natal and thousands of acres of prime cane land. His family claims that when he died each son inherited 1 000 acres of cane. It is said that his greatest regret on his death in 1919 was that he had never had the opportunity to own a sugar mill.[49] There is nobody else quite like the Bodasings in Indian agriculture in Natal; they have something of the status of the Oppenheimers in Rand mining.

In fact, however, there was one Indian-owned sugar mill. The first Indian sugar miller at Glendale was a man named Ramcharan who, as well as grinding maize, sold crude sugar and treacle, of a kind typical of millers' production in India itself, to a largely African clientele. According to a descendant, he came from the same part of northern India as Bodasing.[50] However, he only owned the mill briefly. It then came into the hands of E.M. Paruk. The Paruks acquired the Glendale mill through a foreclosure and greatly expanded it before World War II. They owned it until selling out to Lonrho in 1969.[51] At Glendale, they employed hundreds of Indian millworkers at all skill levels, and hundreds of Indian families served as tenants producing cane for their mill as well. The Paruks, however, were originally Muslim traders from west India, typical "passenger" immigrants.

Fascinating as the story of the Indian agrarian capitalists is, it must be emphasised that it was hardly typical. As we shall see, most of the Indian peasantry in Natal remained extremely poor and found less and less opportunity to advance their fortunes. North-Coombes has pointed out how problematic, for Mauritius, is the rosy image of Indian peasant prosperity based on ownership of small sugar farms. However impressive the gross figures, the individual family produced very little and lived in deep poverty.[52] Lewis effectively analyses the figures for eastern-Cape peasant production in the nineteenth century to similar effect. The golden age of Indian farmers in Natal, a period when at least there was a steady increase in commodity production by Indian farming families, ended perhaps with the severe economic downturn of the first decade of the twentieth century and certainly by the depression following World War I.

By 1920 at the latest, the Indian farming population could roughly be divided into two distinct groups. In what were historically key sugar-growing regions, Indians themselves turned to growing cane, a tendency that began to be noted officially around the turn of the century.[53] North-Coombes dates the shift of Indian small-holders to sugar in Mauritius to the period of World War I and its aftermath, when international prices were excellent. During this phase, the "extension of small-scale cultivation on to marginal land" by hard-working peasants living off tiny margins had an economic logic. From 1921, this period of expansion came to an end and the timing is apt to be very similar in Natal.[54]

However, much of the Indian agriculture in Natal focused on peri-urban market gardening, particularly in the rich if flood-prone alluvial valleys near Durban. Our Blackburn source beautifully epitomises this development in a family story:

> A visitor from Springfield gave a glowing account of the nearness of Springfield from the town of Durban — the rich soil, plenty of water and firewood. My great-grandparents went to Springfield and found that the Springfield Flats were like Heaven on Earth for growing crops. Everything that a peasant farmer required was there.

The specific conditions of farming in these two distinct zones needs to be explored more fully, in the context of the declining capacity of Indian family agriculture to expand in the inter-war years.[55] Sugar farming at first sight seems the more impressively autonomous path but it was the market gardening, because of its consonance with urban and industrial activities, that held more promise in the long run.

* * *

The second decade of the twentieth century witnessed a large-scale conversion to sugar on the part of Indian farmers in the first category. This may have gone hand in hand with continued overall growth in production and land ownership. However, in terms of both acreage and number of farms, the 1920s marked the end of the period of growth. The number of Indian-owned farms in Natal reached 2 575 in 1920/21 and declined slightly to 2 545 in 1925/26.[56] In 1945, 1 229 Natal Indian cane growers farmed (and largely owned) 71 620 acres of land.[57] The number was 1 604 in 1961, 1 835 in 1970/71, 1 817 in 1979/80 and 1 713 in 1988/89. Acreage was also relatively stagnant. Growers farmed 68 485 acres in 1954, 56 992 in 1961 and 61 040 in 1970/71 with little further increase thereafter.[58] Over a long period, reported conditions of cane production and farming life remain relatively unchanged; the half-century between 1920 and 1970 was essentially a half-century of stagnation in Indian agriculture. After World War II, this began to be perceived by the authorities as a "problem" and as a result, a number of excellent social science studies were made of Indian agriculture on the North Coast of Natal. With the exception of the first major study by Gavin Maasdorp, which belongs to a liberal academic tradition, they are constrained within the political limits of what it was respectable to say in the context of racial segregation, limiting their broader value to later scholars despite the importance of the research contained within. One problem, moreover, is that by taking the ethnic category "Indian" wholesale, they do not distinguish sharply enough between the mass of Indian rural producers and the handful of successful Indian rural capitalists.[59] I have profited from this research substantially nonetheless, and have also been fortunate in having the benefit of interview material with Indian growers as a counterweight or check.

The context, it should be underlined, was by no means one of stagnation in the sugar industry. During the inter-war years, white cane-farmers were able to expand acreage and productivity as land values rose due to heavy state support.[60] Indian farmers, by and large, became stuck with, what has been noted above, "poor ground at a high price."[61]

Nonetheless, during this period cane growing became a monoculture for most Indian farmers at any distance from the Durban metropolitan market. In a survey of the Verulam-Tongaat region in the early 1960s, 118 of 154 farmers farmed only cane whilst a mere 19 farmed no cane at all.[62] A slightly later survey found that there was no correlation amongst Indian farmers between the size of farm and the use of land, apart from the tendency for very small holdings to be used for non-agricultural purposes entirely.[63] This latter survey, a massive one, reported that in 1969 no less than 78,7 per cent of North Coast Indian-owned land was under cane. A third survey reported that 62 per cent of such farms cultivated only sugar and only 11 per cent did not cultivate sugar at all.[64] This domination was noticeable, if less extreme, even very close to Durban.[65] Small farmers practised more intercropping, presumably because they continued to farm for their own use to some extent, and because they could apply more labour per piece of ground.

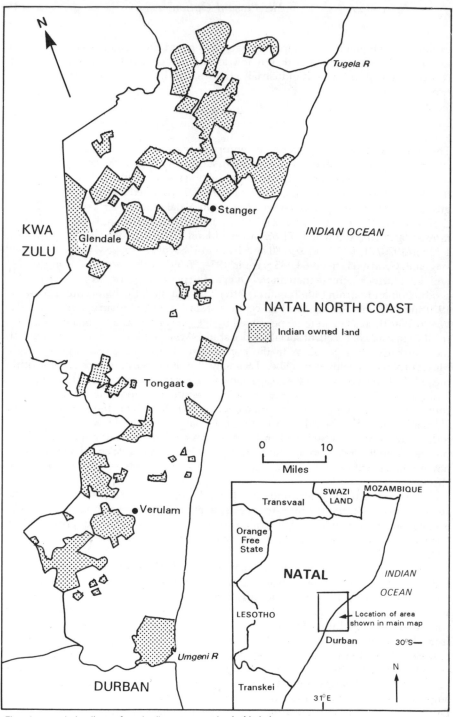

The rise and decline of an Indian peasantry in Natal

(B. Freund, "The Rise and Decline of an Indian Peasantry in Natal."
Journal of Peasant Studies 18 (2) 1991.)

Sugar's dominance is particularly remarkable if we recall the small amount of cane which Indians are recorded as growing at the turn of the century. The one exception to be noted is the continued significance, at least past World War II, (especially on the South Coast below Durban) of a second industrial crop, tobacco, where a co-operative movement made marketing more economical. Tobacco production amongst Indian growers also declined massively in the 1960s, however.[66] According to Indian farmers themselves, this decline was linked to the activities of the control board.[67]

There are several reasons for this shift to an industrial crop. Cane is more adapted to marginal land and the vagaries of rainfall in coastal Natal than most other crops.[68] More importantly, the creation of a marketing and milling network tied heavily to the availability of credit, exactly in that sphere of exchange where exploitation threatened most severely to squeeze the Indian peasantry, made it possible for the farmer to get a small but steady return for his crop. Thus even if other crops, for instance vegetables, yield a bigger return per acre, cane remains the most practicable crop for the smallholder away from the city.[69] The creation of the sugar-quota system in 1936, regulated largely from within the industry, confirmed this possibility and promoted the development of monoculture even while seriously inhibiting the overall growth opportunities for Indian cultivators.[70]

At the same time, while the amount of land that Indian farmers own has remained basically stagnant, from the inter-war years land increasingly began to be divided among heirs, and the average size of landholdings has diminished. Often the death of a landholder was followed by lengthy litigation during which the land deteriorated.[71] Particularly closer to Durban, smallholdings gave way to dwarfholdings with limited economic possibilities.[72] Fragmentation in itself caused absenteeism and out-migration.[73] Especially in the more remote corners of the North Coast, community life could not be so easily sustained and the most important social linkages became those between family members, involving those no longer resident on the farm.[74] In fact, for reasons of familial solidarity which depended on the possibility of equal inheritance for maintaining the peace, representatives of Indian farming communities (apart from the pre-war South African Indian Congress which then represented the most successful elements) wanted to exclude Indians from the provisions of legislation that might block "unbeneficial" fragmentation of the landholdings.[75]

Most Indian farming in Natal remains unproductive and lacking in modern technology, and most farmers are poor men. In 1975, it was estimated that 81 per cent of Indian farmers had incomes of under R1 000 p.a. and some 62 per cent under R500.[76] A little earlier, one-third surveyed were indicated as illiterate.[77] While Natal Indians at the start of the 1970s constituted more than 20 per cent of all sugar growers in the province, they owned only one-twelfth of the cane acreage and produced only one-sixteenth of the sugar, a considerable decline from a generation earlier. Their yields were far below those of white farmers on average.[78] One comparison from the early 1960s put the mean Indian farmers' income (itself twice the median) at no more than one-tenth the mean white sugar grower's income.[79] Particularly after World War II, the average age of Indian farmers rose, and increasingly incomes were supplemented with wage work off the farm.[80] How did the incomes of Indian cane farmers compare with other categories of Indians with limited education and formal skills? By the early 1950s, it could be said that while independent farmers lived better and had larger incomes than the declining number of Indian fieldworkers on white-owned sugar farms, they earned less money under harsher living conditions than the skilled and even semi-skilled workers in the mills.[81]

In the course of the capitalisation of cane country after World War I, when Indian farmers held land that was relatively desirable, the tendency was for whites to buy them out. In exchange, they moved to the steeper and dryer land on the edge of African reserves.[82] Indian farmers largely owned their own land but lacked facilities for irrigation, fertilizer, electricity and capital improvements.[83] The majority lacked the ploughs, harrows and especially tractors essential for profitable development.[84] Access to fertilizer and the effective use of fertilizer was poor, compared to white farmers.[85] Around 1970, less than one-third of Indian cane growers could reap or transport their own cane.[86]

The most crucial requirement for cash crop farmers is access to credit. According to David Rix, himself employed in agricultural extension to Indian farmers, they came to rely above all on sugar mills (69 per cent) and private individuals (65 per cent) for loans. Only 21 per cent got bank credit.[87] It was largely the top class of Indian farmers who could get bank loans.[88] The rest depended on transporters and millers (and independent usurers, themselves richer farmers or shopkeepers) who absorbed much of the potential profits.[89] In the early 1960s, for instance, the Natal Indian Cane Growers' Association estimated that its members were obliged to pay interest at a minimum rate of 10 per cent to mills and private lenders as their only source of credit for fertilizer or implement purchases.[90]

The particular needs of sugar cane, especially at harvesting time, meant also a growing dependence on the hired labour of even poorer African workers (to an important extent women by the 1960s) and on labour contractors to provide it.[91] Such workers could not be economically employed on a permanent basis by small Indian producers and most African farm workers commuted from the nearest reserves (Maphumulo or Ndwedwe on the North Coast) or were temporarily housed on Indian farms. The limited access of poor Indian farmers compared to affluent white sugar growers to this extremely cheap labour was another important constraint to accumulation. In the Greyling study of Indian farmers on the North Coast, approximately half of those surveyed, 1 322 farmers, hired some 7 636 labourers of whom 91 per cent were African and 27 per cent women.[92]

Over time, smallholder agriculture yielded more and more workers to town, both as commuters and as permanent immigrants. Moreover, linked to this is the declining commitment of the Indian bourgeoisie to agriculture. The ownership of land and production of sugar-cane is highly skewed in favour of a few big landowners; the few real success stories in Indian agriculture, including that of Bodasing, have also been linked to sugar monoculture. In the early 1960s (for the Verulam-Tongaat area) while 59 per cent of farmers controlled under 20 acres, the top 1 per cent of growers owned over 200 acres apiece.[93] If 62 per cent of Indian farmers surveyed in 1975 made under R500 p.a., 4 per cent made over R3 000.[94] The 1936 sugar-quota system distinguished between A growers and B growers, the latter including almost all Indians, who received poorer prices for their sugar, but had to pay a percentage of their revenues to the Sugar Association. Indian growers at the time were deeply divided; the most successful supported the quota system from which they profited and the small growers refused to join the the new Natal Indian Cane Growers' Association, which accepted the quota system and organised separately for some years.[95]

However, there is no evidence to suggest that this differential became drama-tically more marked with time. The agricultural fortunes of the pre-1920 era have not been followed by later success stories of any magnitude. It was moneylenders, transporters and labour contractors who became best placed to make profits from Indian agriculture. The stagnation of Indian small farming was accompanied by the relative stagnation of the bigger farms.

It is possible to view this picture of stagnation through two lenses, one emphasising the racist strictures of the segregation era from Union in 1910 onwards, which made the legal ownership of land in South Africa dependent on membership in a particular racial group, and the other emphasising the actual course of capitalist development. Both are significant, but the argument here is that perhaps the latter outweighed the former; in any case, they intertwined. In two ways, segregation did play a crucial role in discouraging the development of Indian farmers. For one thing, it made the further acquisition of land more difficult. In 1923 the recently passed Durban Land Alienation Ordinance, legalising the institution of racially exclusive restrictive covenants concerning land transfers, was extended to the entire province of Natal. In 1946, the Asiatic Land Tenure Act actually restricted outright the ability of Indians to purchase land, and the Group Areas Act from 1950 resulted in Indians losing land that was proclaimed for whites only.[96] By this time, however, the advance of Indian agriculture had long since been halted.

Secondly and probably more importantly, in the very era when the state was becoming deeply committed to supporting and assisting white farmers who pos-sessed the franchise, it did virtually nothing for Indian farmers apart from the granting of quotas for cane production from 1936. Indian farmers had no access to state credit institutions or assistance in the recruitment of labour or equipment purchase. They were excluded from membership in the Marketing Boards.[97] Moreover, Indian-proclaimed land, because of its artificial scarcity, acquired a money value that could not actually be realised by the farmer, further discouraging investment.

Nonetheless, it is probably the more acquisitive and capitalist-orientated Indian farmers who forfeited the most as a result of intensifying racism. For the majority of Indian peasants, capitalisation of the land, i.e. the rising money value of land, itself directly squeezed the peasantry. The bonds of poverty would not have been loosed simply if more land were available legally. The problem was rather that of the cost of improving the land and labour conditions. Inexorably, as land became more valuable and developed in conjunction (necessarily) with state assistance, the smallholder became more marginal. As Indian peasants withdrew from agrarian commitments, moreover, they produced relatively less sugar and their general economic importance declined.

✳ ✳ ✳

In the 1970 census, the largest single grouping of Indian farmers resident in Natal were in the Durban-Pinetown area. Some few belonged to the North Coast cane-farm rubric that we have been examining, but many were market gardeners and their numbers had been yet far larger a generation earlier. As early as the 1880s, the Wragg Commission had reported that Indians had virtually displaced whites in growing fresh produce for the urban market in Natal.[98] In a number of important respects, the market gardeners farmed in a different way to the rural cultivators of the North Coast, and they were far less clearly to be categorised as peasants. To begin with, they were not generally owners of land. In 1930, market gardeners were more than twice as numerous as cane farmers, but owned far less than one-tenth the amount of land.[99] The average size garden was less than two acres.[100] Except on steeper ground, notably Stella Hill where plots were far larger, vegetables rather than fruit dominated market gardeners' production in Durban.[101] In 1942, the borough of Durban contained some 2 326 acres of Indian-farmed market garden, excluding Cato Manor.[102] The most thorough student of the gardeners, I. G. Halliday, characterised the holdings by their "scattered nature and small size."[103] Most market gardeners leased land, either from private landowners or, more usually , from the Corporation or South African Railways and Harbours.[104] Even where they owned a small patch of ground, it was apt to be for living space, while they planted their fruit and vegetables elsewhere.[105]

Superficially, this paucity of land would suggest that market gardeners were apt to be even poorer than sugar farmers, given the desire for landownership that existed. It is true that very few indeed were ever able to accumulate capital significantly in this way. This sector, unlike cane growing, virtually lacked a kulak or capitalist farmer element. However, market gardening had its attractions for the poor with its potential of "quick returns" and cash payments on the barrel-head, and consequently it lured many ex-indentured workers and their children away from the canefields early in the twentieth century.[106] Land such as the Springfield Flats, which formed a little valley near the mouth of the Umgeni river, the South Coast Junction/Clairwood/Bayhead area that stretched south of the harbour, and the low-lying countryside south of the Umgeni mouth and north of the Greyville race-track, was often very fertile.

Access to customers was relatively easy if the household head could dispose of enough labour, even though members of the extended family had to spend long hours distributing and marketing the produce.[107] Typically, the early morning Squatters' Market served the needs of the market gardeners of Durban. In 1938, the Squatters' Market sold some 1 000–1 200 tickets to individuals on a Saturday morning for the right to sell produce.[108] Even the Cliffdale farmers from the Mist Belt marketed their own wares in Durban daily during the season.[109]

Above all, small-scale agriculture could be combined with other activities, suitable either to an uncontrolled urban periphery or to wage work in town. Market gardening could be part of a larger and more diverse household economy; within a complex of economic activities, it provided social security as much as a viable occupation.[110] From the 1920s, market gardeners' sons began to walk to work in Durban factories in large numbers. Especially near the expanding factory-zone south of the harbour, post-war gardeners were part-time gardeners; industrial work was distinctly more remunerative when available.[111]

The ownership, or inexpensive leasing, of land formed the basis of a relatively cheap way of life around which a dense social nexus developed. Gardeners lived in wood-and-iron shacks, sometimes quite sprawling, with little in the way of amenities or sanitation, a poor water supply (at best a communal tap) and no electricity.[112] What little cash was accumulated was placed under the mattress or buried in the ground, perhaps to be invested in a child's education or the purchase of a small bit of land on which to build a shack.[113] Although, in the 1940s, Indians in the region of Durban were statistically more likely than whites to own a home, however humble, their diet was poor. Consumption of butter or fruit was a luxury. The peripheral Indians of Durban lived on beans, cheap bread and poor cuts of meat.[114] Despite the low income of market gardeners, in general it was essential to hire temporary African labour for harvesting (at wages so low Indian men would not accept them) and, for lighter work such as weeding and planting, Indian women were sometimes hired for even less pay.[115]

While Indian market gardeners were not initially particularly affected by the increasing difficulties Indians experienced in purchasing land in Natal, they were in time the victims of the capitalisation of land values and the development of capitalism in South Africa. Improvements in transport and state assistance (such as favourable rail rates) were crucial in allowing for the competitive importation by white farmers of a variety of vegetables to Durban from inland destinations by rail, and later, road.[116] The costs of marketing ate heavily into garden profits.

In 1931, the Durban municipality succeeded in substantially expanding the region under its control. This was done both in order to allow for economic development and to control or eliminate undesirable, illegal and untaxed activities of all varieties and by inhabitants of all colours. The flat land where Indians grew vegetables was desired for industrial expansion, and eventually the possible range where market gardening could flourish became more and more limited.[117] Moreover, the most desirable, low-lying land was also subject to disastrous floods from time to time. In 1905, 137 people, of whom 113 were Indians, died when the Umhlatuzana stream flooded.[118] Rising waters also threatened the Eden of Springfield. The great Springfield flood disaster of 1917 caused many to abandon the fertile Umgeni River plain.[119]

In certain areas, white residential housing, taking advantage of the Group Areas legislation, also expanded at the expense of market gardeners. Just inland from the Berea Ridge, where perhaps the greatest concentration of Indian peri-urban land-ownership was found in Mayville/Cato Manor, market gardening gave way to shack renting, especially with the great expansion of the African urban population during and after World War II. This provided more remuneration for less effort than farming. Finally, the whole of peripheral Indian Durban, under the impact of urban design policies directed from Pretoria, was forcibly shifted towards the new and massive working-class townships to the south-west and north-west of the city. This coincided with the remarkable industrial growth rates of the 1960s which mopped up Indian unemployment and undermined the earlier complex survival patterns combining cultivation with wage work. Hence today only scattered remnants of market gardening have survived.

The conditions of market gardening, under which producers owned little land, and had to work very hard for small and unreliable rewards by marketing what they grew, held in itself little possibility for sustaining much prosperity, however much it impressed observers with the industry of the gardeners and the value of the inexpensive produce for the urban consumer market. In fact, the most appealing aspect had been the way in which it facilitated entry into the urban economy for Indian families. Halliday wrote as far back as 1940 that "it was rather interesting however to note the number to whom 'farming did not pay' and very few wished their sons to follow in their footsteps."[120] In practice, the shift towards industrial employment must have been welcomed by most who made the change. Industrial employment, in fact, has long since been seen as the more secure way to make a living.[121]

✳ ✳ ✳

In 1936, of all Indians in gainful employment in Natal, 36,8 per cent were working in agriculture, a figure that of course included canefield and mill workers. By 1951, this had fallen to 20,3 per cent — manufacturing and services had both overtaken the agricultural sector. A further fall to 12,0 per cent in 1960 and then to 4,8 per cent in 1970 saw agriculture overtaken in employment figures by construction and transport as well.[122] The number of Indian employees in agriculture (including the self-employed), had then shrunk to 2 140.[123] This meant that Indians were less involved in agriculture than in any of the other three South African racial categories, white, African and Coloured. Youths felt isolated on the farms, particularly if they had no access to cars or lorries, and were anxious to leave for town.[124]

The early years of National Party rule after 1948 may have marked the nadir of relations between Indian cultivators and the South African state, with the passage of the Group Areas Act (1950) and the consequent uncertainty about the rights of Indian property owners. South Africa's massive labour recruitment system excluded Indian agricultural employers from using African workers as did whites.[125]

However, after 1960 the situation improved in some respects with a change in the party's policy towards Indian South Africans. National Party doctrine had retained the pre-World War I ambition of Natal whites to ship the "unassimilable" Asiatic population back to India; conditions were intended to discourage their integration into South African society. By this time, though, hopes that any significant proportion of the Indian population would emigrate to India had vanished. The Verwoerd government accepted that the Indians were in South Africa to stay, perhaps as junior partners of the whites in the deteriorating security situation, and proceeded to try to fit them into the framework of apartheid.

State propaganda made it clear that some kinds of Indians still represented an unhealthy element in the population. There were too many Indian traders and too many Indian workers who were informally skilled but not legally qualified. What were needed were men and women who could be fitted into the burgeoning South African economy and idealised social order: nurses, policemen, sailors, skilled craftsmen, manufacturers. The right sort of farmers belonged to this category. The government publication most directly aimed at the Indian population, *Fiat Lux*, contained many articles from the late 1960s, aimed at improving the quality of Indian agriculture and encouraging Indian farmers.

While this shift can clearly be denoted from 1960, in practice it was halting and gradual. There certainly were limits to this encouragement of Indian enterprise as well. The Group Areas Act remained in force until 1991, and reform had to operate within the constraints it allowed. A few Indian entrepreneurs obtained control of land through white front-men, but this was not easy. The frontiers of white ownership continued to be policed in the 1980s and attempts to evade the law through the use of white "nominees" required making them available at very short notice when the government inspectors threatened to appear.[126] However, especially once the apartheid regime entered its reform phase in the 1970s, the state has been increasingly prepared to create favourable conditions for the maintenance of Indian farmers on the criteria that have applied to whites since the days of the Pact (1924–33) and the Fusion (1933–39) ministries of the inter-war years.

Agricultural extension officers were assigned to Indian areas and eventually Indians themselves trained in this work, after a diploma course was introduced at the M. L. Sultan Technikon in 1973.[127] From 1972, the Sugar Association offered extension services to Indian cane growers[128] Indians were permitted to belong to the national, regional and crop-specific farmers' associations.[129] The facilities of the Land Bank were made available to Indians and eventually Indian land assessors were appointed so as to make loans more readily available by the end of the 1970s.[130] The Agriculture Credit Board of the South African Sugar Association loaned money at low rates to farmers, although not for land purchase and in amounts insufficient for mortgage and improvements.[131] Disaster-fund aid became available as well and, following Cyclone Demoina in 1983, for the first time the South African state provided significant assistance to a fairly large number of rural Indians.[132] The institution of the House of Delegates in 1984, however, came after the major shift in policy and has added rather little to it.[133] According to Indian farmers themselves, the arrival of sanctions and the exclusion of South African sugar from the Canadian and United States markets also had a positive effect in convincing the Sugar Association to promote more equal conditions that no longer favoured big growers. Thus, a programme to expand sugar growing for ethanol manufacture, partly sanctions-busting in intent, was made available to all growers and sugar prices equalised.[134]

The growing willingness of the South African state to intervene benignly in Indian-owned farming needs to be qualified in one important way, however. It is a willingness restricted to those who can be transformed into capitalist farmers on the South African model, just as earlier measures in favour of "poor whites" were discarded for those policies that would help those who could help themselves in a capitalist environment. For top Indian farmers, conditions have certainly improved. The Bodasing interests have substantially increased their production of sugar-cane over the past fifteen years. They and some others have found the means to invest in improved equipment and farming methods. The Natal Indian Cane Growers' Association overtly addresses its members as a community of rural bosses in discussing (fearfully) the possibility of African farmworkers' unionisation.[135] The one Indian-owned sugar mill at Glendale had offered a fairer deal to Indian growers in various respects over a long period of time. However, according to Indian farmers themselves, when it was sold to the multinational Lonrho, access to credit and to modern facilities, for instance for irrigation, actually increased.[136] The most successful Indian farmer in Cliffdale has been able to avail himself of African convict labour.[137] For the market gardeners who remain, the move from the Squatters' Market to the modern produce market in Clairwood that took place in the 1970s, increased the salience of middlemen, and represented a convergence of the local state's ostensible aim of hygiene and efficiency, with national state policies. It was disadvantageous to the marginal producer reliant on low expenditure.[138]

However, the decline of the Indian peasantry as a whole has not been reversed.[139] Facilities such as Land Bank loans and disaster relief have been organised in such a way as to largely exclude the smallholder.[140] From 7 per cent of South Africa's sugar in 1961, Indian growers now produce no more than 4 per cent. The kinds of measures the state has introduced have neither aimed at helping, nor been able to do much for, the "middle peasant" (who is neither dependent on exploiting labour nor exploited within the productive sphere).

Despite the significant differences between them explored above, by 1960 market gardening and cane growing shared in common the reality that they had become in large part *economically residual activities*. For the smallholder, no capital has been made available for land or infrastructural assistance. Legislation assumes a long-term intention to squeeze out the least efficient grower who makes poor use of the soil.[141] While the desire to retain land remains, the Indian peasantry has essentially been incorporated into a much bigger wage-earning class and is disappearing from the Natal population as a distinct element of any size. On the North Coast and elsewhere, African cane growers have become economically far more important than Indians.[142]

The peasant road for Natal Indians represented an historic diversion that demonstrated their ability to carve out their own byway. Capital was only interested to a limited extent in converting that byway into a significant road towards economic development in Natal , and then only in an early phase, concluding at latest by the depression following World War I. In the canefields of littoral Natal, it was a cul-de-sac, a sector that failed to grow and that only continues to have a future in the context of a deracialised community of capitalist farmers. On the urban periphery, it represented a transitional existence on the way to proletarianisation of a distinct type; a way of life which we shall explore further in the following chapter. By contrast, it is possible that the conditions under which apartheid is finally dissolving in the 1990s are exactly right for the expansion of an African smallholder class in Natal, precisely because of the different political salience such a class potentially possesses in contemporary South Africa.

The example of the Indian peasantry, however, suggests caution in predicting any considerable potential in capitalist accumulation through peasant farming, especially in sugar. Research amongst African cane growers suggests that their production depends on exploitative and much-resented credit relations with sugar mills which guarantee transport and purchase at a fixed price. In Glendale, where Lonrho bought out the Paruks in 1969, the mill creates a situation in which, given a lack of access to capital and land (especially on the part of women household heads), sugar can only supplement migrant wages, rather than form the basis for accumulation. Vegetable and fruit producers cannot compete in the urban market with the low prices that can still be profitable for capitalist estates, at least given the present credit structure, and therefore grow only subsistence crops. Whether any means are found to overcome these blockages will determine whether African producers are able to surpass the efforts of the Indian peasantry in the past.

FAMILY ECONOMY
Women participated in the domestic economy and in petty commerce.

(Local History Museum, Durban)

SQUATTERS' MARKET

(Studies of Indian Employment)

THE MARKET GARDENERS
Petty commerce was also an extension of the domestic economy (*c.* 1920).

(Local History Museum, Durban)

THE EDGE OF TOWN
Shacks in the fields, South Coast Junction.   *(Studies of Indian Employment)*

THE EDGE OF TOWN
In the joint family, working-class women worked hard at multifarious tasks.

(Iain Edwards)

FISHERMEN
These seine fishermen are depicted on Addington Beach, the southern section of Durban's "Golden Mile." *(Studies of Indian Employment)*

PATRON AND CLIENT
Striking workers consult the pre-1946 Natal Indian Congress stalwart, A.I. Kajee.

(G. H. Calpin, *A. I. Kajee*)

3

The Edge of Town: Durban and the Indian Working Class, 1900–1930

Durban is one of the three great urban agglomerations in South Africa, together with the Pretoria-Witwatersrand-Vaal Triangle conurbation in the southern Transvaal, and greater Cape Town. Its economic foundation as a city derives from its status as the principal port in the country, and particularly as the principal port serving the mining core of the country. Durban's advantage lay in its location on a large, shallow sheet of water, the Bay of Natal, which is joined to the Indian Ocean by a narrow channel. In the nineteenth century, this channel was not deep enough to allow sea-going vessels into the bay, but continuous improvements eventually provided adequate access to the harbour. In 1904, the first mail-steamer crossed the bar and entered the bay directly.[1] By then it was possible to travel by train from Durban, ascending stage by stage through the hills of Natal, to reach the escarpment and the highveld of the South African interior, this line having been opened in 1895.[2]

This was the essence of Durban's economy: the harbour, the railway and the commerce between the mineral-rich South African interior and the outer world. It was therefore a service economy to an important extent. This lent itself naturally to a further development, the establishment of sea-side tourism for the whites of the Transvaal, bolstered by the always warm climate and the popular Durban race-courses.

Durban also served as the natural centre of the Natal littoral, dominated as it was by the sugar estates. Sugar milling itself was an important town industry but also provided the basis of industrial food manufacturing more generally. Cane spirit was not the least of its by-products. As Katzen pointed out, sugar processing itself generated a demand for machinery (the initial focal point for a metal industry), bags, sacks, wood, paper and other relevant equipment.[3] Thus the early metal-working firm Dorman, Long, whose antecedents go back to around 1900, began by constructing sugar mills.[4]

29

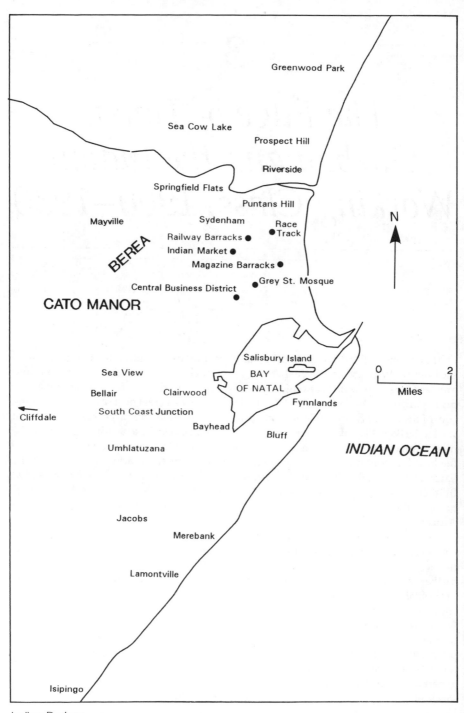

Greenwood Park

Sea Cow Lake

Prospect Hill

Riverside

Springfield Flats

Puntans Hill

Mayville

Sydenham

Race Track

Railway Barracks ●

Indian Market ●

Magazine Barracks ●

BEREA

Central Business District ●

Grey St. Mosque ●

CATO MANOR

N

Sea View

Salisbury Island

BAY OF NATAL

Bellair

Clairwood

Fynnlands

0   2
Miles

Cliffdale

South Coast Junction

Bayhead

Bluff

INDIAN OCEAN

Umhlatuzana

Jacobs

Merebank

Lamontville

Isipingo

Indian Durban

Durban held two advantages for potential manufacturers. It was a good location for those whose natural raw materials had to be brought into South Africa from overseas, and for those who could make use of Natal's agricultural base in sugar and, later, wattle. Thus the paint industry, dependent on imported ingredients, centred in Durban.[5] Another import-dependent industry was soap, dominated by Lever Brothers which began to manufacture in Durban in 1908.[6] The Rand had a much larger consuming population, however. The port and railway allowed Durban industry to sell nationally but it was very significantly outweighed by the Rand, particularly in the inter-war years, as a site of manufacturing orientated to mass urban consumption. From after World War I it was decisively outdistanced by the Rand as a manufacturing centre:[7]

TABLE 3.1 Provincial percentage of national industry

	1915/16	1922/23
CAPE	37,4	35,8
Western Cape		18,2
Port Elizabeth		4,1
TRANSVAAL	29,9	37,3
Rand-Pretoria		33,2
NATAL	25,9	22,6
Durban		12,0
ORANGE FREE STATE	4,2	4,4

Source: Bill Freund, "The Social character of Secondary Industry in South Africa 1915–45," in Alan Mabin, ed., *Organisation and Social Change* (Johannesburg; Ravan, 1989).

Under these circumstances, Durban developed into a very diversified industrial centre during the first quarter of the twentieth century, but lacking in mass production industry, however, and without a capitalist class led by a clear manufacturing strategy. By the start of the century, the city had become the site of carriage-building, wagon and ship repairs, sugar and coal-mine machinery manufacture, and wrought-iron making.[8] The pre-World War I years saw the foundation of a range of manufacturing establishments: the boat builder Henry Spradbow, a variety of timber firms such as Hunt, Leuchars and Hepburn, the Coedmore quarry, Ohlsson's Brewery, the Lion Match Company, Charles Wade and Son, a Birmingham engineering firm, the city abattoir, South African Fertilizers, Kynoch's Explosives in nearby Umbogintwini and the whaling station on the Bluff, the original ships' landing place, were amongst the best-known early companies.[9] The war witnessed rapid growth, including the foundation of Thomson, Savage, the military-clothing supplier, and Natal Cane By-Products, designed to provide industrial uses from molasses and other cane products.[10]

Durban manufactured as follows in the post-war years:[11]

TABLE 3.2   Manufacturing in Durban

Year	Number of firms	Average no. of workers	Output per worker
1929/30	585	36	£ 8 648
1939/40	850	40	£11 728
1949/50	1161	57	£18 148

Source: May Katzen, *Industry in Greater Durban I: Its Growth and Structure*, (Pietermaritz-burg: Natal Town and Regional Planning Commission, 1961).

By 1924/25, fixed capital in Durban industry reached a value of £4,5 million and the value of machinery, tools and plant £2,1 million. Those figures had doubled by 1939/40.[12] Figures show that Durban's contribution to South African industry reflected the variety of these impulses, coming from the port, from local agriculture and from the Durban consumer market:[13]

TABLE 3.3   Greater Durban's contribution to national industry

	1924/25	1937/38
Food/Drink/Tobacco	32,0%	28,1%
Chemicals	21,6	15,3
Building/Construction	11,4	8,3
Metal/Engineering	9,8	11,8
Wood/Furniture	6,3	4,6
Printing/Paper	4,9	4,6
Clothing/Textile	3,9	6,5
Non-metallic minerals	1,7	2,1
Transport equipment	1,5	1,5

Source: Katzen, *Industry in Greater Durban.*

This diversified, but to some extent interrelated, economy,[14] contained many niches serviced by an extremely diversified work-force, whose history militated against its acquiring a common sense of itself as a class and strongly lent itself to the trappings of ethnic identity. At the same time, the transport and commercial sector dominance exposed each niche to aspects of a common South African urban culture in ways that crossed the familiar lines of ethnic identity.

* * *

The urban heart of the city formed on the north end of the bay in the nineteenth century, and early industrial growth occurred on the inland shore. Paralleling the north-south line of the bay rose a long ridge which whites called the Berea. On the sea side of the ridge was the heart of urban colonial implantation, the desired residential core of the new city. Elsewhere too, north, south and inland, whites favoured the breeze-touched hillsides for their suburban residences.

By contrast, the core of Indian Durban lay elsewhere. Behind the business district lay a cheaper, denser and more lively zone where Indian traders catered for the custom of all races. At its heart was the Grey Street mosque around which were alleyways full of petty traders and small-scale manufacturers, jewellers, watch-makers, tailors, and scribes serving the illiterate.[15] This area, which had some of the classic feeling of a ghetto, was the residential heart of Durban for the passenger Indians and their descendants, and Muslims formed the largest part of its population. M.W. Swanson reports that as early as 1871 this terrain, around the undrained "Western Vlei", was being settled by Indians. It was known as the "Coolie Location" within a decade.[16] Some of the ex-indentured workers gravitated there but this was not really their turf. Many lived north of the city centre in the overpopulated and squalid barracks designed for "coolie" employees of the city and, on a smaller scale, the railways. The Magazine Barracks was an important site of Indian working-class life in Durban, but there were a number of other, smaller barracks, a word used as well for private slumyards.

On the lower slopes of the tawny hills that rise between the streams and the small alluvial plains they form, on the inland sides of the hills and particularly on the plains, the mass of those workers lived. Away from the centre, Durban had the appearance of a string of colonial commercial and residential islands set in a sea of cultivated shacklands. Here Indian families lived in low-slung, wood-and-iron houses, normally outside the municipal borders of the city, in a poorly supervised and defined zone that allowed a multiplicity of economic activity. Already by the 1880s, swampy meadows further and further afield from the centre of the town began to fill up with shanties and garden plots, often rented from whites.[17]

In 1927/28, several years before the expansion of the municipal borders took place (see chapter five), the Borough of Durban had a population estimated at about 123 000, of whom only 21 286 were listed as Indian. However, a series of surrounding communities had a population of just under 100 000 more and of those, no less than 57 000 were Indian.[18]

Table 3.4 Racial composition of Durban, 1927/28

Place	Indians*	Natives	Europeans
Durban Borough	21 286	42 100	59 600
South Coast Junction	13 850	7 250	3 036
Umhlatuzana	2 980	1 150	4 248
Malvern	1 800	1 250	3 200
Mayville	14 000	6 000	3 000
Sydenham	17 000	5 000	2 500
Pinetown	560	383	1 236
Greenwood Park	5 100	2 000	4 000

* Includes Coloureds.

Source: Natal Archives, 3/DBN, 14/4/1, Durban Borough Boundaries Commission

There were considerable advantages to this kind of life, in that largely rural people could take advantage of opportunities that the wealth of the urban economy offered, while avoiding the expensive life of the totally committed urban dweller.[19] Memories of life on the edge of town are warmed with thoughts of high-quality, cheap fish, milk, firewood and other provisions.[20] Although distance from town might add to expenses for some categories of individuals, closer to the centre the possibility of exploitation from landlords was greater.[21] Land for farming was relatively cheaply available and, as we have seen, agricultural activity aimed at the city market was intensely practised.[22] Farming was often linked to small-scale commerce, with household women often doing the selling.[23] It was accompanied by participation in a wide range of activities, including wage labour in the industrial economy. One interviewee, remembering his youth before World War I, recalled walking over the Berea Ridge to town to work in a garment factory. Other members of his family were french polishers, garment workers, builders, knitting-factory workers. At the same time, the family grew pineapples and bananas.[24] Another account records the life of a fisherman who lived in a leased wood-and-iron house near the harbour in Fynnlands but also grew bananas in what is now the black township of Umlazi.[25]

Because of its characteristic and striking cultural features, fishing has attracted some scholarly interest. Established on Salisbury Island in the bay as early perhaps as the 1860s, the fishing village was removed onto the southern mainland at Fynnlands on the Bluff during the Anglo-Boer War.[26] This was a specific community defined in terms of occupation as much as, or more than in terms of Indianness (or its predominantly Tamil character). According to a mid-century observer,

> . . . the appearance of the village clearly indicates a fishing settlement, with fishing nets drying in the sun, or hung up for repairs, derelict boats rotting on the foreshore, shove nets for shrimping, oars and fishing tackle. Salvaged wood is stacked up against the walls of dwellings . . . Generally, the interior furnishings of the dwellings in the village reflect the air of poverty which surrounds many of the fishermen's homes.[27]

A better-built section also existed, with brick houses, on land which was owned in freehold. The accessibility of shellfish, joint seine-netting ventures and the possibility of fishing on small boats was, like market gardening, the basis for an inexpensive way of life (inexpensive because so much could be done without reference to exchange in cash) that serviced the urban economy of Durban and formed the basis for the reconstructed Indian family economy in Durban.[28] It peaked in the excitement of the great sardine and other game-fish runs up the Indian Ocean seaboard of Natal.

Fishing tied together a nascent bourgeoisie of net and boat owners with a broader population with little ownership of the means of production.[29] Nonetheless there was a strong sense of co-operation in the fishing crew and a tradition of inherited family access to positions in a boat.[30] At the same time it meant independence — "I like fishing. I am my own boss. I work for nobody."[31] Fish could be sold profitably right on the beach, although stallholders marketed fish at the Indian Market. However, it meant an unsteady living on its own, especially if it was not tied to that inexpensive context, and more ambitious offspring in the inter-war years tried to escape it.[32]

Indians were not the last to participate in an uncontrolled peripheral space on the outskirts of the city where activities which were outside the law flourished and involved people of all colours. According to the social historian Paul la Hausse:

... shebeens flourished on the outskirts of Durban. There brewers such as Matshikiyana Gumede re-established their trade in Springfield, Sydenham, Cato Manor and South Coast Junction [all areas of dense Indian population]. Durban's Chief Magistrate reported that whites and Indians let rooms to 'unemployed' Africans from 'all parts of the colony' and that rooms let by Indian racketeers attracted the 'riff-raff of Durban . . . to sell this beer' Taking advantage of a loophole in the 'five mile ruling' of the Native Beer Act, and the uneven policing of the peri-urban areas, hundreds of workers moved across the Borough boundary to drink at these shebeens every weekend.[33]

Shebeens, moreover, were linked to dagga smoking and to prostitution.[34] Part of the enjoyment of the cheap life on the Durban periphery was fishing, which was in no way confined to fishermen communities. Nothing is more characteristic of the life of Indian workers in Durban than fishing from the sand or off the rocks onto the steep coastal shelf of the Indian Ocean. Fishing could provide a supplement to the diet, and an escape from the crowded house, as much as, or more than, a sporting challenge.[35]

The most crucial element in the construction of this peri-urban society was the extended family. To a white observer, the vast majority of poor Indians lived in squalid shacks whose disorder defied any sense of structured purpose. However, those wood-and-iron shacks in fact were ideally suited to the needs of their inhabitants in some respects. They could be built, repaired and extended cheaply with little reference to the construction industry.[36]

According to the 1904 census, only 13 per cent of Indian households in the vicinity of Durban were made of brick. By comparison 27 per cent were made of wattle and daub and 58 per cent of wood and iron. This compares to 63 per cent, 1 per cent and 22 per cent respectively for white households. That census reported a large number of Indians living in very cramped spaces but equally, a large number of houses, more than 800, or perhaps 15 per cent of the total, which contained five rooms and more.[37] Their sprawl reflected the joint family structure whose re-creation must have represented the single most important task of Indians coming out of the indenture experience.[38] Joint families, according to anthropologists who have studied India, have as their core partnerships between males, usually brothers or fathers and sons. They make particular economic sense for businessmen and artisans.[39] In the South African case, the relationships established may not always have followed this pattern, but they certainly represented some efficient pooling of resources aimed at making the family, by means of specialisation, an effective engine of accumulation for its members.[40] Hilda Kuper considered in an anthropological study of Indian life in Natal that "wealth belongs to families, rather than to individuals."[41] The structure of the housing Indians built for themselves in peri-urban Durban reflected the new authority of patriarchal household heads. Building and, if possible, owning a house, was enormously desirable. According to the descendant of such a patriarch, ". . . it was for a house that he planned, worked and saved. For him, the house was the foremost symbol of security and prestige" and had, containing as it would a family shrine, a sacral character.[42]

The family structures, while potentially benefitting all, were hardly characterised by equality.[43] They were instead a set of hierarchies. In particular, they were intended to harness the labour of younger members. Women, especially younger women, occupied the least prestigious place in the household. In particular, they were subordinated to the control of mothers-in-law.[44] This pattern must have been rudely broken to the advantage of younger women amongst emigrants to South Africa, but by the early twentieth century, it had reasserted itself to a significant, if undetermined, extent. Local dramatist Ronnie Govender's plays reveal, along with a good deal of sentimental retrospective on family life, not only the great extent to which control over women held a place in men's lives, but also the frequency of violence against women amongst poor men.[45]

I have argued elsewhere that whereas Indian women were often employed as agricultural and domestic workers in the colonial economy in the nineteenth century, there was a tendency towards redeployment of their labour to the general benefit of the family in the new setting.[46] The pattern that ensued was, at first sight, one of confining women to the household. This was in fact a means through which Indian families and occupational groups have historically acquired prestige.[47] In reality, however, it covered up the actuality that women's work was a mix of domestic and unpaid productive labour vital to the range of activities in which the family engaged; activities that would include commerce, agriculture and wage labour. In exposing this fallacy, a feminist writer on India reflects that "women's work is defined as non-work, as a natural extension of their anatomy, or as a 'natural resource.'"[48] In fact such work can be strategised in many different directions, including entrepreneurial activity and wage labour.[49] "Usually one form of subsistence production is not sufficient to guarantee survival but a combination of several is required . . ."[50]

An acute white observer noted in 1903 that "a free Indian made his wife and children work as well as himself."[51] The result was a context that powerfully affirmed the family economy in the new continental surroundings. For women, it was difficult to live outside the family setting. It was in their interest to make the broader family enterprise work. The view of an anthropologist studying Tamil speakers in Sri Lanka is apposite: The family institution "keeps women in a double-bind situation, because the family not only exploits and oppresses; it is also only through the family that women can expect support and protection."[52]

Life for a woman alone was certainly very difficult. When bad fortune forced a woman to sustain herself, perhaps with descendants, she had to resort to one of a narrow range of possibilities. One writer remembered the existence in Cato Manor of a woman exorcist.[53] Slightly less exotic possibilities included midwifery and the arrangement of marriages.[54] In India, midwives were typically poor widows or deserted women whose employment was organised by their prospective customers' mothers-in-law; they were considered little better than "inferior menials," especially in the countryside.[55] As with African women on the Reef and elsewhere, taking in washing was another option.[56]

The conventional picture of the Indian household in India centres around dowry as the basis for legitimate marriage. When Tinker noted the presence of brideprice amongst overseas indentured Indians, he assumed it derived from the scarcity of Indian women outside the sub-continent. However, in practice, in poorer households in many parts of India, especially the south, brideprice is common and reflects the extent to which a woman is considered to be entering the household in order to sustain it financially through the sweat of her brow.[57] Her role is defined, though, in terms of subsistence.[58]

∗∗∗

To what extent was the establishment of a familial order part of a process of *community* formation? Networks formed outside the family creating a sense of neighbourhood. Relationships — for instance between landlord and tenant — might combine exploitation with cultural and credit links that bound people together in terms outside the cash nexus.[59] Men would gather to play games of chance and to drink (often on credit) in a masculine world independent of the family.[60] They would sit over *thanni*, a form of cards resembling bridge.[61] Gambling, for instance forms of betting on numbers, flourished.[62] This shaded into a less respectable world that attracted many Indian males, a doubtful milieu where fighting, drinking and vandalism could be noted on the part of men who "gamble with Natives and drink cheap wine."[63] There was thus the possibility of intense integration into religious, linguistic and family networks and some possibility of escape from these tightly woven webs.

Temples and shrines dotted the landscape. Rambling homesteads were fitted to provide for domestic shrines appropriate to memorials and sacrifices.[64] Rituals which focused on specific divine incarnations, typical of village India, arrived early. After 1900, visiting scholars brought more philosophical and reformed versions of Hindu belief, particularly to those of north-Indian origin with claims to a higher caste background.[65] The Barracks (and no doubt peripheral areas, one of which is still famous for its fire-walking ceremonial) witnessed a variety of Hindu ritual performances, Tamil religious dramas and six-foot dances.[66] These were activities that were seen and participated in by the whole community, men and women.

Rarely were neighbourhoods comprised only of people speaking the same home language.[67] Indeed, predominantly Hindu neighbourhoods often contained Muslims and Christians. They also could not really be defined in class terms. Indian writers always talk about the doers and the shakers of society, the "lahnees,"[68] whether whites or those within the Indian world, but class interpenetration powerfully reinforced bonds of commerce and service that linked people up and made the community a resource-rich human network.

If caste had at most a shadowy importance, language and religion survived as important social building-blocks. Intermarriage across these lines, as we have seen, was rare. More difficult to explain, but more important from a general South African perspective, was the development of a sense of Indianness. For one thing, the spatial concentration of the Indian population in and around Durban, a very segregated city, was very intense if far from absolute.[69] The urban periphery did contain people of all colours, but the social networks that reinforced Indianness, partially through religion and through language, were very powerful. There was much to link the immigrants from north and south India together in terms of common cultural discourse.

One might imagine the gap between all the ex-indentured and the descendants of the merchant class would have been greater. In the nineteenth century, for instance, the latter were often favoured with the appellation of "Arab" and there are seeds for the development of this grouping into a separate racial category. Working against this, however, was the extent to which traders, even if they were Muslims, were linked to other Indians. It was the presence of the indentured workers as potential customers that had lured them to Natal. The merchant class was vital as providers of credit and sometimes shelter or employment. The biography of the Muslim Indian community leader, A.I. Kajee, is full of minor references to clients and employees with south-Indian names.[70]

If relationships were exploitative at times, they could also be benevolent. The working class gained from the significant presence of Indian charitable institutions, well established by the 1930s.[71] Gerdener estimated that by 1952 some 44 such organisations had been formed either by Indians or as a joint white-Indian effort.[72] Many of these had no specific religious or regional character. Moreover, they were inured from India to being part of a broader social world that included both Hindu and Muslim. An important minority of the merchant class, including M.K. Gandhi himself, were in fact Hindu. Of course, the intense sense of racial nationalism developed by the whites of Natal powerfully reinforced the sense that "Indians" were a common category of people with whom it was only natural for law and custom to deal as a race apart.

The question of relations with Africans is much shadowier. In a number of texts rich in memory of life in peripheral Durban, I have been surprised at the complete non-appearance of Africans, that is at the extent to which the community is remembered as Indian.[73] The evidence of relationship is clearer for the countryside, where Indians often became fluent Zulu speakers and very occasionally sex and marriage took place across a cultural divide. There was very little indeed in the way of assimilation of Indians into African social structure, however. Peripheral Durban included a significant number of Africans with wavering commitments to the city and the urban economy. Here, especially on the inland side of Berea Ridge, Cato Manor Farm was the site of the most mixing between African and Indian. Africans were tenants of Indian landowners, customers of Indian shopkeepers, and neighbours, although there was a strong tendency, here too, towards neighbourhood clustering.

On the other hand, Indians constituted a distinct labour market as we shall see. In the workplace, the work was done by racially and gender defined work groups. The problems of coping with white dominance in the more desirable sectors of the working class will be touched on below. With regard to Africans, it is important to stress that before World War II, the African population in Durban was heavily male, overwhelmingly migrant, and had a limited commitment to the urban economy. In certain sectors, such as domestic service for private households, rickshaw pullers and dockers, African migrants were the dominant force. However, in other spheres, they were scarcely to be found. If Indians escaped proletarianisation to some degree through harnessing resources on the edge of town, Africans chose instead to combine the advantages of the town wage with the rural resources of a more distant home. This choice was partially governed by the state making it difficult for Africans to own property outside the African reserves.

✳✳✳

The above discussion has tended to focus on the features of Indian life that reinforced conservatism and created an inward-looking ethnic community within which the four-pronged identification of race, language, religion and family, served to define one's place in the world. However, there was another side of Indian life as well which was drawn as by a magnet into a new South African urban culture. This was the brittle, seductive, consumer culture of an affluent colonial port. For many, the specific, often crude and even violent, racism of the locally dominant whites did not take away from the attraction. Survival in fact meant a deference in daily behaviour to whites — who controlled the streets in the centre of town.[74] Nothing is in fact more remarkable about the Indians, and notably the descendants of the indentured Indians, than this bipolar cultural universe which they made their own, a house with one door shut to the world and another appeallingly swung open.

The contrast has never been so well portrayed as in the recent memoir of growing up in Pretoria, Jay Naidoo's *Coolie Location*. Naidoo's background was Tamil — the Pretoria location housed a Tamil teacher who "named, married, buried, drafted out wedding cards, wrote out epitaphs, read the stars and designed the Temple"[75] — but in some respects he belonged to a different world than the periphery of Durban. His location was close to the centre of the Afrikaner capital, Pretoria, and his father was more of a petty bourgeois than a worker; he had a market-stall. But there were plenty of Tamil boys like Naidoo on the Durban periphery who also dreamt of escape from the ghetto. Naidoo spoke an extraordinary Indianised English with distinctive expressions that belonged only to his hybrid world. He portrays his family world and the Tamil school (which he loathed), but also his obsession with soccer, with the cinema and the glamorous world of white women which filled his fantasies.

The first two obsessions, at least, are equally manifest in the pages of the Indian press of Durban. Every week's cinema showings (Indian entrepreneurs opened cinemas in Durban after World War I) were discussed with enthusiasm. At their peak, there were at least twelve Indian-owned cinemas in Durban showing Hollywood films. The Rawat, popular in the early 1920s, was characterised by "hard wooden benches, 'Globe' kitchen chairs and basket chairs for the more discerning."[76]

Soccer and boxing were followed passionately. Benny Singh, the boxing promoter whose father ran a billiard saloon around the turn of the century, lived in a world of jazz joints, ballroom dancing and sport.[77] The venue for much of this activity lay close to, but outside, the densely Indian urban environment around the Grey Street mosque and clustered shops. Gambling on horse-races united Indian men with their counterparts among whites and Africans; it was a major part of the civic culture of Durban.

Soccer was taken up by Indian boys for the first time in the middle 1880s. By 1886, the Indians of Durban sported four clubs.[78] The Bluebells, founded in 1884, were remembered as the first team. Early soccer was associated with service workers, especially waiters, who would have spoken English and closely observed the mores of English working-class men, and with the small community of Indian Christians, although Hindus and Muslims came to take it up with enthusiasm.[79] Early matches took place on the edge of the Indian business district near the Squatters' Market. Sports clubs were very important organisations in which officiation and participation were as crucial as the events on the sporting field themselves.[80]

In the inter-war years, boxing was important both as a sport for Indian boys attracted to urban life, and as a business opportunity for potential managers and promoters.[81] The arrival of Mbata, an African fighter, around 1938, began to alter the earlier dominance of Coloured and Indian boys in "non-European" boxing.[82] In the 1940s African boxers largely took over from Indians as the focus of attention in the press and the promotion business.[83]

Contact with Coloureds, particularly for Christians or Muslims who might share a bond of faith with them, was more intense than with Africans or whites. Indeed, Coloured links with the latter groups in turn created more distant influences on Indians. A set of family papers reveals the extent to which the Christian Indian bourgeoisie married amongst Coloureds and became part of families which included whites. This led to involvement both in "passing for white" and a trickle of emigration, even in the first third of the century, out of South Africa and its system of racial identification.[84]

There were, as well, a small number of Hindu passenger Indians from localities other than the west coast, particularly coming to Natal via Mauritius, like the tobacco farmer and cigar industrialist, Chetty, or the family of Dr Goonam, which also served as models of advancement through commerce and education. Indians in Durban were able through work, through leisure and through observation, increasingly to assimilate aspects of a racially diverse, colonially created, urban South African world while still retaining a basic and in some respects deepening identification with a neo-Indian, home-based culture.

* * *

The existence of windows of opportunity in the cultural and economic sense should not blind us, however, to a basic fact about the existence of Indian life in Durban: harsh poverty and crude discrimination. Towards the end of the inter-war period, a social science literature emerged which focused on Indians as a "problem", partially a response to white racism which wished to exclude a resented and potentially competitive population and partially a response to the very real extent of Indian poverty. A survey as late as 1943/44 estimated that 70,6 per cent of Indians lived below the established Poverty Datum Line.[85] Visiting Durban from Pretoria, a youthful Jay Naidoo was startled at the sight of Indians sweeping the streets and collecting trash, "menial tasks reserved for Africans" in the Transvaal.[86]

That poverty manifested itself in poor diets, high infant mortality rates and diseases of deprivation. Moreover, unemployment seemed to be a particular characteristic of Indian society.[87] Dr Goonam, back from Edinburgh at the height of the Depression, writes as a moderniser and improver about a people prey to ignorance and superstition, in her memories of Indian life in Durban in the 1930s:

> During my home visits, I discovered the depth of Indian poverty. The staple diet was mealie rice, dholl [beans], herbs, potatoes and pickles. Protein was sadly lacking, meat, fish and chicken beyond their reach.[88]

A slightly later account considered as a truism that "protein deficiency is general."[89] Halliday suggested in his 1940 study of market gardeners that they lived in good part on bread, maize meal, and lentils with little money for fruit and vegetables, and butter a luxury. Cheap meat was to some extent available.[90]

At first sight, it seems that Indian workers were squeezed between a white working class that wanted to push them out and a class of black migrant workers who were hardier labourers and prepared to undercut the poor wages Indians received. The actual wage levels of the Indian population were quite pitiful. Contemporary images of Indians as an intermediary stratum between white and African are inappropriate for the period before World War II: most Indians were considered

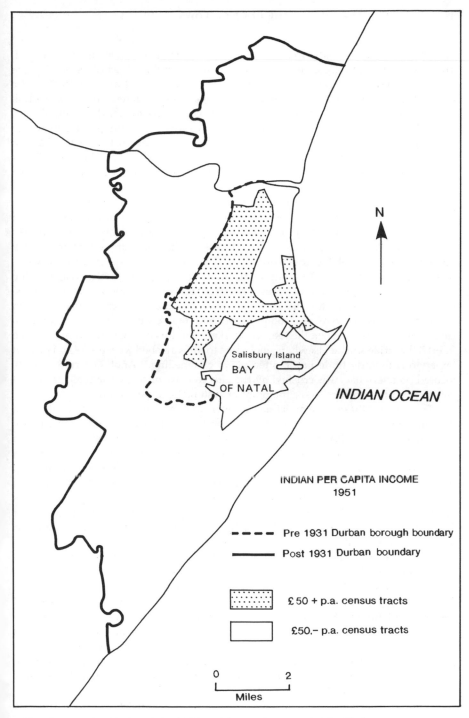

N

Salisbury Island

BAY

OF NATAL

INDIAN OCEAN

INDIAN PER CAPITA INCOME
1951

- - - Pre 1931 Durban borough boundary

—— Post 1931 Durban boundary

£ 50 + p.a. census tracts

£50.– p.a. census tracts

0   2
Miles

Indian income levels correlated with residence, inner and outer Durban

(L. Kuper, et al., *Durban: A study in Racial Ecology*.
London: Jonathan Cape, 1958.)

unskilled and had no real purchase on wages any better than the Africans enjoyed. There is no reason to disagree with Arkin's assessment that "it would seem that the majority of Indian workers who were employed between 1860 and 1910 in the agricultural and mining industries earned wages little different to those of black unskilled workers."[91] Moreover, this situation continued for the large number of Indian labourers through the period after Union as well. According to Katzen, wages per annum for Indian workers averaged £52 in 1924/25, £68 in 1929/30 and £63 in 1934/35. This compares with £39 in 1924/25, £43 in 1929/30 and £43 in 1934/35 for Africans. This does reveal that a differential did exist and that it widened during the 1920s to some extent, but it remained very small. By comparison white wages in this period were calculated at £238, £240 and £201, three to five times as much.[92]

The picture here, however, needs qualification and further development. What did make a difference was that the proportion of labourers was smaller in the Indian than in the African population. Nonetheless, Indian labourers remained very numerous throughout the pre-World War II period. When the indentured cane-workers went on strike in 1913 to support Gandhi's campaign, in particular against the £3 tax, the strike spread spontaneously to other sectors of the Indian working class, indentured and free. Factory hands went out and so did even domestic workers in white homes. They were all "coolies" and had the sense of sharing a common condition.[93] Similarly, when the tobacco workers employed by Chetty went on strike in 1917, the strike spread elsewhere, including to railway-shed workers — and proved impervious to early trade union attempts at channelling.[94] Another strike in 1920, focused on overwork, was crushed by the effective use of scabs relatively easily.[95] It was difficult for workers to see the point of systematic organisation.

The life of those Indian labourers working for the city is relatively well documented and reveals the harshness of conditions. This remained a particularly large group of unskilled workers: as late as 1945, less than 10 per cent of Indian workers for Durban municipality were graded in terms of any skill at all.[96] £2 a month wages were still typical in the late 1930s.[97] Health records reveal the prevalence of tuberculosis amongst them throughout the 1940s.[98] Dysentery and malnutrition were also common.[99] There was little protection for such categories of the population as much-exploited child workers in the tobacco industry.[100] In 1945, it was estimated that 70 per cent of families were seriously in debt.[101] No less than 62 per cent of income had to be devoted to food.[102]

As late as 1945, neither latrines nor shelter were provided for the municipal workers on break.[103] Health and safety conditions were very poor.[104] A 1921 report had revealed that the 707 rooms in the Magazine Barracks contained no less than 3,5 people per room on average. The barracks were notoriously insanitary and overcrowded. Built in 1880, they were considered a scandal and had been condemned as early as 1914.[105] An expansion programme did result in the erection of improved double-storey brick edifices but these were hopelessly insufficient. By 1933, the population exceeded 5 000, with more than 4 to a room. Two-room flats for large families were typical. So were the communal toilets and taps.[106] In 1944, resident numbers had grown further to reach 6 000.[107]

Workers were considered, however, to be under a paternalist regime, bearing the stamp of the indentured era. Allowing for the very poor conditions, rents were kept quite low.[108] Workers, until as late as 1940, received rations in lieu of pay and it was seriously claimed that they would otherwise be inclined to neglect their families.[109]

Even after 1940, rations were offered with fixed payments for basic commodities.[110] Inside the barracks, the city attempted to enforce controls that would prevent the freedom Indians enjoyed on the urban periphery. By-laws prohibited the sheltering of non-relatives in rooms, ordered obedience to the caretaker, limited trade and closed the barracks gates between 7 p.m. and 6 a.m.[111] Those no longer in the employ of the city, including widows, were expected to decamp immediately.[112]

Conditions for railway workers were just as bad. It was said that even in the 1940s, there were literally two bathrooms for 1 000 persons.[113] The Indian press editorialised in 1943 that "the Indian worker on the railway is one of, if not, the lowest paid of all workers in Durban."[114] And this after many years of state policy to eliminate Indian employment on the railways in favour of whites and Coloureds whenever possible; for this reason in fact, few Indian railway workers were anything but labourers. Despite these appalling conditions, it is remarkable that barracks life also contained a dense human texture and was redolent with a feeling of community.[115] Squalor and disease were coupled with close-knit social networks, making for security and a myriad of petty ways of adding to one's income, notably for the wives and children of workers for the municipality.

✳ ✳ ✳

Looking away from this particularly oppressed sector of the working class, however, the Indian working population exhibited a surprising amount of diversity. In 1904 the Natal census captured the following categories of workers amongst Natal Indians:

Table 3.5 Occupations of Indian males with 10+ workers

Durban Borough

Agents	15	
Accountants/Bookkeepers	35	
Barbers/assistants	57	
Barmen	10	
Boot/Shoemakers	42	(compared to 46 white males)
Bricklayers/assistants	55	
Butchers	17	
Carpenters/assistants	103	
Carriers/Carters	160	(compared to 72 white males)
Cigar/Cigarette makers	41	
Clerks	61	
Coachmen/Grooms	33	(compared to 61 white males)
Cooks	214	(compared to 44 white males)
Domestic servants	429	(compared to 78 Indian females and 329 white females)
Dhobis (laundry workers)	274	
Firemen/Stokers	133	(compared to 121 white males)
Fishermen	35	(compared to 27 white males)

Table 3.5 (continued)

Durban Borough (continued)

Fruiterers	70	
Grocers/assistants	28	
Gardeners	122	(compared to 22 white males)
Hawkers	734	(compared to 54 females)
"Independents"	27	
Jewellers/assistants	158	(compared to 67 white males)
General labourers	3 530	(compared to 198 white males)
Natal Gov. Rwy. labourers	19	(compared to 98 white males)
Municipal employees	413	(compared to 92 white males)
Messengers	67	
Ministers/Priests	19	
Mineral water manufacturers	14	(compared to 29 white males)
Painters	28	
Printers/Compositors	33	
Plumbers/Tinsmiths	40	
Police	10	
Produce merchants	26	(compared to 72 whites)
Storekeepers, general	318	(compared to 121 whites)
Store assistants	333	(compared to 390 whites)
Tailors/assistants	92	(compared to 138 whites)
Waiters	299	(compared to 38 white males and 27 white females)

Umlazi district

Bakers/Confectioners	27	(compared to 10 white males)
Barbers/assistants	25	
Basket makers	35	(compared to 5 women)
Bricklayers	31	(compared to 59 white males)
Carpenters/assistants	29	
Carriers/Carters	62	(compared to 11 white males)
Clerks	53	(compared to 187 white males)
Coachmen/Grooms	20	
Cultivators, small	169	
Dhobis	170	
Domestic servants	323	(compared to 58 Indian women)
Farmers/assistants	184	(compared to 186 white males)
Fruiterers	27	
Firemen	31	
Fishermen	63	
Fruit growers	700	(compared to 37 white males)
Farm labourers	3 476	(compared to 463 females)
Grocers	38	(compared to 25 white males)
Gardeners	1 634	(compared to 107 females)

Table 3.5 (continued)

Umlazi District (continued)

Hawkers	162	(compared to 15 females)
Jewellers	53	
Labourers	127	(compared to 38 white males)
Natal Gov. Rwy. labourers	77	
Ministers	18	
Police	10	
Painters	31	(compared to 42 white males)
Printers	25	(compared to 11 white males)
Paupers	13	
Porters	27	
Planters, general	55	
Quarrymen	56	
General storekeepers	176	(compared to 39 white males)
Assistant storekeepers	71	(compared to 49 white males)
Sirdars (overseers)	49	
Teleg. messengers	12	
Waiters	107	

Source: Natal Blue Books, Census of 1904.

Unfortunately for comparative purposes, numbers of Africans by profession were not tabulated. Certainly petty commodity producers and labourers are in the great majority, but individuals who can primarily be counted as skilled labour are clearly enumerated.

Early reports indicate that Indian workers quickly acquired a practical range of skills apart from those they had brought with them from peasant society in the sub-continent.[116] Neame reported at the turn of the century that he could note Indian fitters, turners, carpenters, bricklayers, painters, coppersmiths and wheelwrights, amongst others.[117] The most acute opposition to Indian indentured immigration arose from white Durban when, in 1896, the Tongaat Sugar Company started to import skilled workers on indenture, a move that would have struck at the heart of the protectionist requirements of white skilled workers.[118]

A more tolerated exception lay in service work. The cream of domestic workers were able to put forward an image of multi-skilling that made them invaluable to white employers of the early twentieth century. As late as 1947, an old family retainer was described as follows in a testimonial that reveals an old-fashioned employer's outlook:

> Indian Gengiah (Atchia) is an Indian who anyone can trust implicitly — He was personal servant to the late Hon. J. Baynes and after that to the later Mr. John Grant — This Indian is honest and reliable, a good house boy, an excellent cook, and very capable when in charge of gangs of natives and indians — I have no hesitation in recommending him to anyone.[119]

While Gengiah stayed in a rich man's private service, many such workers shifted relatively readily to skilled service work for commercial enterprises.[120]

In the sugar mills themselves, Indians acquired footholds by stages in more skilled jobs. However, it was typically Mauritian whites and "Creoles" who controlled the most skilled work, that of panboilers, passing it on from father to son. Boilers earned five to ten times the wage of an unskilled caneworker, far more than other skilled categories such as overseers and mule drivers.[121] Only very gradually did Indians penetrate this well-paid category of labour.[122] Even then, whites were far better paid.[123] A periodical biography captures the life of a successful entrepreneur in the metal trade who founded his workshop in 1914, on the Durban periphery near the Umgeni river. He learnt from his father, an ex-indentured worker, who had risen to the position of assistant to the mill engineer at Ottawa around the turn of the century.[124]

The original Defy opened in 1904, making moulded hollow metal blocks with three Indian workers on a staff of eight.[125] By 1908, the Indian press was reporting that some early manufacturers were entirely dependent on ex-indentured Indian hands; however, there was not so much a preference for Indian workers as an inability to find white workers at the wage offered.[126] Industry became steadily more important as a source of employment for Indians. By 1936, Natal Indian workers were primarily divided between agriculture (37,8 per cent), services (20,4 per cent), manufacturing (19,1 per cent) and commerce (16,1 per cent) with agriculture beginning to decline rapidly.[127]

Manufacturing would steadily increase its share amongst Indian workers into the 1970s, becoming the biggest sector by the time of the 1951 census. A sectoral analysis of Indian manufacturing workers in the early period revealed that in 1917, 64,0 per cent were concentrated in food, beverages and tobacco with some 9,8 per cent in chemicals and 5,2 per cent in metals and engineering. By 1929, the first sector had significantly diminished in favour of a range of other industries; furniture, chemicals, metals and engineering, but particularly clothing and textiles:[128]

Table 3.6 Percentage composition of the Indian labour force in select branches of manufacture

	1917	1929	1936
Food, drink, tobacco	64,0%	48,3%	38,0%
Chemicals	9,8	5,6	3,5
Metals/engineering	5,2	6,5	7,8
Clothing/textiles	2,8	12,3	20,2
Furniture	2,5	5,3	4,7
Books/printing	2,3	3,6	3,8
Leather/leatherware	1,1	3,2	5,3

Source: Alan Arkin, *Contribution of the Indians to the South African Economy, 1860–1970.* (Durban: University of Durban-Westville, Institute for Social and Economic Research, 1981)

Indian skilled workers had great difficulty in gaining formal recognition for their skills. The stereotyped view was that they were men of all trades who knew a bit of this and a bit of that and were not really worth the skilled man's hire, more handymen than genuine artisans.[129] Maurice Evans observed, for example, that the children of indentured Indians "often took employment in the less arduous callings, as waiters, cooks, drivers, office boys, etc. They seem addicted to change and some take up one calling after another with intervals of idleness."[130] This could have been said to some extent for white Natalians too, but they were able to use flexibility effectively and direct their children into formally acknowledged skills when business opportunities began to be limited. The pattern continued, too: a survey of the unemployed in the 1930s revealed many working-class Indian men who had learnt a trade but few who systematically practised only that trade.[131]

However, white exclusionism was a crucial feature in their inability actually to get skilled recognition. The colonial economy of Natal, for a long while, did not define "trades so sharply as in England." Natal did not attract many immigrants from Britain but some that did come were able to rise spectacularly from humble origins.[132] As urban society in Natal became more competitive, definitions were tightened.[133] It was in fact useful to have a class of artisans who could be employed in good times — but at a discount — and dismissed when times were hard. Whites considered Indian workers as less skilled in substance, but then they did their best to make sure that this would be the case.[134] The educational requirements of the Apprenticeship Act, as well as the prejudices of employers, were used to block Indian acquisition of prized skills. One of the commonest tales from the memory of working-class Indians in Durban is this one of exclusion from and marginality in a craft.[135]

Whites in Durban had been organising themselves in skilled trade unions since the carpenters, in 1882, and the printers, in 1888, had made a start. Protection of relatively high wages and definition of craft skills was their central purpose and the temptation to establish a racial barrier (perhaps including Coloured with white workers, however) was overwhelming.[136] White workers often refused to allow Indian members into their unions.[137] The folk wisdom amongst Indians was that "the union was there to keep you out."[138] Indians were rarely able to secure apprenticeships; one account actually reports the case of an Indian building contractor unable to register his own workers as apprentices in the late 1920s.[139]

Perhaps the most crucial skill of all is modern education. By 1904, 19,1 per cent of Indian males (and a tiny proportion, only 2,6 per cent, of females) were listed as literate by the census, although it is not clear what the term literacy would have meant to census-takers in this period.[140] The Christian Indian community was vital in the diffusion of interest in and provision for Western education amongst the families of the indentured immigrants. Substantial interest in it began to build up after World War I. By 1928 something like half of Indian boys (but only a small minority of girls) were getting a minimum of schooling; the equipment and structures available for Indian schools were very poor, however.[141] Education before the Depression was a ladder to a better life for only very few poor boys, let alone girls.

Indians began to organise into unions in the World War I phase, in the very period when white workers in South Africa were particularly militant. The first phase of organisation had a strong ethnic character. Early strikes emerged as strikes of Indians, ethnically specific.[142] A central figure was the Revd Bernard Sigamoney, who made contact with sympathetic white trade-unionists and through them, the International Socialist League (an antecedent of the Communist Party of South Africa as a force to the left of the Labour Party) and helped create the "Indian Workers Union" before 1917.[143] Born in Durban, he was a key figure in the popularisation of both socialism and Christianity among the Indian working class and also a great sporting fan.[144] A leading boxing promoter described "Benny" as a man who "would as soon be at a bout as preach a sermon."[145] Sigamoney began his career as a teacher, but trained in England to be an Anglican priest in a phase of life somewhat later than his socialist activist phase.[146] The example of the Christian Indian community, adaptable and attuned as they were to linkages in the wider society, was important; so was the site where union meetings took place — the heart of the ghetto where Indian merchants formed a hive of economic activities, physically very distant from the outlying areas where poor workers mainly resided. Yet the early material produced by Sigamoney and his friends had to be written in Tamil and Telugu.

Sigamoney pointed out that the organisation of Indian workers was necessary precisely in order to promote Indian employment; it was a response to Indian exclusion and to the absolute preference of most white employers for white workers. In the words of his collaborator, the Christian Indian lawyer Albert Christopher, unions were about helping the Indian to rise in "the industrial world."[147] On this basis, despite the radical impulse that came from Sigamoney's ISL contacts, the Indian unions received some sympathetic support not only from the Indian bourgeoisie, but also from the High Commission of the Government of India.[148]

These unions struggled under conditions which were far from favourable, particularly beyond the volatile post-World War I years when whites and Africans were also involved in strike action in Durban. Whites were fearful of their high-wage situations being swamped by Indians without the formal skills. In some trades, for instance those related to metal working and sections of the chemical industry, white skilled workers were fairly successful at guarding their positions effectively. Indians in the metal trades were defined as occupying the lowest skill levels, effectively as tinsmiths who could produce articles for the "native" trade. When bakery vans and motorised delivery of other articles became commonplace, it was considered the prerogative of whites to be the drivers while Indians remained for a time confined to driving horse-drawn vehicles.[149] However, in consumer industries, this exclusion proved more difficult. The furniture trade, with growing employment of Indian workers, was extremely vulnerable to undercutting.[150]

With the partial exception of furniture workers and hotel employees' unions, none of the Indian unions of the 1920s secured recognition. Early attempts at organising municipal labourers to address the question of rations seem to have lost impetus.[151] The furniture workers' union was devastated in a 1925 strike. The laundry workers' union died in the Depression.[152] Other groups where union activity began included the printers, the shop assistants, hotel employees, sugar mill workers, bakers' van drivers and dockworkers.[153]

By the 1920s, the Indian population was a characteristic element in the Durban economy. It formed 25 per cent of the wage-earning population in 1924/25, a percentage which was equalled a decade later.[154] Its customs, its food, its amusement, its religions, were a moulding force in the urban context. The Indian working class entered into relations with the Indian middle class as well as with other elements in the city population. Culturally it exhibited a distinct, in some respects rigidly bounded, community consciousness, but it was also a consciousness that contained windows and doors open to the wider environment. The great success of the Indians on the edge of town lay in combining access to a rather hostile urban environment (dominated by a nervous and arrogant threatened white core population) with a cheap way of life that avoided much of the rigours of proletarianisation.[155]

However, the bourgeoisie of Durban, of whom only a small if very significant section were themselves Indian, showed little acuity in making use of this population, which was certainly cheaper and poorer than the white population but more committed to urban life and orientated to urban skills than the African population, in order to fuel the process of capital accumulation from the city. Instead, establishment views fantasised a city without Indians and hoped many would be induced to emigrate to India. The Indians were a kind of "surplus" and the "Indian problem" often was seen as one of unemployment and redundant population. With the onset of the Depression and under the inspiration of the Pact government, authority saw the answer in firing Indians to give jobs to whites.[156] According to the Town Clerk in 1935:

> Indians are not eligible for membership in the Durban Municipal Employees Society which is a trade union mainly responsible for looking after the interests of its members. *The policy of replacing Indians by Europeans* [my emphasis] has been carried out as far as the Council can, with advantage. There are certain jobs, however, of a "dead end" nature which an Indian values, gives efficient service therein, and is prepared to spend his working lifetime thereat, which would not satisfy nor be carried out efficiently by a European lad.[157]

Indians had a hard struggle to advance in such a milieu.

4

"It is my Work":
Labour Segmentation and Militancy, 1935–1960

> *One (white) man in Grey Street was vainly endeavouring to fill his cart, when a huge crowd of Indians, boys and men, gathered around him and hooted and jeered as the man strove with the pipes. He wisely took no notice of the crowd or of the Indian who claimed that No. 7 was his cart, and no European loafer should be entitled to drive it. "It is my work," the coolie kept reiterating.*[1]

When, after 1933, the industrial economy of South Africa began to recover from the Depression on the back of the increased price of gold, a remarkable phase ensued in Durban. Indian workers became, in the words of a veteran Communist Party activist, "the most militant workers in South Africa during the 1940s."[2] At least in Durban, this was a fair assessment for the period from the mid-1930s to the end of the 1940s. White worker militancy, which had been very significant around the period of World War I, had faded considerably. African workers did engage in a few important strikes after 1939, but these were not sustained in an effective comparable movement.[3]

This chapter seeks to investigate why this militant phase occurred, why it ended, and how to understand its significance. To some extent, a literature addressing these questions does exist. Simultaneous with this phase there occurred a revolution in Indian political life in Natal. Between 1939 and 1945 radicals challenged the leadership of the Natal Indian Congress in a complex series of manoeuvres that Swan has called a "continuous process of amalgamation, dissolution and reamalgamation."[4] In a stimulating but brief discussion, Swan notes that this process of radicalisation was accompanied by the rise of people, of more modest class backgrounds, antagonistic to the "merchant class" which had assumed political leadership and monopolised it in pursuing narrow business interests of their own. The key figures in this process were members of the Communist Party of South Africa. Paradoxically, while radicalisation was powerfully influenced by nationalist politics in India, and in an early phase was actually called the "national bloc" in tribute to this influence, it represented a deeper engagement with, and commitment to, assimilation into South African society.

Swan follows Frene Ginwala in recognising the importance of radical trade-unionism in changing the nature of Indian politics during this period.[5] Some of the most memorable figures amongst the young Turks in Indian politics had made their mark in labour struggles. That trade union activity helped to build Indian radicalism, is acceptable as a general principle, but it fails to explain the absence of a reverse influence. Why did Indian trade union activity neither remain militant nor become part of the politics of resistance to which Ginwala and Swan point? With what impact did the new politics, defined as an alliance of oppressed non-white peoples against the white-run government of South Africa, react on the Indian working class and its organisations?

During the 1980s, when the anti-apartheid opposition radicalised, some members of the new generation effectively took the Natal Indian Congress to task for having abandoned working-class politics in favour of an ethnic tag. The leaders of the NIC, according to critics, had left the mass of Indian workers in the lurch, having lost interest in class issues. In particular, this approach has been characterised by the rediscovery of non-racialism as a strategy and a cause in at least the earlier phases of militant Indian working-class activity of the 1930s and 1940s. Might it not have been possible rather to build up a movement that resisted racial divisions in the work place and had a strongly class character? This is certainly the implication of the thoughtful and impressively researched study written by Vishnu Padayachee, Shahid Vawda and Paul Tichman.[6] Padayachee et al. are very conscious of the growing conservatism of Indian workers from the 1950s and set their concerns within the context of a problematic of racial division that held negative consequences for the future.

While sympathetic to this approach, I wish rather to concentrate on the structural features which make the development and decline of Indian working-class militancy more logical and to a greater extent determined by the actual features of the industrial labour market. I wish to investigate the relationship of militancy and other forms of behaviour to economic and social pressures and changes. As such, this chapter continues to explore themes in an essay that I wrote on the social composition of labour in the industrialisation process on the Rand up to 1945.[7] The purpose of that essay was to try and look at the changing labour market in complex ways that go beyond the crude assumptions of writers who either rely on "market" forces or the "state" to explain economic change. Indian militancy and its decline help to shape the economic and social history of Durban as a whole. Undoubtedly the militants linked to the Communist Party of South Africa and the Natal Indian Congress did abandon the ideal of working-class unity for a more ethnic kind of politics but the structural reasons for their so doing were understandable and quite compelling.

Despite the harsh conditions in which Indian workers were living, even at the end of this period, one can profitably draw a parallel with white workers, workers who had previously been extremely militant but had become incorporated into a mainstream political consensus in which it proved possible to serve the interests of white working-class people to a considerable extent.[8] At first sight, it would seem that the position of Indians and whites had little in common. Not only did Indians suffer from harshly racist attitudes on the part of whites, they also lacked the vote, the possession of which, according to most historians, was crucial in explaining why white workers were able to improve their position dramatically over time. However, Indian workers shared with whites the legal right to strike at all times and to organise in trade unions. Once the indenture system came to an end Indians could, unlike

Africans, change jobs without hindrance in Natal. Moreover, it is important to remember that throughout the twentieth century, white workers have often opted for incorporative trade union strategies with regard to other workers, even while maintaining their own dominant position in the labour market and skill hierarchy, as much and as frequently as they have opted for total exclusiveness.

A major determinant of change before the apartheid era, was the impact of Wage Board determinations, introduced by the Pact government (in which the Labour Party was represented) after 1924. If the Wage Board could guarantee a relatively high wage for the job, Indians would be apt to be excluded from that job. However, Wage Board determinations could at times come to the rescue of the Indian against the competition of "low-wage" Africans. Another related differential was the relatively much more favourable legal position of the Indian worker compared to the African in terms of the right to organise and to strike. This encouraged the Indians to form effective trade unions on their own, or with whites and Coloureds. African membership could only be registered informally or through parallel sections that had no legal right to strike. For capital, this created a long-term temptation to break through closure by taking on non-unionised African workers. As with whites before them, Indians were attracted to militancy in response to this threat, precisely because of their structural vulnerability. Reaching out to African workers had a real strategic logic.

A striking feature of the industrial economy of Durban is the conjuncture of occupation and ethnicity, of job and race. The labour market is highly segmented; workers choose or are assigned positions (at least until very recently) by gender and race. Indeed such segmentation helps to define ethnicity, as well as to be determined by it, in the circumstances of a competitive labour market. Segmentation may be linked to skill, or perceptions of skill. It defines different labour pools that can operate in the market under very different conditions because they exhibit specific strengths and weaknesses. Indians were conventionally associated with particular sectors of the labour market.

In the hard circumstances workers face, a key tactic that can also fit into capitalist strategies is closure for a self-defined group. Capitalists can undercut one group of workers with another; alternatively, they can show support for the claims of a group and earn loyalty through that solidarity. Moreover, such strategies can, and indeed must, change over time in a rapidly changing industrial economy. Underneath what initially appear to be immutable racial or gender categories, the shifting economic terrain constantly threatens the existence of any long-term monopoly of a particular corner of the market. Such a monopoly under threat may be defended fiercely.

A major feature in labour history, and notably in that of Durban, has been the changing of the ethnic or gender identity of a job either in response to scarcity, that is the declining availability of a category of workers for a particular sort of job, or as a result of the desire of employers to identify a new, generally cheaper, source of labour. This kind of change is sometimes accomplished in periods of growth with desirable kinds of social mobility for a collectivity on its way "up," but it can also be linked to struggles under bitter circumstances that divide workers and reduce their share of the product in eras of restructuring. Such changes occur subtly and often in a subterranean way uncaptured by official records. It is rarely easy, without access to personal memory, to trace how and why it happens.

For radicals, there is a temptation to see the segmented labour market as being largely the result of conspiracy on the part of capital.[9] There are certainly numerous and crude examples in the history of Indian workers in Durban that could illustrate that point very well. However, it has to be said that, just as in the extreme case of the Indian caste system, ethnic and racial identity is complex; it cannot simply be created from outside by enemies or manipulators.

Indeed it is typically in very large part moulded from within and asserted in work or occupational categories in robust and positive ways. Indians have, in other words, been discriminated against and exploited through emphasis on ethnic categories in South Africa but (as in the case of white workers far more obviously), they have also *promoted* such associations to *enhance* the economic chances of the group as well. There are a few good South African studies of this universal phenomenon. A striking example is an article by Jeff Guy and Motlatsi Thabane on the association of Basotho with shaft sinking in the gold-mines, a crucial niche in the labour process which they defend with great vigour.[10] A different example, taken from the white miner labour force, was provided by Peter Richardson and Gill Burke studying Cornish miners and miners' phthisis (silicosis) on the Rand early in this century.[11] Keletso Atkins, in a doctoral dissertation that is particularly sensitive to the cultural definitions (and self-definitions) of work, records the wholesale replacement of Zulu *amawasha* in Pietermaritzburg by Indian laundry entrepreneurs using new piped water systems, some access to credit and control of family labour in the 1880s.[12] This is also the gist of the quote that opens the chapter, one that reflects possession of a very humble but still significant niche in the urban labour market at the time of the 1913 strike against the tax on indentured and ex-indentured workers, amongst other grievances.

The age of militancy cannot be understood simply in terms of a striving for non-racial working-class unity. Instead, it needs to be associated closely with assertions of ethnicity, both by and against Indian workers. Up to the 1930s, the relationship of militancy and organisation to ethnicity was largely captured by the problem Indian workers faced of exclusion from jobs, qualifications and unions by whites, particularly when times were bad. Competition from African workers was quite rarely an issue. However, with the revival of the economy during the 1930s and then the World War II years, the African presence in the work force of Durban increased dramatically. Moreover, Africans began to lay claim to domiciliary rights in the city where previously they had formed an overwhelmingly male and transient population.[13] Indian militancy was powered by the pressure that this imposed on Indian workers, caught between white racism and African attempts to secure urban jobs and space. To the extent that Indian workers were identified with the Communist Party's activities and more generally with challenges to bosses in the workplace, capitalist interests lay in threatening Indians with replacement and experimenting with the use of African industrial workers.

Response to this pressure contained several elements. Militants tried to overcome the problem through the formation of non-racial or multi-racial unions to unify the working class around the demands of the threatened group. More moderate and pragmatic unionists aimed instead at incorporationist techniques and even at closure. As with whites, Indians eventually were pushed out of most of the niches where capital did not want them into others where they could be associated with greater skill levels and hold their own.

Radicalised Indian activists found the road forward elsewhere, either in protest, aimed against the removal of Indians from white parts of Durban, that particularly affected property-owners and won wide support from the middle class, or in accepting the strategy of the Communist Party in working with the African National Congress and acknowledging the African national struggle as the key — or first stage — in the struggle for a socialist or non-racial South Africa.

* * *

In their attempt to recover the possibilities of non-racial trade-unionism from the militant era, Padayachee et al. devote particular attention to three strikes, all of which were very important and have been remembered by leaders, participants and contemporaries and to some extent discussed with descendants. A full discussion of these strikes will therefore not be repeated here but a brief recounting is in order.[14] The first was at the Falkirk foundry[15] where some 400 workers went out on strike to protest the dismissal of fifteen Indian and one African worker on 3 May 1937. The strike essentially died after two months when barely one-quarter of the strikers were rehired on the company's terms.

The policy of the company was essentially to dismantle a trade union, organised by Indian Communists, but including numerous Africans. Padayachee et al. stress that management depended on being able to divide the labour force into racial categories as a normal means of maintaining control in the workplace and found the principle of non-racialism deeply disturbing. Coloured and white workers had struck work earlier, engendering the conflict initially, but they did not participate in the main part of the strike and were not locked out. In fact, the white-dominated engineering union whose own strike initiated the conflict, saw the aroused and organised Indian organisers with their new ideas as potentially dangerous rivals.[16]

The strike was a major fillip to radical organisation in Durban as it did bring Indians and Africans out together — although it is important to stress in a ratio of three to one — under radical Indian leadership. It also attracted the attention of the Natal Indian Congress, particularly the skillful politician A.I. Kajee, and the High Commissioner's office which sought to intervene on behalf of Indians. For them the issue was Indian access to the job market and retention of jobs that were characteristically accepted as Indian.[17] Kajee, who was unsympathetic to trade unions in general, pointed out in the Indian press that "we are Indians first and everything else after."[18] The strike was essentially defeated through the employment of white and African (although also a few Indian) scabs in the hiring of whom the Labour Department colluded,[19] but some of the strikers were rehired, with the intervention of the old guard of the Natal Indian Congress, led by Kajee, perhaps being crucial.

Dismissal of thirteen Indian workers in a non-racial trade union, the Natal Rubber Workers' Industrial Union, following a number of some more successful and smaller strikes that were not on a racial basis, precipitated a second major struggle at Dunlop and Co, the British tyre manufacturer, in December 1942. As was Falkirk, Dunlop was a typical firm of the new post-Depression boom, relatively large in scale and involving foreign investment in South African secondary industry. Among Indian workers in Durban, it was well known for its concentration of radicals.[20]

In theory, the dismissals were intended to pave the way for the return of white demobilised soldiers to their factory jobs. In practice, it was to replace Indians and their Communist leadership with migrant Africans. Company pressure got the many white union members, now dependent on company favour, out into a separate white union.[21] Non-union Africans worked throughout and African scabs effectively replaced the strikers. Mobilisation of support for the strikers was impressive, including a protest of 4 000 workers at the City Hall on 17 January 1943. Again, there were attempts at paternalist intervention on behalf of Indian workers *qua* Indians by the Natal Indian Congress. However, the strike was undermined effectively by the use of scab labour from the African countryside, particularly from Transkei.

The failure of this strike resulted in the Indian work-force being removed permanently from this important factory. Dunlop became a model, written about in a Natal Regional Survey volume, of how secondary industry could prosper on the basis of cheap migrant or semi-commuter African labour as had traditionally been the case in the docks and on the mines.[22] Residential compounds typically represented an effective cost and control structure to employers that fitted this strategy. At low enough pay, such a workforce proved attractive in this era to relatively large-scale, low-skill industrial process firms.

The third strike covered by Padayachee et al., "the last major strike by Indian workers in the 1940s,"[23] involved the Laundry Workers' Union. Originally formed in the 1920s, this union had revived and re-registered in 1938 and had come under radical influence.[24] Although non-racial, it was in fact overwhelmingly Indian while most of the numerous African workers in the industry were outside the union. The strike was called in reference to a large range of grievances in December 1945. It was broken after three months through effective use of African scab labour, only a few of the older Indian workers being rehired. A key side-element was that it served the interests of bigger European laundries, which could secure hotel contracts, to use African labour and thus oust small Indian employers who often had relatively paternalistic relations with largely Indian labour forces.[25] This was the strike which cut through the thin fabric of non-racial trade-unionism most forcefully. Padayachee et al. cite the newspaper, *Indian Views*: "The laundry strike has taught a bitter lesson to Trade Union secretaries . . . these secretaries are apt to forget that in the unskilled field the Indian worker is not indispensable."[26] For unskilled work at the motor assembly works in Jacobs, in the sugar mills, on the railway and in the municipality, preference increasingly was for migrant African workers as labourers.[27]

The trends that manifested themselves in all three of these strikes also could be seen in some other industrial contexts. The patronage of conservative community figures was also a feature of the strike of poorly paid railway workers in 1943. This strike affected only Indian workers, and it was also more successful. The state agreed to improve certain conditions of employment for a stratum described as ". . . one of, if not the, lowest paid of all workers in Durban."[28]

The sugar mills provided a logical target for radical trade-unionists. In 1941, sugar mill strikes led by radicals at Mt. Edgecombe just north of Durban and elsewhere, succeeded in gaining African support in an industry with a large mixed work-force, albeit where specific jobs were generally assigned rigidly by race. In the context of the war with its engendered inflation and the imperative of production at all costs, the state mediated and determined a wage increase.[29] This was not invariably effective. In some areas of employment, for instance cigar manufacture and tea plantations, the result of Wage Board awards in favour of Indian workers during the war simply led to large-scale dismissals (in the former case, at the hands of Indian bosses).[30]

Whether the more sophisticated nature of the industry or the pressures of the war were responsible, however, sugar mill workers made gains and their organisation was strengthened. In this phase, it was possible to bring African and Indian workers into the union together fairly readily. The Natal Sugar Industry Employees Union, at the height of its influence, organised the largest number of Indian workers of any union.[31] Yet Lincoln claims that it had an even larger number of African workers in its membership.[32]

However, in the post-war years, the maintenance of unity became more and more problematic. African labour began to replace Indian in semi-skilled employment.[33] "The Indians are gradually being replaced by Africans."[34] In this context, the Indian leadership began to fear African militancy and the union membership became more Indian again. Strikes tended to be on the part of racially distinct work-forces within the industry. According to Lincoln, "the NSIEU had organised almost one-third of all sugar mill workers in Natal; its success had not resulted in the elimination of 'ethnic responses' to the sugarmilling labour process."[35] The price of acceptance into a bargaining format with the bosses, and continued recognition, was acceptance of "being cast as an ethnic union."[36]

In 1952, a strike consisting mainly of African workers took place in Durban at the Hulsar sugar refinery. The refinery had been substituting Africans for unionised Indians and the Indian workers felt threatened and reluctant to support African workers, even though they were union members. Now it was Indians who were the scabs, even though the union formally backed the strikers.[37] This strike marked a key stage in the decline of Indian labour militancy.[38] The union drifted into a defensive and conservative frame of mind. When the South African Trades and Labour Council split in 1955, the NSIEU would join the conservative body SATUC, not the radical, non-racial South African Congress of Trade Unions, aligned to the ANC.[39]

One must finally consider the case of the greatest strike involving Indian workers during the decade of the 1950s which took place in 1956/57 in the rising textile industry at the Consolidated Textiles Mill (Frame's). This firm was perhaps the linchpin in the most significant industrial development in Durban after World War II, development that represented an effective response to unprecedented state protection against imported textiles that had previously dominated the South African market. Here again lay an attempt to break a key union, officially non-racial and with Communist Party involvement. Three hundred Indian workers were fired and replaced with cheaper African labour.

Superficially, the strike was partially successful in saving jobs, but a formal recognition of racial quotas, with a set proportion of African to Indian workers, was the basis of agreement.[40] The whole position of the radical SACTU-linked textile workers' union was undermined and it was effectively destroyed. African workers had refused to participate in the strike and expressed resentment at being excluded by Indians from more skilled work . According to R. Lambert, the Textile Workers Industrial Union's "inattention" to them was decisive in the rift that was created. An African interviewee remembered that Indians were hired by preference and got better jobs while skilled African weavers were kept at "learner" level pay.[41] Moreover, Indian workers who did not support SACTU politics were prepared to scab. In addition to the question of direct costs and workplace power, there was the element of work organisation in a big new factory operation. Frame's was intent on introducing piecework techniques.[42] This key strike seemed to be the last great battle in a distinctive history where struggles over the labour market, defined in racial terms, fuelled an unprecedented militancy among Indian workers that has since been lost.

Another very salient but particular kind of strike characterised this period. This was the political protest stay-away. Such a strike, supported by the Natal Indian Congress, affected Durban Corporation workers, largely although not entirely Indian, in 1950.[43] Some Indians felt forced to strike for fear of attacks from Africans.[44] At the same time, conservative whites demanded the removal of Indians from the city payrolls. Indian individuals were dismissed while the city council was contemplating replacing Indians with Africans on a massive scale.[45]

In the context of the Passive Resistance campaign, initiated by the African National Congress and supported by the NIC, another such strike took place three years later on 6 June 1953. This campaign, partly inspired by non-violent, anti-colonial resistance in India, was intended to utilise the strike weapon as a means of undermining the authority and legitimacy of the state. It was an important stage in the formation of an anti-apartheid movement and superficially presented the possibility of non-racial unity in resistance. Some 300 Indian workers who took part were fired and thrown out of their homes in the Magazine Barracks.[46] These strikes were bitter experiences. According to Lambert, historian of the South African Congress of Trade Unions, they decisively turned Indian workers against political strikes. An initially inclusive reaction, that was built around the idea that the future for Indian workers lay in a common anti-apartheid struggle with the African National Congress, was abandoned in favour of passivity.

One other event from this period requires mention. This was the notorious Durban race riot of January 1949. Beginning with a trivial assault on a young African employee by an Indian shopkeeper in the centre of town, continuing through a phase of almost good-natured looting exclusively aimed at Indian property, the violence escalated over a horrible weekend into an anti-Indian pogrom on the part of Africans in residential areas. As a result, "87 Africans, 50 Indians, one white and four 'unidentified' people died. One factory, 58 stores and 247 dwellings were destroyed; two factories, 652 stores and 1 285 dwellings were damaged."[47] Indian workers were assaulted on the job and Indian-owned factories were attacked.[48] State authorities were very slow to take action although, once they did act, they caused many of the deaths of Africans recorded. ✓

This tragic and violent episode connects to the broader pattern that emerges from the above narrative descriptions of strikes from this period. Edwards and Nuttall have identified the riots as part of a process by which thousands of African newcomers to Durban, irritated at Indian racism and squeezed by a rapidly shifting economy, were struggling to seize space in the city. They were unprepared to accept the conventional ethnic boundaries. Much of the worst violence occurred in Cato Manor Farm, inland from and below the Berea ridge. Before World War II, this had been a lightly peopled district of Indian market gardeners and small property-owners. It then turned dramatically during the war years into Mkhumbane, the home of many tens of thousands of African squatters who depended on Indian-owned transport, bought from Indian-owned shops and paid rent to Indian landlords. "With these shacks went all types of illegal business, illegal trading, like liquor . . ."[49] Collusion by African small businessmen and would-be bus operators was widely alleged, but the pogrom certainly achieved considerable support. Edwards reports that it is still celebrated to the present day in African communities as the victory won against the Indians.[50]

For Indians, the memory of 1949 is extremely painful, not least for those who relate to some idea of non-racial solidarity around a struggle against apartheid. At the time of the riot, the National Party government had been in power for less than a year. The Doctors' Pact, linking up the two provincial Indian congresses with the ANC, had been established in 1947. For Congress activists, the only way to grasp the horror was to assume that white authority was responsible. A typical account, written more than forty years after the event claimed that ". . . it became apparent that repatriation had failed to rid the country of Indians compelling whites to devise other means. Instigating the frustrated Africans was one potent means that they settled upon."[51] A less sophisticated witness believes that the Africans were egged on by whites who hated Indian competition and that the mayor of Durban personally instigated the riots while other whites gave Africans benzine and petrol to destroy Indian property.[52]

The intensity of white racism in this period, and the indifference of the authorities and of many white private citizens until matters progressed to where they might themselves be affected, gives an apparent verisimilitude to such views. But it is only apparent. In reality, there is little or no evidence of a white "conspiracy." Amongst those who supported the pogrom on the African side were the militant wartime labour leader Zulu Phungula and the veteran politician A. W. G. Champion.[53] It was a courageous and impresssive gesture of the African National Congress (which was of course a racially exclusive body itself) to denounce the activities of Africans acting against Indians, but in so doing it probably did not have much support from Natal members.

If co-operation with Africans became more problematic, there was also a magnet drawing Indians into an ethnic politics operating simultaneously. As the next chapter will reveal in more detail, the 1940s were characterised by a sustained attempt on the part of Durban whites to segregate the city and by the city establishment to plan it on racially exclusive lines. Resistance to these plans, which directly threatened the homes of many middle-class Indians and which were taken as a deep racial insult, began in response to the temporary measures known as the Pegging Act. Passed in 1942–43, these measures were directed against so-called Indian penetration of white neigh- bourhoods rising on the Berea above the racetrack, and of the Indian business district behind the city centre. A passive resistance campaign, led by the radicalised NIC, focused on issues of racial discrimination that were not particular to workers or the working class and stressed the united interests of all Indians.[54] Writers such as Swan and Padayachee et al. see this type of movement as being successful in constructing an ethnic resistance identity as opposed to a class or worker one.

The "race riot" enforced this point of view. Apart from simply sheltering in the doubtful benevolence of the white-run state, the only recourse for those who saw themselves as militant opponents of apartheid was to seek alliance with African leaders. This course of action made far more sense to politically ambitious and active leaders than it did to ordinary Indian workers. The 1950s witnessed the rapid decline of Indian worker militancy. In 1955, when the T & LC split, most Indian workers became members of the moderate South African Trade Union Council rather than the Congress-aligned SACTU, which had achieved some success in organising and energising African workers. The main potential for worker militancy had now decisively switched to African workers. By 1962, at which point the ANC had been banned and SACTU was actively involved in recruiting for the underground, it seemed "normal" that the Durban Health Department, completely reversing the thrust of municipal policy a decade earlier, would replace African workers with "more efficient" Indians.[55] In the eyes of the authorities, Indian workers had become the more amenable sector of the work-force and the era of Indian worker militancy was definitely over.

***

From this dramatic history, a number of patterns emerge very sharply. Firstly, it is clearly true that bosses in Durban found it convenient and profitable to manipulate the changing labour market continuously and effectively. A geographer, a generation later, soberly made the point that ". . . race preference has apparently been the choice of the individual managements."[56]

On what might the choice have been based? Their interests lay in negating the possibility of a strong, unified working class, in limiting the influence of the Communists, and also in taking economic advantage of the market to replace one kind of worker with another, cheaper and/or more co-operative. Dunlop was really the classic case. At the same time, it is of some significance that several of the key strikes under discussion occurred at plants that represented large labour forces and relatively advanced technology. The new plants in South Africa might have been more suitable for African operative labour, which had been of little importance in South African industry previously. Hiring Africans enabled management to break through the protective crust of the Wage Act and the apparatus that protected free labour in South Africa from the time of the Pact government. Factories in Durban were becoming larger.[57] On a 1924/25 base of 100, fixed capital per establishment (measured at 1938 prices) leapt from 147 in 1944/45 (lower than before the Depression) to 199 in 1948/49 and 291 in 1953/54.[58] The National Institute of Manpower Research at this time was engaged in promoting the use of African labour and in pushing more expensive white labour out into supervisory and more skilled positions in the name of scientific management.[59]

On the other side of the table, the continued dream of militant trade-unionists was above all to break through the racial barriers to create strong organisations that could withstand such manipulation. This was the real challenge, understood by the most skillful organisers throughout the period, but unfortunately attempts to meet it had little success. The implication of failure was that workers should instead turn to national politics because there was no solution to their problems simply on the union front. Padayachee et al. provide an excellent account of how this way of thinking related to the absence of strong, democratic shopfloor organisation with a life of its own.[60] As a result, the political leadership moved largely away from workplace issues. The disappointing results of workers staying away for political reasons, as in 1950 and 1953, discouraged the class project further.

The manipulation of bosses and the state and the strategies of organisation do not provide sufficient means of grasping why inter-racial militancy faltered and disappeared. One important factor was the growth of African nationalism and self-assertion. In a number of strikes, Africans in trade unions actually came out and supported Indian workers, but the reality of prejudice and of differential treatment where Indians occupied a superior place in the pecking order made it easy to recruit them as scabs. According to Katzen, the average wage ratio in manufacturing between Indian and African, only 133:100 in 1924/25 estimates, rose to figures between 145 and 150:100 in the decade up to 1945/46 where the figure was 145. Then it rose rapidly to 166:100 in 1953/54.[61]

Non-racialism in the unions would have required conscious efforts to reduce these ratios. Yet just as, historically, white workers have rarely supported the strikes of others in South Africa, similarly the Indian workers were rarely interested in the problems of the Africans. Historian Baruch Hirson quotes the Africanist and anti-Communist journal, *Inkundla ya Bantu*: ". . . they exploit African members to further the cause of the Indian and Coloured in getting higher wages and insisting on asking less for the African because he is not recognised."[62] In a memoir on the career of the veteran African trade-unionist M. B. Yengwa, Hirson notes Yengwa's sense of frustration because African workers were never encouraged by Indians to advance in trades and organisations. Yengwa was generally expected, as a labour organiser, to concentrate on organising African labourers in "their place." The idea of an African as a bookkeeper or a typist, part of the Indian's idea of his own space in the labour market, was very unwelcome. Thus *The Leader* opined in 1944 that in genuine skilled work, Indian superiority was such that there was no reason ever to fear African competition.[63] Indian workers were not prepared to follow leaders into a struggle to revise the terms of this pecking order significantly and that, as Africans asserted themselves, would have been essential to saving unity.

At the same time, Indian politicians sought to turn workers into political clients through the normalisation of ethnic identity, even though this identity was presented in terms of an anti-state and radical discourse. Radical petty bourgeois activists convinced beaten trade-unionists that militant anti-racist protest, concentrating on issues such as housing segregation rather than class issues, was the way forward. The radicalised NIC was the umbrella under which this strategy operated.[64] Indian workers at times benefited from effective intervention in their struggles by the Indian High Commission and the NIC, under the rubric of support in the provision of jobs for Indians. The NIC never entirely broke with this world which was inimical to building a different sort of working class, whose predominant loyalties might conceivably lie outside the "community." In turn, radicals were reluctant to make enemies of the Indian bourgeoisie whom they felt could be brought into agreement on the major issues.[65] Sympathetic people with resources were potentially valuable and not to be slighted.

Some attention must be given to the fascinating role of organisers and militants. A symbol of the era was the clever, self-taught tribune of the people, the "bush lawyer" who helped sort out the problems of the poor and uneducated in an increasingly hostile milieu and in so doing made himself a living. This was a time when talented and ambitious youths often found little scope for exerting their ability in conventional channels. In addition to some radicalised sons of the petty bourgeoisie, there were also intelligent men (hardly any women since they were rarely in the wage labour force) who had no chance to escape their poor working-class background. The union and the party became their salvation. George Ponnen and H. A. Naidoo started out as clothing factory operatives in the immediate post-Depression recovery years.[66] The Falkirk strike was a decisive formative influence on their lives and careers.[67] Naidoo recruited L. Ramsundar, a sugar farm boy.[68] R. D. Naidu, a key figure in the Dunlop strike, was a van boy at Baker's, the biscuit makers, in the middle 1930s.[69] Billy Nair, a seaman's son and today a prominent veteran figure in the ANC and South African Communist Party, was brought up in great poverty although he struggled to get some education.[70] V. S. M. Pillai, a Treason Trialist in 1956, had attended Sastri College but left to earn a living, earning a pittance cutting thread off garments in a small factory. He walked out when the foreman demanded that he wipe the floor after his work.[71] M. P. Naicker, who in exile edited the ANC journal *Sechaba*, had been a major activist of the late 1930s and 1940s when still very young. He had left school at 16, and was then unemployed until he became a clerk to a grocer's firm, and later a junior bookkeeper while doing night classes at Sastri College. In fact, night classes of this kind may have been more important than the factory floor in igniting radical ideas.[72]

A trip by Edward Roux in 1934 to Durban may have linked the commitment of such men to the reviving South African Communist Party. They were its life and soul in Durban. When the party revived secretly from the mid-1950s, if they were still active in South Africa, they got swallowed up into a politics of Congress movement support work. As Ginwala and others have written, they were partly at least radicalised by the poor conditions of many Indian workers, by their union experience and specifically by confrontations in the context of the labour market (although their ranks included some sons of the old merchant class as well, it should be noted).

However, they did not simply take orders according to a far removed party line or decree. No doubt the failures of the militant years that have been recounted were crucial in redirecting their activities. When R. D. Naidu told Padayachee et al. that even Dunlop was a "rich lesson," the lesson was surely that the activist must take his militancy elsewhere, to join the CPSA and give up on trade-unionist struggle in its own right. Swan interprets the passive resistance struggle of 1946–48 as an attempt to build up an Indian nationalist resistance that would feed into a multi-ethnic alliance against the white state spearheaded by the CPSA.[73] My reading of the Indian press suggests that this is already foreshadowed in the movement against the Pegging Act in 1942–43.

The success of this movement was remarkable in seizing control of the established Indian congress movement and pointing it in an unprecedented way towards resistance and towards alliance with Africans. However, the difficult truth is that the ordinary working-class Indians, even those who had been strongly involved in such struggles and identified with the "national bloc" in the late 1930s and early 1940s, were not inclined to follow on the same road. Lambert argues that what he terms "political unionism" on the part of SACTU, which focused on consciousness-raising "factory committees" that made propaganda for the ANC and the SACP from the late 1950s, enormously increased African interest in trade unions but probably Indians became disaffected.[74]

Militancy in the Indian cause did not flow easily into support for a Congress Alliance and the politics of the ANC, given the circumstances of job rivalry and Indians feeling threatened by Africans claiming what they had long seen as "their" jobs. At best, the NIC leadership could try to talk about Africans and their leaders as mistreated people who deserved sympathy, and who were waging a different if allied struggle; they were also a nationality oppressed because of their colour. Indian activists outside the leadership could actually be racists themselves. As the substantial activists moved into a different level of consciousness about South African problems, they simply left behind them most ordinary Indian workers.

Mr. M., the subject of an unpublished paper by Columbia University post-graduate student, Dhianaraj Chetty, makes a perfect exemplar. A garment factory worker and son of a clothing cutter, he had been a passive resister and had gone to gaol in 1946. He identified strongly with the Natal Indian Congress and had once been a shop steward. He also identified with the SACP (while pointing out that ordinary workers were not recruited as members) and as a youth used to sell the *Guardian* to Indian workers. Mr. M. did not, however, like Africans whom he considered spiteful and envious people unable to compete in skill levels with Indians. He did not really understand or accept the policy of the NIC-SACP leadership of alliance with African politicians. Considering himself a man with "leanings towards the NIC and the Left," however, "even to this day, we had that tiff with Farouk Meer [a well-known NIC activist of long standing]. We told him if you want to rub shoulders with the Africans, you can do it."[75] My reading of *The Leader* in the 1940s found no mention of the famous 1947 Doctors' Pact and only the most infrequent and vague references to "non-European unity."

An interview with an elderly, but not prominent, veteran of this era, very proud of the militant past (although never a Communist Party member), also suggested that, outside of a small, sophisticated clique of leaders, the radical era was a response to *Indian* poverty and *Indian* problems. It was a response to the realities of power in a labour market that could be manipulated against workers as Indians and lacked any wider vision. "Natives," as he still called them, do not figure prominently in his story.[76] As the introduction to this volume points out, oral evidence reveals more about what memory wishes to hide than to recall. As this was particularly the case on this issue it has consequently been put to less use than might be hoped.

For much of the period covered in this chapter, Indians confronted harsh conditions in the labour market. A premise of Indian militancy had lain in the bitter struggle to hold on to and acquire jobs that whites wanted to reserve for themselves. Whites blocking Indians from skill recognition and acquisition were a dominant feature of the Durban economy as we have seen. In the Depression years, they elbowed Indians out of jobs with state assistance.[77] In 1942, there were only 18 properly indentured Indian workers under the Apprenticeship Act. In 1952, it was written that "the Indian is excluded very largely from the skilled trades, he is not always admitted to the membership and protection of trade unions, fixed wage rates prevent him from undercutting the European labour, and he nearly always lacks the minimum educational background or the educational qualifications which are necessary for apprenticeship training."[78]

Yet the very contradictions which spawned militancy also fed at the same time into a different social and economic reality. In practice, it was not possible for the Indians to be pushed out of key niches in the industrial labour market in favour of whites, whatever white popular opinion may have been in favour of. Ginwala quotes a famous statement by the general secretary of the South African Typographers' Society who claimed that Indians were incorporated into his union to prevent undercutting and to reduce their numbers and this very strategy was so successful that it was leading almost to their elimination.[79] In practice, this state of affairs did not last for long. Whites were simply not numerous enough to keep such a situation intact in times of economic growth in expanding trades; bosses could not always be contented with hiring workers who cost more. The notoriety of the typographers' union's racism, it has been suggested to me, was in direct proportion to the early and continual presence of Indian workers skilled in the printing trade.[80] Indians never even came close to being eliminated from printing.

As the upliftment of whites took place and white unemployment was mopped up, Indians, whose command of English and formal schooling years was on average improving relatively rapidly, were able to advance gradually through these decades into better job grades and skills. Closure broke down as whites could not fill the posts and Indians were able to begin to advance, whatever the formal attitude towards them of their fellow white workers.

A particularly important instance was that of the garment trade which employed so many Indian workers. From 1933 when South Africa went off the gold standard and mining began to boom again, the clothing industry, especially the cheaper end of the market for men's clothing relying on male Asian workers, took off in Natal.[81] In Chapter Six, the circumstances of this conjuncture will be explored.

5

Destroying Communities: The Impact of Group Areas, 1950–1980

The greatest event in the post-war history of the Indian population of Durban, including the working class whose history we have been trying to conceptualise, was the forced removal of the majority from their existing homes into purpose-built townships which contained both state-owned and private accommodation. Recent popular history has characterised the Group Areas Act of 1950 as "doom at the stroke of a pen."[1] According to a 1954 estimate, some 75 000 Indians would be moved after the proclamation of segregated "group areas;" in fact, the numbers ultimately involved were certainly very much higher.[2] In the heyday of apartheid policy making, it appeared that perhaps 80 per cent of all Indians in Durban would be forced to move.[3] For the whole Indian population of Durban, the process was one that reminded them of their vulnerability to the power structure, defined in racial terms, of the city and the country, and one that would alienate them further from that power structure. At the same time, the creation of legally constituted Indian group areas would have a major role to play in shaping economic structures in Durban, and in the development of consciousness, cultural, social and political.

Large as was the scale of Indian removals, it was only one aspect of forced removals. The rapidly increasing African population was simultaneously being resettled in new townships located further afield, mainly under the administration of the KwaZulu homeland. Few whites were forced to leave their homes, but many benefited from the availability of relatively cheap land for home purchase and rent as well as from an improved infrastructure, above all a superb highway system.

Two trajectories came together in the making of Group Areas. The first was white racism, the desire to define Durban as a city built around a white core. Indians were to be expunged from this core with little say on their own position in the urban environment. However, at the same time, the Group Areas idea was closely allied to notions of progress, hygiene and modernity. For the bureaucratic planners of Group

Areas, restructuring the Indian population in terms of family life, definition of class contours and creation of new sources of jobs needed by the national economy, was to be complemented by an improved and more modern physical environment. As such, it was an undeniable good. They aligned themselves with the massive movement to reconstruct working-class housing in Britain and other European countries at the same time, a movement which certainly had major parallels and affinities with processes in South Africa.[4] It has even been suggested that the colonial and extra-European terrain was something of a model for the most up-to-date capitalist town planning in the metropolitan countries. Modern Durban was to be reconstructed on the basis of the clearance of slums.

It can be argued that this vision of modernity was not only tied into racial ideology, but that it also pursued a physical reconstruction of the city which was inimical to the flourishing of networks of small enterprise. Such networks appeared to be a symbol of backwardness, dirt to sweep under the rug or to eliminate.[5] Ironically, with hindsight this may have been a disastrous thrust in terms of the prospects of late twentieth-century capitalism, where heavily protected "modern" industries, imitating those in the most advanced countries and restricted to serving local consumers, are becoming less and less viable and are unable to provide many jobs. Economic relationships and forms that once seemed archaic might have been the key to economic development in this context. The South African state and the most powerful business interests in the 1940s and onwards rejected such networks as backward, however, and sought to undercut their survival.

While officials thought that they were engaged in the noble art of slum clearance and urban beautification and refused to consider the racist implications of the form this was taking, their anti-Group Areas antagonists emphasised the racist aspects of the reconstruction of the city and ignored the problem of slum clearance.[6] Not only did they not comprehend the bureaucrat's urban vision, they also did not really consider the housing needs of many poor Durban residents. To an important extent, this reveals the dominance of bourgeois and petty bourgeois concerns within Indian politics.

Perhaps the most valuable and influential detailed study on the subject of Group Areas is John Western's *Outcast Cape Town*.[7] Much of what Western says is very relevant to Durban. However, it may be useful to put the emphasis rather on what was *different* when comparing Durban to Cape Town. Western concentrates most of his attention on Coloureds (and a handful of Indians) who were evicted from a predominantly white suburb, Mowbray. Mowbray offered all its population convenient access to jobs and a myriad of small shops. Small-scale housing and intense social networks limited the danger of crime. Groote Schuur Hospital and other social amenities were very close and transport to the centre of Cape Town easy and inexpensive. Coloured Mowbrayites seemed to feel encadred within a larger Cape Town identity, and some were even successful in having themselves reclassified white after experiencing the pressure for removal.

For Coloured working-class people, therefore, removal to state-constructed rental accommodation on the Cape Flats, with its extraordinary levels of violent crime, was a grim experience with little positive to offer. The objection, however, can be made that the pre-removal situation of many Coloured Capetonians, including a large number of squatters already on the Flats, was so much less favourable that the Mowbray situation cannot really be generalised to all of Coloured Cape Town. It is also true, according to Western, that for an important section of lower middle-class

Coloureds who were able to become homeowners in defined class-bound suburbs on the Flats, views on Group Areas removals were rather more ambiguous or even positive.

By contrast, in Durban, the bulk of working-class Indians already were "outcast." Before 1930, as we have seen, and to some extent to their own advantage, they lived beyond the city limits and they certainly did not enjoy easy access to the centre. The principal study of the impact of Group Areas in Durban, written at an early stage of the process, stresses the extremely high level of racial segregation in the city even though heterogeneous neighbourhoods did exist on the borders between different areas.[8] Although home ownership amongst Durban Indians was widely diffused, the access to even such basic amenities as piped water and electricity was poor, and affordable council housing, even if racially segregated, did have some appeal.

Finally, even if more honoured in the breach and very flawed, the opposition of the Cape Town City Council to the imposition of Group Areas legislation, which Western stresses, should be mentioned. By contrast, in Durban, the council had never liked or accepted Indians as an inherent part of Durban, and they shamelessly spearheaded and directed the drive towards segregation, acquiring an opprobrium amongst Indians in Durban which has lasted to the present day. In 1957 the mayor of Durban frankly pointed out that apartheid "was the traditional policy of the burgesses of Durban and their urban representatives long before the Nationalists came to power."[9] //

The passage of the Group Areas Act, as Mabin and others have stressed, far from being any sort of break in South African urban history, was part of a thrust, dating back to the early days of Union and before, for racially defined segregation of the city. In 1922, even before the arrival of the Pact government in Pretoria, the Durban Town Council initiated the passage of a provincial ordinance which enshrined the right of property owners to put racially exclusive clauses in deeds covering future sales.[10] Neighbourhood covenants and the activities of real-estate agents kept parts of the city exclusively white. Thereafter two forms of state interference proved of particular significance. One was the process which led to the expansion of the municipal boundaries, an expansion which would lead the way to the restructuring of the city along new lines. The other was the passage of the Slums Act and its application to pre-war Durban.

The expansion of Durban beyond the Old Borough in 1931 represented an important challenge to the way of life of the heterogeneous population on the periphery of the city, particularly to Indians, who were estimated in 1927/28 to form 60 per cent of the total in the annexed zone.[11] If one looks in more detail at a small corner of this periphery, on the northern backslopes of the Berea, called Puntans Hill, the disordered margins become perhaps more real. It was estimated that there were 150 houses in good condition there, of which 120 were owned by "Europeans;" these were mainly in the most elevated section. One hundred Indian-owned dwellings were described as being in fair condition. Then there were 160 shacks inhabited by Indians and "Natives" and described as slums. Many Africans were quarry workers. They and others lived in shanties by the roadside at the bottom of the hill. On lower-lying sections, some sugar-cane was grown. While there were almost as many African as Indian adults resident in the district, almost three-quarters of the resident children were Indian.[12] Thus the family residents of the area were largely Indian.

This kind of uncontrolled area was defined as a problem by the city fathers. Weak,

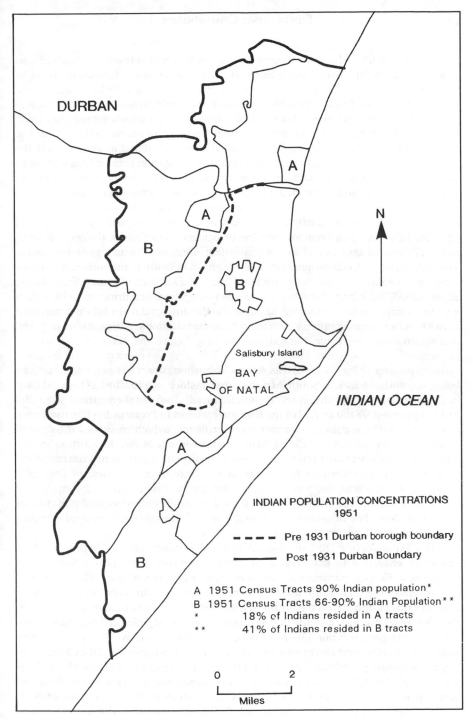

DURBAN

N

Salisbury Island

BAY
OF NATAL

INDIAN OCEAN

INDIAN POPULATION CONCENTRATIONS
1951

- - - Pre 1931 Durban borough boundary

Post 1931 Durban Boundary

A 1951 Census Tracts 90% Indian population*
B 1951 Census Tracts 66-90% Indian Population**
*   18% of Indians resided in A tracts
**   41% of Indians resided in B tracts

0   2

Miles

Indian population concentrations, Durban 1951

(L. Kuper, et al., *Durban: A study in Racial Ecology.*
London: Jonathan Cape, 1958.)

small municipalities such as those in Sydenham, Umhlatuzana or South Coast Junction offered little here compared to the well-developed Durban Council and its dependent structures. The question was rarely put of control *over* Indians (as opposed to Natives) directly. However, from the view of the state, the periphery was the site of illicit activities of every description.[13] Taxes were low and difficult to collect. Small businesses were difficult to regulate. Health hazards (such as malaria-breeding swamps) and poor road construction and other services needed to be remedied. An informant remembered how the family laundry business operated on an unregulated basis beyond the Borough boundaries. Incorporation (apart from mechanisation) was the device, through the agency of the Health Committee, that destroyed the business.[14]

To Durban industrialists, the periphery represented desperately needed level ground. Land was required for industrial expansion, particularly after economic activity began to take off in the middle 1930s, and some of the most favourable possibilities for such expansion, such as the land at Bayhead on the southern end of the Bay, were thickly and inconveniently peopled by Indian shack-dwellers. In addition, the white population could no longer be effectively housed on the seaward slopes of the Berea ridge alone. The urban planners sought to create solid white population zones that linked up the Berea with somewhat less desirable slopes and lower land into which the whites could expand.

Consulted about annexation, the Natal Indian Congress reacted in a rather hostile fashion. Representatives had expressed concern about the racist nature of borough licensing, the incumbent introduction of rates for which voteless Indians would have no representation, and the likely increase in taxes that would squeeze the small property-owner.[15] To take a phrase from the Natal Indian Congress at a somewhat later date, shortly after the passage of the Group Areas Act, removals would represent a "disruption of our economic life."[16] The inexpensive life of the Durban poor on the urban periphery could no longer be afforded by the city establishment. After annexation, numerous unlicensed traders were effectively closed down and "the more serious crime of selling yeast to natives" substantially dealt with.[17]

Moreover, in some areas, such as the Umgeni estuary not very far from Puntans Hill, thick population densities were forming and more conventionally defined slums were coming into being. There was also the problem of the squalid and miserable workers' barracks, above all the Magazine Barracks north of the city centre, which existed in defiance of the planners' ideas of how a modern city should develop. Built in 1880, the Barracks had been condemned as far back as 1914, to no avail.[18] Two-room flats housed large families in insanitary conditions. Other miserable accommodation housed railway and harbour workers elsewhere in Durban. A 1937 report described such housing at the Point to which Indian waiters, cooks, hospital attendants and others were forced to repair. This housing was also more expensive than the Magazine Barracks, and it was claimed that workers there were desperate for public housing to be made available.[19]

In response to this kind of situation, the Slums Act was devised in 1934 and applied nationally. Its most acute observer, Susan Parnell, has written that "in instigating slum clearance projects in the 1930s, the Johannesburg Council had set three objectives. First, to ensure industrial expansion, second to guarantee the removal of any menace to public health, and finally to enforce residential segregation."[20] Parnell points out that stating such objectives was a different matter to realising them within the bureaucratic structures that existed and the cost constraints of the 1930s; policies were applied piecemeal and in more pragmatic ways than might be imagined. The poor, moreover, did not disappear and the housing question was not amenable to solution through such measures.

However, it is important to stress the growing prominence of a discourse about slums and slum removal in the 1930s, and to reiterate Parnell's point about the way in which this discourse was married to the drive towards segregation.[21] It is a striking feature of Kuper et al.'s account of Durban in the 1940s and 1950s that the planning for segregation was often organised through what was called, in sanitised language that evoked technocratic neutrality, a "technical sub-committee." A major theme in the history of South Africa in the twentieth century has been the conjoining of capitalism and segregation/apartheid.[22] In a seminal and widely known article by Martin Legassick, the view was expressed that "the specific structures of labour control which have been developed in post-war South Africa are increasingly functional to capital."[23] This is a difficult view to sustain for the period after 1970 but in the years of the long boom, from 1933 to 1970, it is resonant; such functionality seemed plausible to actors in the state and in business.

In Johannesburg, considerable segregated public housing was constructed in response to the slum question. Durban was by no means in the vanguard in this area. Yet by 1935, the borough was proud of having already demolished 752 dwellings.[24] In Durban all-white council housing was, in fact, created. Lamontville was established for the supposedly tiny section of respectable urbanised Africans.[25]

The enormous housing needs of the Indian working class were, however, largely neglected. Only on the eve of World War II was a small, "sub-economic" housing estate created for poor Indians in Springfield Estate. The quality of this housing was spartan, if not lamentable, and the scale on which it was constructed was quite small.[26] During the war, the estate lacked electricity and street-lighting, sanitation was poor, and thereafter many houses had to be restructured or torn down. It was often difficult to persuade shack-dwellers to consider moving there. Residents found the asphalt floors dismal and were unhappy that no purchase scheme existed.[27] Indeed, after the war the attitude of the Council at first was to devote all its attention to white housing needs and simply to ignore any objections raised by Indians.

Indeed, perhaps very understandably, few Indians imagined that removals would be coupled with any programme of mass housing construction.[28] A sympathetic councillor, S.J. Smith, pointed out in 1938 that the Indian community feared that the Slums Act would be applied for "political reasons, racial reasons and other reasons than that of slum clearance."[29]

During the 1940s, measures aimed at containing so-called Indian penetration, the Pegging Acts of 1942–43 and the "Ghetto" Act of 1946, became a major focus of Indian community activism that cross-cut race lines. The penetration scare particularly involved middle-class housing, on the lower slopes of the Berea above the Indian business core in town, into which some Indian families were moving; resistance to it focused on racism and property rights. As late as 1953, an indignant Greyville Indian Ratepayers' Association recorded that ". . . under guise of providing housing for the homeless Indians, the Council seems to be working hand-in-hand with the Government to clear Durban of all non-whites and make it a wholly white area."[30]

The environment was one of intensified white racism.[31] In 1936, for instance, a Hindu ritual ceremony at the beach was disrupted by a violent attack on the part of a

Special Service Battalion, effectively a militarised force of unemployed whites. The beating of men, women and children went unpunished. The post-war climate was worse, if anything. The Indian press hinted at the existence of vigilante groups aimed at punishing Indian men who might be found ogling white women.[32] It was a cliché that few whites sympathised with the Indian victims of the 1949 riot, and many were even happy to abet African attacks on Indian shops and individuals. It is very difficult to substantiate such a cliché, but its existence is a reflection of widespread white attitudes. In 1947, a poll was taken of white municipal voters to obtain approval for some segregated Indian representation on council. It was turned down by a vote of 15 066 to 1 639, or some 90 per cent against. The Kuper et al. study of Group Areas segregation in the 1950s conveys a sense of the constant (if not always successful) white pressure to prevent any significant white property being made available for Indian Group Areas.

At the same time, the 1949 riot bloodily revealed growing African assertiveness in the urban context. The core of African settlement in Durban, Cato Manor Farm, was largely Indian property. As that settlement developed, it became commonplace to find situations such as the one on the edge of Hillary at the southern end of Cato Manor where Africans dwelling in no less than 100 shacks were paying rent to a Mrs. Ranjalai. The rent was £5 per annum and was collected by "her induna."[33] Such arrrangements collapsed or were dangerous for the landlord in the wake of 1949. In sections in and on the fringe of Cato Manor, such as Mayville, there was a very substantial and concentrated Indian population. While these inhabitants were bitter at the potential loss of their homes, they were also frightened by the events of 1949 and not entirely hostile to removal to a safer place. The riots, of course, represented a powerful argument in favour of the white Establishment view that segregation was the key to "peaceful race relations."[34]

In these circumstances, Indians themselves confused the desire to save neighbourhoods with the struggle against Group Areas to a certain extent. In the wake of the riots, the Cato Manor Ratepayers' Association at first called for repatriation of Africans from Cato Manor, the institution of curfews on them, and a ban on the construction of shacks.[35] The 1950 annual conference of the Natal Indian Congress "opposed the expropriation of Indian-owned [but not in fact occupied] land in Cato Manor for the purpose of a temporary African housing scheme" only to agree to such a scheme a year later because "if the shack development in the Cato Manor area is not checked, then the shack settlements will overflow into adjacent areas now occupied by Indians."[36] A decade later, the Mayville Indian Ratepayers' Association, pointing out the contrast between themselves and African tenants, requested that Cato Manor be made a "model Indian town."[37] Clairwood residents, perhaps only because they thought it would fit the prejudices of the authorities, described their neighbourhood as a "veritable Group Area of our own choosing and a model of self help and separate development."[38] Concerned at the distance between the centre of town and Chatsworth, the Durban Indian Municipal Employees' Society suggested in 1964 that instead of removing Magazine Barracks residents to Chatsworth, it might be better to eject Africans from Lamontville and replace them with Indian workers.[39] To some extent, conservative leadership amongst the Indian bourgeoisie abandoned any real struggle against removal and instead tried to ensure more favourable terms and arrangements.[40]

Despite the general anger at the threat of removals, the leadership of Indians in

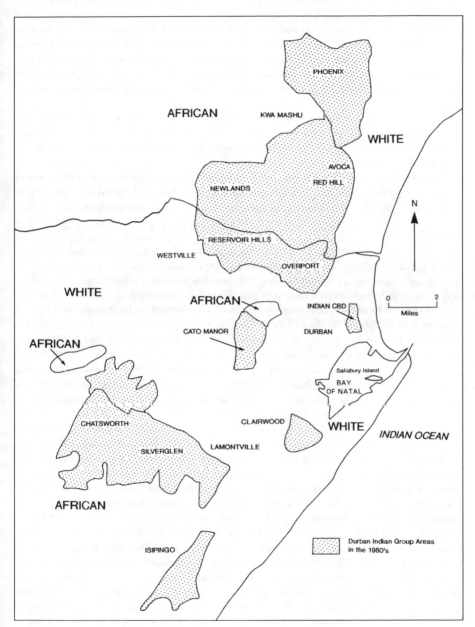

Indian Group Areas in the 1980s

Durban had no answer to the problems of exploitation and rack-renting in the slums. Indeed some of the Natal Indian Congress dignitaries from the pre-1945 period were themselves slumlords who made large amounts of money from their properties.[41] P.R. Pather, leading light in the post-1945 breakaway conservative Natal Indian Organisation, was unusual as a "community leader" in emphasising in a 1955 article that "portions of the Magazine Barracks, the slums at Jacobs, Umgeni Newlands and Merebank were a blot on the name of the Durban City Council."[42] The latter two locales were the sites for large resettlement shack areas that awaited further municipal housing construction.[43]

Once it became clearer that land and houses would become available for Indian settlement on a large scale, the reaction amongst Indian people was in practice a very divided one. At one end of the spectrum, were individuals who owned substantial property in predominantly white areas, who felt justifiably the harsh sting of racism.[44] At the other, were those who felt delivered from the worst abuses of landlords and were very grateful for the availability of houses which might be improved and purchased over time.[45] According to testimony collected in a popular history:

> We were happy to move to Merebank. We had moved from Durban North to Rippon Road. From Rippon Road we moved to Wireless. Because of industrial development we were forced to leave Wireless. We saw our houses bulldozed while we stood there. Our things were out on the street. From [t]here we moved to Jacobs. We were forced to leave Jacobs because of industry. But we were happy to leave. The house had no ceilings. We had to cover our heads and sleep because the dust and sand kept getting in. The Merebank house was a neater house to live in.[46]

Quoted in the *Leader* on the possible expulsion of Indians from the central business district, the heartland of the Muslim trader class, the comment of a youth from this category gave expression to class antagonisms: "I like the Group Areas. For the first time we have a home of our own. All my life I have been living with my parents in a hovel we call a home, paying exorbitant rents to a well-known businessman in town."[47]

In practice, many people fell between these stools. There were numerous rather poor Indian home-owners who lived in shacks but had invested something in their properties. It is remarkable that Indians owned homes in larger proportions than whites in the Durban of the 1940s.[48] Again, however, some of these were so indebted in terms of repayments that it is not entirely accurate to see them as home-owners.[49] Others rented on short leases.[50] A pair of Indian researchers pointed out that "a great deal of Indian shack dwelling is no more than 'hoveldom.'"[51]

While some people were delighted to have access to better quality homes or home-ownership for the first time, others were concerned about the loss of access to very cheap housing. The municipal workers in Magazine Barracks lived in squalid and overcrowded surroundings, but their rent was very low. As late as 1964, rents were as low as 87 cents per month (for a two-room flat with electricity and water) compared to between R2 and R10 in Chatsworth township, apart from the cost of utilities and transport.[52] Removal made the availability of casual work in town much scarcer. Yet according to one survey, some two-thirds of removees claimed to be "satisfied" in Chatsworth, a notably higher figure than for those who had come from Cato Manor.[53]

At the same time, large numbers of Indians lost relatively high-quality property in such areas as the lower slopes of Sea View and Bellair, south of Cato Manor, and the pleasant heights above the central business district and the racecourse where Indian penetration had been so resented.[54] (And even at the upper end of the housing scale, new neighbourhoods were less well serviced than otherwise comparable white suburbs.) A particularly unpleasant aspect of the removals from the Bluff and the southern suburbs was the sense that the state placed the interests of the white working class before anyone else. Moreover, since whites received the lion's share of land in Durban, Indian land, just as in the countryside, was relatively scarce and overvalued.

For the Indian middle class, the state made available for the first time distinct neighbourhoods modelled on white suburbia. By 1950, the Indian press was containing advertisements for modest new homes for purchase in an "exclusively Indian" suburb, Umhlatuzana. Later Red Hill, on the edge of Durban North, and Silverglen, in what later became Chatsworth, were added to the list. In the 1960s, Reservoir Hills and the Indian section of Westville, which adjoined property where a university college was created for the Indian community, contained lots suitable for more well-to-do people. North of Durban, a section of beach was made a residential area for Indian property owners at La Mercy. A small, white middle-class suburb, Isipingo Beach, was in time proclaimed for Indian occupation. This was the most substantial transfer of built-up urban land out of white hands in the whole Group Areas process in South Africa. For some individuals, certainly, these zones contained attractive possibilities. From the late 1950s, in the increasingly less politicised Indian press, large advertisements bearing new home offers jostled oddly next to declining amounts of news about Group Areas protests.

In some cases, purpose-built housing replaced poor settlements of agglomerated dwellers in temporary accommodation as in Merebank, vaguely known at first as "Marine Settlement."[55] By the end of the 1950s, a reconstructed Merebank offered numerous cheap houses made of breeze blocks and roofed with asbestos, for which purchasers had ten years to pay.[56] However, the most important community of working-class Indians was in Chatsworth, south-west of the white core of Durban as now defined, constructed on 500 acres of banana farmland much of which was already thinly peopled by Indians.[57] Indeed, the expansion of Indian townships itself drastically reduced the available space in some sections of peripheral Durban for market gardening and other rural activities.[58]

Planned from 1960, Chatsworth opened in 1964. By 1980 Chatsworth consisted of eleven neighbourhood units containing 7 000 "sub-economic" and 14 000 "economic" houses.[59] It was not accidentally built as a kind of buffer between white residential areas and the large new African township of Umlazi constructed on mission land. Both Kuper et al. and Western have emphasised the attempt to use natural features such as rivers, and major impediments to movement such as railway lines and highways to differentiate Group Areas, as well as the tendency to create Coloured and Indian population buffers between whites and Africans. Chatsworth was intended to house 165 000 people, but perhaps held 250 000 at its peak.[60] By the late 1970s, many more people crowded into the small houses than the official planners' allotment.

At first, Chatsworth was a grim place to observe. A Principal Planning Officer in the Durban Town Engineer's office, L.G. Vinton, said himself that it had a "military and inhuman look."[61] This certainly reflected the extent to which town officials and planners designed Chatsworth according to their own ideas with little consultation or thought of requirements unfamiliar to their own preferences. A study of the construction of Phoenix suggested that town planning in Durban is best understood as being ". . . determined by a 'bureaucracy-centred coalition' entered into between the senior bureaucrats and their Council supporters," with the former as the real generators of significant schemes.[62] A Phoenix activist pointed out to me that, despite the fine language in planning discourse, in the first years of settlement the lack of even basic amenities, apart from the houses, was glaring.[63]

However, Chatsworth offered Indian residents extensive possibilities for upgrading and for home purchase over time.[64] Sales were allowed for those occupying property for seven years and tenancies could be taken over by heirs. In its early phase, rented accommodation was relatively cheap.[65] It has often been used as an indictment that city officials "colluded" in the expulsion of Indians to Chatsworth and elsewhere, but it is probably this collusion that also explains how the planning of new settlements tended to fit well with the industrial expansion of Durban.[66] A survey from 1974 pointed out that Chatsworth, well located from the point of view of the rapid industrial expansion on land south of the city for worker-commuters, had low levels of unemployment.[67] A striking feature of resettlement in Durban was the wholesale removal of communities to physically new locales. Thus the fishermen settlements, first displaced in favour of port-based industry, were removed *en masse* to a section of Chatsworth called Havenside in 1963, in part through the intervention of A. I. Kajee.[68] Some Cato Manor people were also able to establish themselves as groups in another network of settlement.[69] Ratepayers, according to this report, were involved in negotiating compensation rates and plans. Another example was the distinctive community of "Zanzibaris," Muslims of obviously African origin who were assimilated by the state into association with Indians and also consigned as a community to a particular section of the new township.[70]

The most spectacular example lay in the removal of the 6 000 inhabitants of the Magazine Barracks, whose working component were employees of the municipality. Plans to remove this apparently classic slum population went back a long way. By the time of World War I, the barracks had been condemned as insanitary. In 1933, there were plans to remove the population to Cato Manor.[71] Thereafter, focus partly fell on upgrading and improvements, particularly because the city had such meagre plans for urban renewal in general, apart from the white population. Improvements did occur — double-storey brick structures were erected by 1933 — but they were coupled with ever greater population densities.[72] A population estimated at 5 089, or almost four persons per room, actually rose to about 6 000 by 1944.[73] Many were really only kin to council workers.[74] Attempts were made in the 1930s to restrict the barracks to sober, clean, well-behaved families with no more than two children, and then only to employees, but the policy proved unenforceable.[75] Removal of Magazine Barracks residents (no longer viewed by the city fathers as potential radicals) to Chatsworth took place finally in 1966.[76]

The other important site of working-class settlement was north-west of Durban in the Indian portion of Newlands and, particularly, Phoenix. "A rough place"[77] with a smaller component of detached middle-class suburbia, Phoenix was first demarcated in 1964, just as Chatsworth was opening up. It was provided with an overarching plan, considered to be the equivalent of a British New Town, in the middle 1960s, and finally founded in 1976.[78] Early projections were for a "self-contained," isolated, "Indian City of the Future."[79] Its initial core population arrived from Tin Town, a shack settlement of people from the northern side of Durban, and from poor settlements along the

Umgeni in the context of dislocation following a flood. In an echo of the extremely violent street life of the new townships on the Cape Flats, the raw settlement was characterised at first by gang activity and high levels of crime.[80] The early settlers were joined by most of the remaining population of Cato Manor; by people from nearby Riverside and Asherville south of the river; by those living, sometimes in shack settlements, on the edge of the sugar villages of the North Coast; and by a large overspill of Chatsworth inhabitants on the list for housing with the council. Phoenix has been a harsher place than Chatsworth; slower to take on urban services, and affected by more crime and anti-social behaviour. There was no equivalent industrial expansion in the 1970s on the ribbon of lowland north of the Umgeni to anchor a working class with factory and commercial employment near to home. South Africa's industrial boom had stopped, and even when growth occurred it did not lead to the expansion of factories employing large numbers of workers.

The patchwork process of removals tailed off after 1980 and was never completed. Some Indian families remained, even in Cato Manor, in good part by dint of their fierce resistance to removal. Cato Manor was "proclaimed" for, but never really settled by whites; it became a huge empty green-and-brown hole in the centre of Durban. The City Council had in fact lost interest in its prospects as white suburbia. It seems likely that its proclamation as white stemmed from Pretoria notions of creating a secure white block extending down the hills of Natal to the centre of the city, in defiance of any other planning rationality.[81] One remnant of South Coast Junction-Bayhead, once the largest single concentration of Indians (especially working-class Indians) around Durban, known as Clairwood, fought a long and to this day successful battle to avoid expulsion by expanding industry.[82] Plans to expel the Indians entirely from the so-called Indian Central Business District around the Grey Street mosque were never carried out. Thus by contrast with Cape Town, where by far the largest part of the population inhabiting the edge of the business district — District Six — were entirely expelled, leaving a strangely (and dysfunctionally) empty urban core, the centre of Durban retained a large, intensely urbanised population on its edge.[83]

By the middle 1980s, however, Phoenix was as large as Chatsworth and the Indian working class of Durban was primarily to be found in one or the other township. Poised above Phoenix were the vast African settlements of Inanda, once an African mission station whose sections nearer to Durban had become very intensively populated. A wave of violence in 1985, in some respects similar on a smaller scale to the 1949 riots in Cato Manor, affected the still important Indian shop and landowning community of Inanda. As a result, several thousand people came, at first as virtual refugees, and settled in Phoenix.

Underlying the entire Group Areas experience (Group Areas ceased to be legal entities in 1991) was the extent to which changes in the physical environment drastically altered the balance in family life and orientation amongst Indian people. As Chapter Three suggested, the Indian "community" in reality consisted of networks of community linked together through dense human contacts that tied into family relationships and a myriad of economic connections. There is frequently a sentimental association of the idea of *community* with homogeneity and total, organic harmony. This is not the way the word is used here. *Community* relations invariably embrace (but perhaps to the outsider, mask) conflict and inequality. It is the sense of network and the mediation of relations through networking that gives the concept of *community* some value.

Residents of particular areas had built mosques, temples and schools which now had to be abandoned, or could only be reached through a special journey. The Indian population of Durban had been quite highly segregated, but it had not internally divided up physical space on class lines so sharply. The new townships were by contrast clearly demarcated, particularly between sections with homes for sale and council housing; patronage in access to resources and land was of limited value. For example, emigration to Chatsworth divided the fishing-boat owners and captains, who began to move into new business opportunities, from the fishermen, who were more clearly identifiable as workers, where previously the community had been tangled up.[84]

Even more dramatic in effect was the impact on the life of the joint family.[85] In the new purpose-built housing, the patriarchal homestead, which had gone together with home construction linking up room onto room in a mushrooming shack or tin-and-iron construction, no longer fitted the built environment. The state was in fact quite explicit in promoting construction that suited commuter-workers living directly on wages and in nucleated, small family structures.[86] One of the informants who most impressed this author pointed out that, despite the many practical advantages of life in Phoenix, he often still dreamt of the complex, patriarchal homestead in Clairwood where he had grown up and the way of life it represented, although he chose never again to visit the physical site of his grandfather's homestead.[87] Unsurprisingly (and of course, as in other parts of the world) the impact of removal could be devastating on the elderly. The centrality of the family issue is brought out in a quote by a well-known anti-apartheid activist from the Witwatersrand, writing about the equivalent process in a Johannesburg neighbourhood:

> These removals were done in the name of separate development — they were supposed to create conditions in which different groups could preserve their own culture and their own identity. But the great irony is that they have in fact broken down traditional ways of life. They have forced families into a single mould, the mould of the typical family you would find in any other urban industrial community in the world.
> . . . It was a patriarchal family and the father was a single authority . . . they are forced to go to Lenasia but some of the city values have rubbed off on them and they don't go to the cheaper housing areas . . . The father finds he has high monthly instalments to pay off on his house, high maintenance costs. And his wife now rents modern furniture, refrigerator, television . . . Suddenly the girls are encouraged to go on to one of the commercial colleges which have opened and they become clerks and typists. They become independent of the family and the father's unquestioned authority falls away. The traditional patriarchal Indian family is being affected profoundly by these resettlements and I can see it will eventually emerge as a modern family like any other modern industrial family with all the strained relations of three generations living together.[88]

"Worries of a patriarch," the reconstruction of Indian social interaction within the context of the new, "modern" economy of urban South Africa is the subject of the final chapter of this study.

MALE BONDING
Factory managers at cards. (Institute for Black Research)

MALE BONDING
Youths on the Bluff. (Institute for Black Research)

EDUCATION
A classroom in Cato Manor, 1940s.

(Iain Edwards)

WHITE DOLLS, BLACK DOLLS
Indian midwives in training under clinical supervision, Borough Health Department.

(Local History Museum, Durban)

THE 1949 RIOTS
Indian youths fraternise with a couple of Africans.   (Local History Museum, Durban)

THE 1949 RIOTS
Inspecting the damage.   (Iain Edwards)

CHATSWORTH
Women and children in the new state-built township. (Local History Museum, Durban)

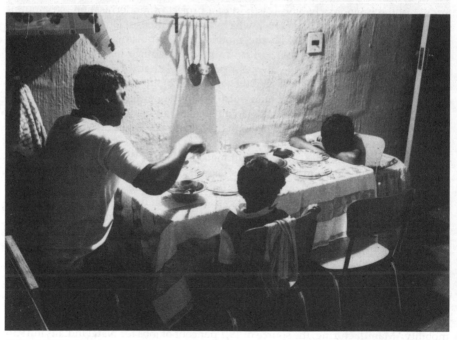

CHATSWORTH
Nuclear family life in a small space. (Institute for Black Research)

6

Insiders and Outsiders: The Working Class of the Apartheid Era, 1960–1990

The destruction of the dwellings in which Indians of all classes in Durban lived, it was argued in the previous chapter, was part of a project of modernisation of economic forms, of life-style and of manners in which the city fathers of Durban believed. This chapter continues by portraying the modernising impulse as one which Indian working-class people were able to turn to their advantage in important respects, despite the fact that they were always made to feel that they were not first-class citizens of the city. In return, however, their own way of life was changed in significant ways. They became both insiders and outsiders in the new era.

The material foundation of these circumstances lay in the unprecedentedly long and consistent period of economic growth that began at the end of World War II and lasted for twenty-five years. Moreover, particularly in the 1960s and 1970s, the growth of Durban was more rapid, for the first time since World War I, than that of South Africa as a whole. Despite the arrival of significant numbers of immigrants from Europe, the white population was quite unable to provide the skills necessary to service this growth and the employment gaps into which Indian workers could move were very substantial. Unemployment, the scourge of Indian family life during the inter-war years, persisted as a major phenomenon throughout the 1950s, but then subsided rapidly after 1960.[1] In particular, unemployment in the new working-class townships around Durban, was low by the end of that decade.[2] Indeed, "Indian" labour shortages began to emerge.[3]

Bell has argued that the success of relatively low-wage industry in Durban itself enabled Indians to acquire more skills, and improved their access to education through the stabilisation of the labour market which they could use for further mobility.[4] Manufacturing, the source of 19,1 per cent of jobs for Natal Indians in 1936, provided 31,4 per cent in 1951, 37,7 per cent in 1960 and 41,9 per cent in 1970.[5] In Durban-Pinetown, according to Bell, Indian employment was 53 per cent in

Table 6.1 Spatial distribution of manufacturing employment in South Africa

	1956/57	1961/62	1967/68	1972	1979
Pretoria-Wits-Vaal Triangle	46,0%	45,3%	46,3%	44,7%	43,8%
Cape Town	16,2	16,2	15,7	15,6	14,3
DURBAN/PMB	12,5	12,7	13,2	13,6	13,8
Port Elizabeth/Uitenhage	4,9	5,9	5,9	6,1	5,3

Source: John Stanwix, "Capital Accumulation, Crisis and Spatial Manufacturing: A Study of Spatial Shifts in South African Manufacturing with Particular Reference to Natal," M.Com. thesis, University of Natal, Durban, 1987

manufacturing in 1970 and just short of 53 per cent in 1980.[6] At the close of the prosperous 1960s, Indian industrial workers were still mainly semi-skilled at best. They could be classified as 74 per cent process workers, 20 per cent supervisors, 4 per cent trained artisans and 0,8 per cent apprentices.[7] The proportion of skilled workers thereafter increased very substantially.

Although opportunities for Indian workers opened up in various branches of industry as well as in other sectors of the economy, the key areas for expansion lay in the textile and clothing industries. Some parts of the Durban economy were not as open to Indian advancement.[8] Dunlop, which remained a major employer, avoided employing Indian workers into the 1980s. The new automobile assembly industry, focused from 1963 around Toyota, largely avoided Indian workers. It was particularly around some parts of the consumer-goods industries that the Indian working class in Durban found plentiful job opportunities.

By 1979, Natal was the site of only 21,3 per cent of manufacturing jobs in general but of 38,8 per cent of jobs in clothing, 38,3 per cent of jobs in textiles and 50,1 per cent of jobs in footwear in South Africa.[9] In particular, Durban became the major centre for manufacturing lower- to middle-quality levels of clothing and particularly men's and children's clothing.[10] The clothing industry grew from fairly modest beginnings before World War II. "Japanese shirts" made from imported Japanese cotton cloth were sewn on machines in small shops even before the Depression.[11] During the inter-war years, the garment trade clustered on the Reef where the greatest market for ready-made clothes was to be found. The very success of the Garment Workers' Union there during the 1930s in raising wages and improving conditions for workers, particularly white women, led to employers searching in other parts of the country and among other working-class communities for conditions where exploitation was less hampered.[12] In the post-war years, as a result, much of the industry moved to the coastal cities of Cape Town and Durban. At first sight, Durban was not a propitious site for expansion. Its white and Coloured women garment workers were better paid and worked shorter hours than elsewhere in the country.[13] This is where Indian male labour came in.

In 1939 there were 39 clothing manufacturing firms in Durban, of which 17 employed under 50 workers.[14] By 1950 there were 70 manufacturers with more than 10 employees and some 4 000 workers; in 1970, there were roughly 150 manufacturers and 22 000 workers.[15] Indian workers, who by this time understood English well, increasingly speaking it as their first language, and were prepared to accept the discipline of industrial labour, were a very desirable component in this industry.[16]

Table 6.2 Percentage composition of the Indian labour force in select branches of manufacture

	1917	1929	1936	1946
Metals, engineering	5,2%	6,5%	7,8%	6,6%
Food, drink, tobacco	64,0	48,3	38,0	27,0
Clothing, textile	2,8	12,3	20,2	26,2
Books, printing	2,3	3,6	3,8	5,3
Furniture	2,5	5,3	4,7	6,7
Chemicals	9,8	5,6	3,5	4,2
Leather, leatherware	1,1	3,2	5,3	10,5

Source: Arkin, Contribution of Indians

In the clothing industry nationally, Coloureds and Indians rose as a percentage of the total work-force from 67 in 1936 to 83 in 1946 and 89 in 1955.[17] The bosses' clichés of the era, quite different from an earlier generation, suggested by the 1960s that ". . . the Indian worker is generally regarded as being particularly suited to work demanding initiative and quick thinking, especially process-minding, while the African worker seems to show more aptitude for routine repetitive work."[18] It was now believed that he showed "greater facility than the Bantu for skilled manipulative work and clerical employment but lacks the physical strength and stamina of the Bantu."[19] Yet Indian male workers in Natal were earning less in the 1950s than African machinists in the Transvaal.[20]

Wage levels became set at a level that effectively undercut garment production on the Reef, but which allowed for substantially improved wages and benefits for a growing industrial workforce of Indian men in Durban. Bell reports that Indian wage levels have been only two-thirds those for Indians in the Transvaal.[21] Company histories remember this factor well as a motive for moving to the Durban area.[22] "Indian males . . . were more satisfactory and cheaper to employ than the European women previously employed in Johannesburg."[23] Yet in Durban according to Katzen, between 1945/46 and 1953/54, while African wages rose on average by 38 per cent, Indian wages rose by 58 per cent.[24]

The textile industry has a slightly different history. Dependent on imported raw materials to an important extent, this highly protected industry flourished behind tariff barriers after 1945 and had its core in Durban as the port was a useful site for production even while much of the production was sold on the Reef.[25] Alan Hirsch has ascribed its location in terms of the relation of port to market on the one hand and the availability of a large pool of cheap labour on the other.[26]

Two important structural features of this participation need as well to be earmarked. One was the emergence from the stratum of small merchants and tailors of a significant class of Indian industrialists in the garment trade. In 1948, one estimate suggested that there were 10 Indian-owned clothing factories employing 600–650 workers. This rose to 32 factories employing approximately 2 500 in 1958 and 82 factories employing 6 500 by 1968.[27] Although the Indian trading bourgeoisie had been diversifying into industry since the turn of the century, such diversification had been on a small and rather irregular scale previous to the 1940s. One who later became particularly successful referred to this as the era of the "small back-street undertaking employing half a dozen girls at a few sewing machines."[28] Cut, make and trim (CMT) operations, prevailed in the early days.[29]

Thus the Paruks, one of the most important entrepreneurial families in Durban, began manufacturing in an outhouse of their Montpelier Road home shortly after World War II. They produced boxer shorts and playsuits for children, which they sold in their shops. For this backyard operation, they could not obtain a licence. As they expanded production, they removed to the densely peopled Indian business district in the centre of Durban on Alice Street where mobs destroyed the stocks in the 1949 riots. Finally, Reunion Clothing was established south of Durban in 1955.[30] By 1970, they employed 550 workers, two-thirds of whom were Indians, and sold most of their output to the Transvaal conurbation, while starting to branch out of the lowest levels of the market.[31]

By 1969, Indian industrialists had created a division of the Natal Chamber of Industries.[32] The result was hardly one of particularly attractive conditions, because Indian capitalists on average were forced to operate more marginal operations and obliged to cut costs at worker expense with particular intensity. Indeed, the most successful Indian industrialists came to move their operations out to the edge of KwaZulu where a very low-wage, usually female, African workforce could replace better-paid, more urbanised and mobile, Indian and African workers — a manoeuvre employed by many white entrepreneurs.[33] Thus the A.M. Moolla group, by the late 1980s, owned 8 factories, of which 4 were in "border areas." The most important one, in Hammarsdale, employed some 1 000 workers, 80 per cent of them female, and of the 1 000 only about 45 were Indian and 20 white. The unskilled majority earned considerably less than in town.[34]

Of Indian workers, a significant percentage now came to be the employees of Indian bosses.[35] Forced by their more marginal circumstances to pay less, it was a commonly held view that "working for an Indian boss was hardly a boon."[36] Yet such Indian bosses conceived of themselves as operating in a paternalistic way with regard to Indian workers that cross-cut the antagonistic lines that the racial divide imposed and may have resulted in the consistent granting of small favours that acknowledged common membership in a racially defined community.[37] Supervisors tended in such operations to be Indian only. The managerial stratum provided role models for factory workers who did actually occasionally succeed in transforming themselves into entrepreneurs.[38]

A second, distinctive structural feature that emerged on a large scale in the 1960s, was the entry of significant numbers of Indian women into the factory, especially the garment factory.[39] Such women were not easily accepted as free agents in the marketplace, for believers in the mind-set of Indian paternalism, and fears of immoral activity subversive to the good family order on their part, were rife.[40] However, in practice, their entry into the formal work-force reflected not only their rapidly growing command of English and exposure to formal education, but also a family strategy governed by fathers and husbands, rather than by the women themselves. There is no comparison in Durban to the situation in India where women, participating in the construction of a family income, became themselves the dominant proletariat in a key national industry.[41]

So much of the current literature on women workers assumes the link between militancy, independence and employment, which goes back to Engels and his contemporaries, that it seems worthwhile to stress that very often women workers are not easily able to turn their power to earn wages into any substantially different sense of themselves in the world. An excellent study of women factory workers over four generations in a conservative Latin American milieu captures this situation well and deserves quoting at length:[42]

> But the history of the workers of Fabricato reveals equally a process of looking for autonomy, of placing in question the limits imposed by the business and the family. For the two first generations, the individual strategies are significantly determined by the family strategies that coincide in turn at a higher plane with the politics of the enterprise. The social status of the woman, defined in the first place by the family, is represented through a particular modality, that of the girl's prolonged spinsterhood which serves as a true financial resource for her family, as can be confirmed in the comments of the renowned historian of the French working class, Michèle Perrot: "The history of women's work is inseparable from that of the family, of the relations between the sexes and their social roles. The family, more than the labour participation which it conditions, is the true anchor for the existence of women and their struggles, the brake or the motor for change therein." For women, prolonged spinsterhood and labour, equally prolonged, at the Fabricato factory, are the result of a family decision which consists of assuring a stable revenue to the family in a phase when the father is no longer capable of doing so. This family determinism prevents the conversion of wage labour into a source of independence for the woman.
>
> The domestic status of the workers is present equally in the politics of the enterprise. Since the industrial revolution, women come into the factory along the lines of function conferred on them by a particular domestic status, situating them in one of the following categories: daughters of working class families during a phase that precedes their marriage or partnership; single mothers, abandoned wives and widows obliged to replace their man or husband in his traditional role as financial support; wives or partners trying to complement the salary of their men. The productive status of all three categories is defined in relation to domestic status and in general, their presence in the factory is considered temporary, complementary or exceptional. In the case of the first historic generation of Fabricato workers, the workers tended to prolong their work commitment, thought of as temporary, in their capacity as daughters, bringing home a salary to the family.
>
> In industrial structures, the marginal status of the woman is directly linked to her domestic status and to the idea that her work is always temporary, provisional or complementary. Around this conception rests the division of labour between men and women with branches, sectors of production and particular jobs reserved exclusively to women, to which corresponds a salary and a social status inferior to that of men.

Fatima Meer's study of women factory workers in Durban singles out Indian respondents and reveals that the major economic decisions as to the women going to work are made by male household heads.[43] "We have to work. If we did not work our families would be in a fix. We just don't know what would happen. We wouldn't be able to buy clothes; we would not be able to pay our hire purchase instalments."[44] Or, as a male informant, perhaps reflecting the active power in most families, told me "if our wives don't work, we've had it."[45]

In Meer's survey, some 60,4 per cent of Indian women at work in the factory were married and another 29,6 per cent were living in a family setting but unmarried; most with children were able to draw on family members for child care.[46] Estimates of the proportion of the family wage here and elsewhere earned by women varies from one-third to two-thirds.[47] Of Meer's Indian women, 25 per cent thought men should be paid more than women for the identical job, just under 50 per cent thought women should always be fired first in a recession, just under 80 per cent thought that unemployment was more serious for men than for women and 81,5 per cent believed that men needed jobs more than did women.[48] These figures were notably higher than those for Coloured or African women surveyed. A contemporary survey indicated a large amount of passive acceptance of work conditions by Indian women in factory employment.[49]

A few features of the Colombian example, for instance the frequency of common-law unions or the prolongation of spinsterhood, are not typical features of South African Indian women workers' experiences. But the powerfully laid out general perspective on the relation of domestic work to wage work is most suggestive. It applies to Indian women workers in good part, who do still represent a first, or perhaps second, generation of wage workers. Luz Arango notes, however, that in Colombia, as the sociologist moves to study the third and fourth generation, the findings are that women workers tend to challenge this structuration and begin to utilise work as a source for emancipation.

In Durban, it is much less clear so far whether a similar claim for gradual emancipation can in fact be made. For Indian unlike African women, earnings usually form only a portion of the family wage. Indian women earn the same for the same job but they are more apt to be promoted into better positions.[50] It can, however, be suggested that the character of home life has altered with the shift of women to wage labour; the implications for changing community and family structure will be discussed below.

The final structural feature which is marked in the Durban clothing industry was the emergence of an effective but anti-radical and only fitfully militant trade-unionism, typified in the clothing industry by the Garment Workers' Industrial Union (Natal). Certain other groups of Indian workers, notably the municipal workers, the sugar refinery workers and the furniture workers, also became significant in shaping a tradition of unionism that contrasts markedly with what we have considered in Chapter Four. It is a tradition whose importance grew as the militant non-racial tradition, often linked to the Communist Party, declined. Radicals were present amongst the garment workers but never successful, perhaps in the end underscoring the effectiveness of Indian working-class participation in this industry as a form of incorporation into those structures of South African mid-twentieth-century capitalism acknowledged by the state and the business world as legitimate.[51]

The figure of an English workingman, James Bolton, looms large in this history. Bolton, a figure long excoriated by the South African Left as a racist and reactionary, arrived in South Africa as a foreman-upholsterer in the furniture trade in 1928, was at one phase a city councillor, and died in 1964. In 1934, he was the key figure in the founding of the Garment Workers' Industrial Union (Natal).[52] Originally involved in the struggle to save the white furniture craft workers' jobs, so typical of the South African industrial scene of the 1920s, Bolton quickly came to understand that it was essential to proceed through policies of inclusion and incorporation while rejecting the radical impulse. The union initiated struggles in the 1930s which significantly improved the situation of Indian workers in the industry in Durban, while still allowing for labour costs that would look profitable compared to those in Transvaal factories. Honestly run, gradually promoting Indian, Coloured and female officials, and offering genuine benefits, the GWIU was to be a central force in the reconstruction of the Indian working class away from the desperate conditions that prevailed in the militant era of the 1930s and 1940s. Imitating one and then another approach of the historically white trade unions, the union tried first to prevent undercutting from Africans as a new component in the work-force, through exclusion, and then shifted towards incorporation, generating a parallel trade union for Africans.[53] By the end of the 1970s, the GWIU was the largest component in the "moderate" Trade Union Council of South Africa after the equivalent union, mainly catering to Coloured women workers, based in Cape Town.[54] Such unions organised perhaps 20 per cent of economically active Indians, including many who received some benefit, but were paid at low levels.[55]

Table 6.3   Trade unions with significant Indian membership, 1952

Trade Union	Total membership	Indian membership
Building Workers	1966	600
Non-European Bus Workers	330	330
Furniture Workers	1007	971
Garment Workers	4184	2518
Liquor & Catering	3236	2500
Sugar Industry Employees	2742	2742
Textile Workers	1069	976
Leather Workers	2606	2100
Typographers Union	1766	960

Source: T. Gardener, "Socio-economic Position of the Indian," ms., South African Bureau of Racial Affairs, *c.* 1952

By 1962, the Durban municipality, which had a decade earlier been threatening Indian workers with mass dismissals, was replacing Africans with "more efficient" Indians.[56] The Durban Indian Municipal Employees' Union — DIMES — could take a militant stance against what it felt as discrimination, or in favour of moderate improvements in the workplace, but it did not shake the overall economic order on which municipal services rested.[57] Such Indian workers could however feel "protected" from competition with African workers.[58]

Outside the strictly industrial sphere, but with major implications for the job market, however, the policies of the state itself altered to the benefit of Indians. The crucial turning point came in 1960. Before that point, National Party policy insisted on labelling Indians as aliens who could never be assimilated into South African society and emphasis was placed on making repatriation to India attractive to the surviving ex-indentured workers and their children. Until 1947, militant Indians, however concerned for their rights in South Africa, actually believed that the successes of the nationalist movement in India, with which they strongly identified, would directly benefit their situation locally. This view dissipated in the 1950s and coverage of sub-continental politics and affairs dwindled markedly in the Indian-orientated press.

After 1960, the state changed policies fairly dramatically, conceding that the Indians constituted a permanent portion of the South African population.[59] One consequence was the investment in large working-class townships around Durban and other centres where Indians lived. However, there was also a willingness to rechannel Indians into economic activities where the state wanted to encourage their active participation. The apartheid era was one of rapidly increasing educational opportunities on a segregated basis for Indians.

Indian education had always depended to a significant extent on the contribution of Indians themselves. In 1946 only 15 per cent of the education vote in Natal was designated for Indians; by 1964, it had risen to 37 per cent, but the cost of land and buildings was still usually met by Indian communities and education was neither free nor compulsory.[60]

An important shift occurred with the transfer of Indian education to a separate ministry of Indian affairs in 1966. According to the first minister, W. A. Maree, "The take-over of all Indian Education, beginning in Natal in April, 1966, will I am convinced, herald a new era for the Indian Community of the Republic of South Africa. The particular needs of the Indian community will be especially and adequately catered for and the present somewhat narrow educational field will be considerably expanded."[61] Compulsory education for Indians, once a demand of Indian militants, was in fact introduced in 1973.[62] Now there was a growing willingness to train Indians for particular careers, and to promote mass secondary education. This culminated in the development of a teacher training college at Springfield and a university designed for Indians in Durban, which would feature education in such fields as pharmacy and engineering.[63] The recipients of these benefits came to resent bitterly remaining limitations and the elaborate system of controls over their lives. Into the 1970s, Indians had formally to get permission from the state, for instance, to move from Natal to another province. Thus the university particularly became a key site of political opposition, but the economic importance of the broad range of jobs and careers now opened to Indians cannot be gainsaid.

Throughout the 1950s, Indians were virtually excluded from apprenticeships and the full acquisition of skills in the South African working class. Thereafter, not only was skill acquisition opened up, but training courses at the M. L. Sultan Technikon and the university college (later the University of Durban-Westville) were specifically designed to attract Indian boys into new areas. In 1959, M. L. Sultan only registered "a handful" of apprentices, mainly in the furniture trade, while the number by 1973 was 708, including the building and engineering trades.[64] During the 1970s, significant numbers of skilled Indian workers emerged.[65] This made possible unprecedented mobility, symbolised by the constant home expansions and improvements character-ising Chatsworth and other Indian working-class areas.

It remained largely true that Indians were placed in a position where they could not compete with whites, except by offering services at a lower cost, and they were not frequently welcomed into positions where they would exert managerial authority over whites. The continued segregatory element in the apartheid system ensured that Indians of all classes felt a sense of antagonism to and distance from whites.

Nonetheless, the new advantages were tangible and real. Expression was given to this situation by the new political structures. The South African Indian Council was created in 1964 to allow Indians some power over affairs relating to their own community. Economic opportunity was part of its brief. It included a trade union representative in its membership. The Indian Industrial Development Corporation, for instance, lent money to Indian industrialists from 1977. Here, too, lay the origins of a significant complement of Indian civil servants. In 1983, the so-called tricameral constitution was inaugurated, giving Indians the vote in a separate chamber of parliament. While this provided little say in the running of national affairs, it was another stage of co-optive and advisory structuration that served as a source of patronage and community resource allocation.

* * *

Changes imposed by life in the new townships also held major implications for working-class Indian society in the Durban region. The attitude of Indian working-class communities perhaps revealed the flexibility of people with immigrant roots; this factor was crucial in making these townships viable. At first cry, a sense of loss of human networks in which material life had formed, prevailed. Youths formed gangs in the absence of a viable street culture.[66] Resources were poor and it took a long time for schools to be erected, health facilities to be built and neighbourhood ties to form. The built environment lacked attractive public spaces. The illegal liquor outlet replaced the community-supportive shebeen.[67] Crime was a significant factor, particularly in Phoenix and particularly in its early days. It was a world where "you gotta mind your own business."[68] However, there has been an overwhelming emphasis on constructing new communities.[69]

The evolution of Chatsworth into a network of neighbourhoods in which people took great pride and formed extensive new kinds of human contact was universally noted by informants to me. "People have bettered themselves" was the verdict of a pastor who came there from Puntans Hill.[70] "Chatsworth," said an elderly informant, "is becoming better than Overport."[71] At first, many denizens lived as sub-tenants or in spare rooms, garages, basements and the like, but by 1983 a survey estimated such people as only 16 per cent of the total.[72] Phoenix has been less successful because it is newer, because it emerged at a time when economic growth was starting to falter seriously, and because its population tended to be poorer from the outset. Yet here, too, the commitment of anti-apartheid community activists, despite deep hostility to the philosophic underpinning of racial Group Areas, to struggling for a better living environment and their intense sense of loyalty to Phoenix as home, struck me as an interviewer forcibly. The lesser success of Phoenix has, moreover, been paralleled by the rise of private sector suburbia catering to Indian families on its periphery.

Housing was now structured along lines of class-based neighbourhoods and constructed in a way that was inimical to group families organised around the authority of the patriarchal head. Only a small proportion of income could be earned in this physical environment, apart from wages, salaries and pensions and other such grants.[73] The House of Delegates MP for Phoenix himself reported that the joint family system was "destroyed by Group Areas."[74] The new townships "split up the families."[75] The extended family certainly survived as a cultural ideal, an idiom, after all there remain advantages in the family as a unit of trust, but it now lacked physical substance.[76] It was forced against the odds to exist in physically non-continuous space. Within the family, power shifted away from the patriarch. An informant reported a haunting story of such a patriarch from Clairwood now forced to shift, Lear-like and impotent, between the households of his three daughters.[77]

A 1978 survey suggested that 80 per cent of Indian families were "basic" nuclear families, with or without some extended members, and most of the others merely accommodated grandparents. The formally constituted, negotiated, joint family has become relatively rare. That survey indicated that some two-thirds *prefer* living in a basic family.[78] For previously junior and relatively exploited members of the family, growing financial independence and greater privacy were in fact highly desirable. There are counter-tendencies. Families do extend houses in the old way sometimes, and sales outside the family are not very frequent. Yet the dissolution of older bonds is worth stressing.

Closely tied to this was a growing self-definition in terms of consumerism. The family became the seat for possession of cars (poor transport to work and the availability of shops, not good even in Chatsworth, made this an extremely important if costly investment) as well as other consumer durables around which family entertainment operated. The female factory worker whose wages go largely to sustain running the family car is not uncommon.[79] A 1970 survey of Indian readers of the *Daily News*, showed that two-thirds of the respondents owned a radiogram (phonograph), half owned a refrigerator, three-quarters owned an electric stove and one-third possessed a car.[80]

The nucleated family was the key site of material and ideological life. In a 1978 survey of Indian households (of which half had as prime earners unskilled or semi-skilled workers) 84 per cent had male household heads and, of the remainder, 85 per cent of the heads were widows.[81] Family size diminished from 1945 (but rapidly from the 1960s), hand in hand with the growing prospects for mobility and good health on the part of children. Yet there was far less time for the complex and gracious rituals of Indian family interaction.[82] The family suffered from indebtedness and also the tensions that went with the enormous amount invested in it in terms of happiness: reality that goes against the ideology includes alcoholism, the growing divorce rate, frequent family violence and murders, and a high level of tension for lack of social alternatives.[83] By 1986 there were 1 029 divorces compared to 7 414 marriages amongst "Asians" recorded in South Africa (1975: 265 for 7 938 marriages); a divorce rate close to one in seven in flagrant contrast to the extremely conservative conventional image of the Oriental family.

Only an intense, in-depth study of social change within the new townships would bear fruit effectively in the understanding of cultural change. However, a few shifts can be suggested. An obvious point is the dramatic decline in Indian languages first as the normal language of communication and now, amongst those born since 1960 especially, even the ability to understand these languages.[84] By 1978, a study reported that in urban Natal, 96 per cent of Indians between the ages of 15 and 35 were literate in English.[85] According to Mesthrie,[86] speakers of the principal Indian languages once spoken by the working class have declined as follows in number:

Table 6.4 Speakers of Indian languages in South Africa

	1960	1980
Tamil	141 977	24 720
Telugu	34 483	4 000
Hindi	126 067	25 900

Source: R. Mesthrie, *Language in Indenture: A Sociolinguistic History of Bhojpuri-Hindi in South Africa* (Johannesburg: Witwatersrand University Press, 1991).

Indians in Durban have become English speakers, probably a factor of considerable importance in the range of economic opportunities open to them that gives them a tremendous advantage over Africans who remain primarily Zulu speaking, even though a distinct South African Indian English speech pattern continues to be a tie that binds.

One cultural phenomenon that has received some attention has been the rapid spread of fundamentalist Christianity amongst working-class Indians in Durban. Gina Buijs has made a fascinating study of the most important new church, the Bethesda Pentecostalists, with a membership estimated in 1983 at 40 000, predominantly drawn from amongst the descendants of ex-indentured workers from south India.[87] This church originated before the arrival of Group Areas (in the 1920s in Pietermaritzburg, introduced at the Magazine Barracks in the following decade), but it has spread extensively in the new physical terrain. Buijs argues that the pioneer converts were, as in the case of the urban explorers of sport and the cinema in a slightly earlier era, often service workers such as Pastor Frank Victor, a Durban waiter. "Those who became evangelists, leaders or pastors in the organisation had usually come from jobs in service industries, such as a waiter, chef or factory worker."[88] Evangelical Christianity in this form harmonises with and shows an appreciation of some aspects of Indian culture, such as the prestige of family structures (and Oosthuizen has suggested that, in some measure, the church is a substitute for the family-based community)[89] or the survival of such symbolic cultural features as the wearing of the *sari*. At the same time it incorporates members into a universal organisation that encourages thrift, education and social mobility and communicates in English. Austerity of Christian practise accommodates a tolerance for exorcism and speaking in tongues. While rejecting overly lavish ceremonies and parentally arranged marriages, the church projects a very conservative role for women and strongly upholds abstinence from sex for the unmarried.[90] It rejects as sinful all kinds of activities that have been a hallmark of secularisation and acculturation to the Indian working class — the secular cinema, smoking, drinking, gambling, "worldly dress" — although promoting participation in sport.[91] The Bethesda Pentecostal Church has been careful to avoid any kind of political hostility to the state; it is clearly a force for social and political conservatism. In hard times, such churches are crucial as sources of charity for the desperate.[92]

Less studied is what has been called "neo-Hinduism," a Hinduism largely purged of the older dependence on caste as the basis of society and other elements inappropriate to participation in modern South African society, although containing elements of what Buijs calls "folk Hinduism" which retained beliefs in older forms of medicine, demon possession, etc.[93] If a symbol of the new outlook of urban Indians in Durban half a century ago was a virtual love affair with the cinema, today, the continuing home-based appeal of sentimentally romantic Indian films, best watched at home on video and thus linked to the continued cult of family identity and loyalty, the continued popularity of Indian popular music, etc. can be taken as tokens of a new kind of ethnicity. It is an ethnicity divorced often from the specifics of language and even of religion but linked effectively to the realities of residential segregation and an apparently opportunity-laden but anomic society where it is not easy to forge new and meaningful loyalties.

$$* * *$$

While at first, rents and services in purpose-built Indian housing in Durban were relatively reasonable, the recovery of costs by the state imposed waves of dramatically increasing rents and, especially, service charges. The first phase in 1969 eliminated the extremely low "sub-economic rents" of early days.[94] The new rates bore heavily on many Indian families, some of them wistful for the inexpensive life that enabled survival on the urban periphery in the old days.[95] A composite portrait suggested that "We were moved because the place had to be cleared for whites or because they said we were living under slum conditions. The houses they gave us were better but the rent is high and we must pay so much for transport as we now live far from town."[96] A survey after the 1983 election revealed that some 61 per cent of Phoenix tenants saw high rents as a serious problem, compared to only 14 per cent concerned with transport, or 13 per cent concerned with crime and violence.[97] The threat of evictions (and to a lesser extent shutting down electricity), especially in the hard times of the middle 1980s and early 1990s, was a major source of tension and fear.[98] Conditions were particularly difficult in Phoenix to where many of the poorest Indian families with the lowest incomes were removed at the end of the whole Group Areas programme.[99] By contrast, the quality of housing is less often a major source of complaint.[100]

The family was squeezed by a combination of these demands and the internalised pressures of consumerism. At first sight, this yielded a prospect of new Indian working-class radicalism. After many years in which repression and relative prosperity had seemed to marginalise radical political activity, a revival of the Natal Indian Congress (re-formed in 1971) seemed to herald renewed attempts to galvanise working-class opinion, partly around new issues that focused on economic pressures in the municipally owned townships. The Durban Housing Action Committee, formed in 1980, targeted on the tenant-residents of Indian townships, but was also active to some extent amongst Coloured tenants. Only in the small African areas which had not been incorporated into the KwaZulu homeland, was such activity relevant amongst Africans. The plan was to coalesce such practical complaints and build them up towards a broader political vision. The relatively low turn-out (below 30 per cent of registered voters) by the Indian population for the tricameral election in 1983 seemed to be a triumph for this strategy.[101]

However, this triumph may have been more apparent than real. According to one survey of 150 Phoenix dwellings, while only 16 per cent of those queried had a positive view of the election, a larger number had no view or were simply uninterested than actually expressed a negative view; some 66 per cent could identify no organisation interested in their problems.[102] To a large extent, the material complaints of Indians in

Durban reflect particular circumstances that require redress in terms of the fiscal crisis of the state, but will only with great difficulty unite those who own their own property, those who rent but have reasonable and steady incomes, the poorest of homeowners, and shack-dwellers. From 1980, a first major rise in rentals led to boycotts and resistance that encouraged anti-state activists.[103] It was possible as well to look to the poor transport situation and to expose the implications of creating a separate Indian city detached from Durban and its resources. In 1988 again, there was considerable success in mobilising city tenants across race lines in protest against a new significant wave of rent increases and service charges, often a very large share in the expenses of the poor, but it was not a success that could create a new kind of politics.[104] In 1991, unskilled employees of the House of Delegates (the parliamentary chamber representing Indians) launched a spectacular strike, superficially showing militancy reminiscent to some extent of the commitment of half a century earlier, but faced now with the context of recession and a state no longer able to finance services on an increasing scale.[105]

These movements have had a somewhat ephemeral character, and do not show any definite build-up towards reconstructing urban politics in Durban. The political affiliations in different communities continue to reflect originally racially constituted constituencies, and different ideas of what sort of country South Africa is, as well as different material circumstances. Admiration for activists prepared to stand up to City Hall does not necessarily translate into positive support for the Natal Indian Congress, still less for the African National Congress.[106] Politically, there remained an unresolved division between the politics of non-participation and the desire to obtain services and patronage through participation. A 1992 poll suggested that 53 per cent opposed and 35 per cent favoured existing Local Advisory Councils being incorporated into the existing white Durban City Council.[107] Such a move would have been unthinkably liberal to whites in the racist climate of a half-century earlier but at this stage was dismissed by radicals as a sop to buy off Coloured and Indian support and prevent "majority rule" and a presumptive African majority in local government.

This political quandary reproduces itself notably in the new trade-union movement that has surfaced since the middle 1970s. The cautious and non-militant trade unions to which Indians largely belonged, developed and expanded "parallel" structures for Africans, and then declared themselves non-racial, but were unable to capture the support and enthusiasm of African workers.[108] They have gone into decline or dissolved, unable to retain these structures into the current era.

The new unions, most of which came together in 1985 into the Congress of South African Trade Unions, became involved in trying to win the support of various categories of Indian workers. A number of observers have commented on the significance of incorporating non-African, and notably Indian, workers into those unions. This kind of incorporation often has a strong material logic. Apart from the sheer weight of numbers of Indian workers in Durban, the high skill levels of some gives them a critical workplace salience. Moreover, there remains an important submerged tenth of the Indian population of Durban that is bitterly poor, so poor that during the 1980s it looked with some admiration and envy at the gains of the more militant African unionised workers.[109]

Effective unions have certainly found it possible to win and hold Indian members.[110] However, to do so has required reaching Indians through Indians, with politicised and committed individuals often playing a key role.[111] Indian workers often have deeply internalised self-images of diligence and acceptance of authority, and this applies particularly to women; the historic fears of being undercut by African workers also run deep. In particular, pro-African National Congress politics, have not been acceptable to Indian workers who continue to understand the unions, most of the time and outside crisis situations, in terms of practical benefits rather than as a cultural component of a new hegemonic approach to South African society.[112] By contrast with many African workers, the unions are not a substitute for a sense of community which comes, if at all, from a family or residential base.[113]

One African organiser for the paper workers' union commented that "Indian workers are not integrated into the union — they don't attend locals or BECs, so they are not familiar with union policies or strategies."[114] To deal with the problem, he could only think of approaching Natal Indian Congress or "community" leaders. Such individuals are often committed to COSATU and its political allies, but their standing amongst ordinary Indian workers is less certain. A recent analysis of COSATU indicates that while the Indian Garment Workers' Union members, now swallowed up in the South African Clothing and Textile Workers' Union, have remained unionists, they are now much less interested in participating or becoming shop stewards.[115]

In material terms, the in-between character of Indian South Africans as a whole is now easy to indicate in figures. In 1984, 42 per cent earned R16 000 p.a. compared to 83 per cent of whites, but only 14 per cent of Coloureds and 5 per cent of Africans. At the bottom of the scale, only 13 per cent earned under R5 000 p.a., a figure significantly higher than the 3 per cent of whites, but very much lower than the 48 per cent of Coloureds and 62 per cent of Africans.[116] Mass secondary and technical education has been a key to very extensive upward mobility.[117]

Indians remain frightened of Africans, who are poorer and have claims on resources that might threaten and endanger their own gains. To what extent an ideology of "non-racialism" will bring people to redefine their identity in other than racial terms, the future in fact of ethnicity in a "new South Africa," is quite uncertain.[118] In April 1994, a four-year transition period, at the outset of which Group Areas were abolished, culminated in the first general election based on universal franchise in South Africa. The actual results of the election were only made available in terms of provincial totals. Consequently, assumptions about how the Indian working class voted depend on extrapolation from polls, and from the opinion of informed and anonymous individuals involved in the election process. Polls predicted that the National Party would get a significant majority of the Indian vote. Individual opinion suggested, in the context of a large turn-out, that this is precisely what did occur. The National Party, which received approximately one-tenth of the Natal vote, ironically now depends on its provincial Indian supporters and it is in Chatsworth, and even more in Phoenix, that this support was particularly strong. Moreover, a significant minority of the Indian vote, especially perhaps in Chatsworth, remained loyal to the tricameral parliament politician Amichand Rajbansi and his Minority Party. An educated guess suggests that perhaps one-quarter of the Indian vote in Natal at best went to the African National Congress. That vote disproportionately came from younger, more educated middle-class Indians. Sources suggest that the class line was important in determining the Indian vote.

Memories of racial exclusion, of being cast as outsiders in the city, are long and continue to enflame a minority of committed activists, particularly those who have come together since the mid-1970s at the University of Durban-Westville, and who constitute the core of a new generation of Indian radicals in South African political and intellectual life. By contrast with the average Indian voter, Indian intellectuals and activists, some from working-class backgrounds, are extremely prominent as parliamentarians, cabinet members and other foreground figures in the new post-apartheid political scene.

This remarkable ethnic dichotomy reflects a distinctive perspective and its ambiguities, a perspective shaped in large part by the particular working-class history which has been the subject of this volume. The only conclusion to which one can come at present is that Indian workers exhibit a mixture of attitudes. They look out on South African society from a unique position, experiencing it both as outsiders and as insiders. Their own vigour, the plasticity and ingenuity of their cultural and material response to circumstance, has been applied to the peculiar institutions of South Africa to shape the rooms in which they dwell and the windows through which they look out on the broader world.

The vision of racialism joined to modernism has faded and a new South Africa, perhaps a new Durban where small-scale, unregulated activities become widespread and new kinds of social and economic associations proliferate, may be emerging. The descendants of the indentured workers will probably adapt themselves anew to the changing scene and help, in important ways, to shape it. Studies of working-class life and labour have often been studies of proletarianisation as a totalising project, of the "making" of a working class as though this were a process of setting in concrete. This section of the South African working class experienced complex relations with the rest of the population and its history exhibits change, flexibility and mobility. To what extent the Indian working class will succeed in maintaining its historic distinctiveness is quite unclear; equally, the extent to which mobility will reduce its ranks to a far more marginal section of Durban society and economy is hard to predict. Its history thus far, however, sheds light on the formation and development of the South African city and the struggles of its inhabitants to determine its character and turn it into their home.

NOTES

Preface

1. Michael Storper and Richard Walker, *The Capitalist Imperative: Territory, Technology and Industrial Growth* (New York and Oxford: Basil Blackwell, 1989), p. 225.

Chapter 1
A Passage from India: Indentured Immigrants Come to Natal, 1860–1911

1. I have discussed this system and its impact in "The Cape under the Transitional Governments 1795–1814," in Richard Elphick and Hermann Giliomee, eds., *The Shaping of South African Society, 1652–1840* (Cape Town: Maskew Miller Longman, 1989), pp. 324–57.
2. See, for example, David Brian Davis, *The Problem of Slavery in the Age of Revolution 1770–1823* (Ithaca: Cornell University Press, 1975); Robin Blackburn, *The Overthrow of Colonial Slavery 1776–1848* (London: Verso, 1988).
3. Jan Boeyens, "'Zwart Ivoor': Inboekelinge in Zoutpansberg, 1848–69," *South African Historical Journal* 24 (1991), pp. 31–67.
4. Robert Hughes, *The Fatal Shore: A History of the Transportation of Convicts to Australia 1787–1868* (London: Collins Harvill, 1987).
5. For Mauritius, see Hugh Tinker, *A New System of Slavery: The Export of Indian Labour Overseas 1830–1920* (London: Oxford University Press, 1974), pp. 44–45.
6. For an excellent comparative and theoretical discussion, see Robert Miles, *Capitalism and Unfree Labour: Anomaly or Necessity* (London: Tavistock, 1987).
7. Tinker, *New System of Slavery* remains a standard introduction to the subject.
8. See Keletso Atkins, "The Cultural Origins of an African Work Ethic and Practices: Natal, South Africa 1843–75," Ph.D. thesis, University of Wisconsin, 1986, for Natal Africans with regard to colonial labour demands.
9. For a useful history of the colonial sugar industry in Natal, see Peter Richardson, "The Natal Sugar Industry, 1849–1905: An Interpretative Essay," *Journal of African History* 23 (1982), pp. 515–27.
10. M. D. North-Coombes, "Indentured Labour in the Sugar Industries of Mauritius and Natal 1834–1910," in Surendra Bhana, ed., *Essays on Indentured Indians in Natal* (Leeds: Peepal Tree Press, 1990), pp. 62–63.
11. Tinker, *New System of Slavery*.
12. Maureen Swan, *Gandhi: The South African Experience* (Johannesburg: Ravan, 1985), p. 26.
13. Maureen Swan, "Indentured Indians: Accommodation and Resistance 1890–1913," in Bhana, *Indentured Indians*, especially pp. 121–22.

14. Jo Beall, "Women under Indentured Labour in Colonial Natal 1860–1911," in Cherryl Walker, ed., *Women and Gender in Southern Africa to 1945* (Cape Town: David Philip, 1990), pp. 146–67 and "Women under Indenture in Natal," in Bhana, *Indentured Indians*. See also Tinker, *New System of Slavery*, pp. 201ff.

15. See North-Coombes, "Indentured Labour," p. 39. Compare with John Edwin Mason, "The Slaves and their Protectors: Reforming Resistance in a Slave Society, the Cape Colony 1826–34," *Journal of Southern African Studies* 17, 1 (1991), pp. 104–28.

16. Eric Foner, *Free Soil, Free Labor, Free Men: The Ideology of the Republican Party Before the Civil War* (London: Oxford University Press, 1970).

17. See *Natal Government Gazette*, supplement, 20 September 1887: Wragg Commission [hereafter NGG WCOM], evidence of James Saunders, p. 100; Killie Campbell Africana Library, Durban [hereafter KCAL], KCM 32545, Marshall Campbell papers.

18. A. J. Arkin, *Contribution of the Indians to the South African Economy 1860–1970*, Occasional Publication, no. 14 (Durban: University of Durban-Westville, Institute for Social and Economic Research, 1981), p. 46.

19. See Frene Ginwala, "Class, Consciousness and Control: Indian South Africans 1860–1946," D.Phil. thesis, Oxford University, 1974.

20. Swan, *Gandhi*, pp. 65–66.

21. Jo Beall and M. D. North-Coombes, "The 1913 Disturbances in Natal: The Social and Economic Background to 'Passive Resistance,'" *Journal of Natal and Zulu History* 6 (1983), p. 65.

22. Maureen Swan, "The 1913 Natal Indian Strike," *Journal of Southern African Studies* 10, 2 (1984). See also Beall and North-Coombes, "The 1913 Disturbances."

23. Swan, "The 1913 Strike," pp. 256–57.

24. Swan, "Accommodation and Resistance."

25. Beall and North-Coombes, "The 1913 Disturbances," p. 59.

26. See North-Coombes, "Indentured Labour."

27. L. M. Thompson, "Indian Immigration into Natal (1860–72)," *Archives Yearbook for South African History* 15, 2 (1952), chapter 5.

28. Tinker, *New System of Slavery*, p. 313.

29. For an excellent analysis see Jonathan Crush, "Uneven Labour Migration in Southern Africa: Conceptions and Misconceptions," *South African Geographical Journal* 66, 2 (1984).

30. Tinker, *New System of Slavery*, p. 331.

31. NGG WCOM, p. 69.

32. Beall and North-Coombes, "The 1913 Disturbances," p. 67; Swan, "The 1913 Strike," p. 241.

33. Tinker, *New System of Slavery*, p. 120.

34. *Ibid.*, p. 215.

35. [Gonarathnam] Goonam, *Coolie Doctor* (Durban: Madiba, 1991), p. 11.

36. Tinker, *New System of Slavery*, p. 120.

37. *Natal Blue Book* [hereafter NBB], 1883, Report of the Protector of (Indian) Immigrants (with reference to the circle of Stanger), p. FF57.

38. Joy Brain, "Religion, Missionaries and Indentured Indians," in Bhana, *Indentured Indians*, pp. 209–26. But see Alleyn Diesel and Patrick Maxwell, *Hinduism in Natal: A Brief Guide* (Pietermaritzburg: University of Natal Press, 1993).

39. Diesel and Maxwell, *Hinduism*, pp. 63ff.

40. Tinker, *New System of Slavery*, p. 209. On this see Gina Buijs, "The Influence of Migration on Ethnic Identity: An Historical Analysis of the Disappearance of Caste among Indian South Africans," Paper presented to the Conference on Ethnicity, Society and Conflict in Natal, University of Natal, Pietermaritzburg, September 1992.

41. See for instance Swan, *Gandhi*, p. 19.

42. S. Rampersad, "Biography of Jaichoo Nanoo," History III essay, University of Durban-Westville, n.d.

43. Rajend Mesthrie, *Language in Indenture: A Sociolinguistic History of Bhojpuri-Hindi in South Africa* (Johannesburg: Witwatersrand University Press, 1992), p. 8. For the memory of an

indentured employee of Marshall Campbell, who was closely questioned on his caste background when he did seek to marry, see Documentation Centre, University of Durban-Westville, G.P. Reddy papers. For the continued interest in caste on the part of Hindu *passenger* Indians, see the evidence of an indentured clerk, George Mutukistna to the Wragg Commission. NGG WCOM, p.191.
44. Mesthrie, *Language in Indenture*, p.56.
45. Tinker, *New System of Slavery*, p.211.
46. Mesthrie, *Language in Indenture*, p.17.
47. *Ibid.*, p.240.
48. Tinker, *New System of Slavery*, p.210.
49. For an economic analysis see Vishnu Padayachee and Robert Morrell, "Indian Merchants and *Dukawallahs* in the Natal Economy *c.*1875–1914," *Journal of Southern African Studies* 17, 1 (1991), pp.71–104.

Chapter 2
Heaven on Earth in Springfield Flats: The Peasant Option

1. The historian who has best captured this period of South African history is Charles van Onselen, *Studies in the Social and Economic History of the Witwatersrand 1886–1914: New Babylon, New Nineveh* (Harlow: Longmans, 1982).
2. For the Natal economy in the nineteenth and early twentieth century, the most convenient guide is Bill Guest and John Sellers, eds., *Enterprise and Exploitation in a Victorian Colony: Aspects of the Economic and Social History of Colonial Natal* (Pietermaritzburg: University of Natal Press, 1985).
3. D. Hobart Houghton and Jenifer Dagut, *Source Material on the South African Economy 1860–1970*, vol.3 (Cape Town: Oxford University Press, 1977), p.297; Andrew Duminy and Bill Guest, *Natal and Zululand from Earliest Times to 1910: A New History* (Pietermaritzburg: University of Natal Press and Shuter & Shooter, 1989), p.431.
4. Colin Bundy, *The Rise and Fall of the South African Peasantry* (Berkeley and Los Angeles: University of California Press, 1979); Jack Lewis, "The Rise and Fall of the South African Peasantry: A Critique and Reassessment," *Journal of Southern African Studies* 11, 1 (1984).
5. M.L. Morris, "The Development of Capitalism in South African Agriculture: Class Struggles in the Countryside," *Economy and Society* 5, (1976).
6. Richardson, "Natal Sugar Industry."
7. Mervyn David Lincoln, "The Culture of the South African Sugarmill: The Impress of the Sugarocracy," Ph.D. thesis, University of Cape Town, 1985, p.197.
8. Tinker, *New System of Slavery*, p.234.
9. North-Coombes, "Indentured Labour."
10. Anne Vaughan, "Cane, Class and Credit," 1990. This is the subject of her forthcoming Ph.D. thesis. Departmental paper, Department of Economic History, University of Natal, Durban.
11. North-Coombes, "Indentured Labour," see also Tinker, *New System of Slavery*, pp.34–35.
12. Interview with K. Naidu et al., 20 November 1990.
13. *The Leader*, 19 July 1941.
14. L. Neame, *The Asiatic Danger in the Colonies* (London: George Routledge, 1907).
15. Sir John Robinson, *A Life-Time in South Africa* (London: Smith, Elder & Co., 1900), pp.76–77.
16. Neame, *Asiatic Danger*, p.138.
17. *Ibid.*, p.30.
18. For a recent, useful general survey see Joy Brain, "Indentured and Free Indians in the Economy of Colonial Natal," in Guest and Sellers, eds., *Enterprise and Exploitation*.
19. According to the Resident Magistrate, Pietermaritzburg; Surendra Bhana and Joy Brain, *Setting Down Roots: Indian Migrants in South Africa, 1860–1911* (Johannesburg: Witwatersrand University Press, 1990), p.65.

20. Interview with K. Naidu et al., 20 November 1990.
21. Rampersad, "Jaichoo Nanoo."
22. According to the Wragg Commission, between 1860 and 1885, 26 954 indentured workers arrived in Natal from India but only 1 716 returned to India and already some two-thirds of the Indian population in Natal were free by that date.
23. NBB, 1882, Umlazi Division Annual Report, p. GG35.
24. NBB, 1882, Protector of Immigrants' Report, p. FF35.
25. Cited in *Indian Opinion*, 24 April 1908.
26. NBB, 1904, Protector of Immigrants' Report.
27. NBB, 1894–95, p. B21; NBB, 1890, Protector of Immigrants' Report, p. A14.
28. R.J. Davies and J.C.C. Greyling, *Indian Farming on the Natal North Coast*, Report no. 39 (Pietermaritzburg: Natal Town and Regional Planning Commission, 1978), p. 25.
29. Neame, *Asiatic Danger*, p. 35. Frene Ginwala found a figure of 14 000 acres in the Verulam-Tongaat area alone in 1900 from the Lands Commission, "Indian South Africans," pp. 85–86. Perhaps 6 per cent of cultivated land in Natal was farmed by Indian tenants and landowners.
30. NBB, 1899, Protector of Immigrants' Report, annexures, p. A42. The accuracy of such figures is not to be highly rated and the figures are probably underestimates, as in other official reports.
31. NGG WCOM, p. 82; NBB, 1882, Inanda Division Report, p. GG46; NBB, 1883, Reports for Lower Tugela Division, p. GG16; for Inanda Division, p. GG25; for Alexandra Division, p. GG45; NBB, 1885, Inanda Division Report, p. B10; NBB, 1887, pp. B18–20.
32. NBB, 1887, Inanda Division Report, pp. BB18–20.
33. *Indian Opinion*, 25 November 1906.
34. Henry Slater, "The Changing Pattern of Economic Relations in Rural Natal, 1838–1914," in Shula Marks and Anthony Atmore, eds., *Economy and Society in Pre-industrial South Africa* (London: Longmans, 1980).
35. Davies and Greyling, *Indian Farming*.
36. See Lewis, "South African Peasantry." For the trekboers, see P.J. van der Merwe, *Trek: Studies oor die Mobiliteit van die Pioniersbevolking aan die Kaap* (Cape Town: Nasionale Pers, 1945) but, for the view that they too were intensively market-orientated, S.D. Neumark, *Economic Influences on the South African Frontier 1652–1837* (Stanford: Stanford University Press, 1957).
37. Padayachee and Morrell, "Indian Merchants."
38. NBB, 1892–93, Inanda Division Report, p. B53. Particularly further up the coast, Indian landholdings tended to be somewhat larger.
39. *Indian Opinion*, 14 September 1903.
40. In *Indian Opinion*, 23 December 1906.
41. Natal Archives, MSC/137/SUPREME COURT. [From V. Padayachee collection.]
42. J.C. Coulson, *Richmond: Its People and History* (Richmond: Women's League Institute, 1986).
43. *Fiat Lux* 2, 1 (1967), p. 3.
44. V. Chetty, History III essay, University of Durban-Westville, n.d. This essay obviously relates family history and claims that the first Chetty owned 5 000 acres of tobacco land near Spitzkop.
45. R. Moodley, "Biography of Pugavanam Moodley," History III essay, University of Durban-Westville, n.d.
46. *Fiat Lux* 18, 4 (1983).
47. N.A. Naidoo, History III essay, University of Durban-Westville, 1984.
48. Not all indentured workers were labourers, despite the great hostility of white working-class Natalians to the indenture of skilled men. Perhaps Indian success stories often involved such individuals.
49. In 1983–84, two descendants of Bodasing wrote History III essays on family history which are deposited at the Documentation Centre, University of Durban-Westville. Obviously the business history of the Bodasings would make an extraordinary tale.

50. Group interview with K. Naidu et al., 20 November 1990.
51. N.R. Kandosamy, "A Short History of the Glendale Sugar Mill," History III essay, University of Durban-Westville, 1985.
52. North-Coombes, "Indentured Labour."
53. NBB, 1900, Protector of Immigrants' Report, p. A14.
54. North-Coombes, "Indentured Labour," p. 54.
55. To some extent, the distinction being made here has an ethnic resonance. While the majority of North Coast farmers were Hindi-speaking immigrants from northern India, around the city of Durban and on the South Coast, the large majority originated from south India. J.J.C. Greyling, "Problems of Indian Landownership and Land-occupation on the Natal North Coast: A Socio-geographic Investigation," Ph.D. thesis, University of Natal, Durban, 1969, vol. 1, p. 47. Information about Durban and the South Coast from V. Padayachee; see also the survey in University of Natal, Department of Economics, *Studies of Indian Employment in Natal*, Natal Regional Survey, vol. 11, (Cape Town: Oxford University Press, 1961) p. 32.
56. S. A. Waiz, *Indians Abroad Directory* (Bombay: 1934).
57. Natal Indian Cane Growers' Association [hereafter NICGA] Annual Report, 1945.
58. Figures from the annual reports of the NICGA.
59. For instance, in 1962/63, some 2 per cent of Indian sugar-cane growers did have an income equivalent to the mean net income of white growers. Davies and Greyling, *Indian Farming*, p. 144.
60. William Beinart, "Transkeian Migrant Workers and Youth Labour on the Natal Sugar Fields 1918–40," Paper presented to the History Workshop, Johannesburg, 1990.
61. Interview with K. Naidu et al., 20 November 1990.
62. G.G. Maasdorp, "A Socio-economic Survey of the Indian Community in the Tongaat-Verulam Region," M.Com. thesis, University of Natal, Durban, 1966, pp. 134, 172. See also the shorter version published by the Economics Department of the university in 1968 entitled *A Natal Indian Community*.
63. Greyling, "Indian Landownership," vol. 1, p. 217.
64. David Rix, "Indian Agriculture on the North Coast of Natal: Technical Aspects," M.Agric. thesis, University of Pretoria, 1972.
65. Greyling, "Indian Landownership," vol. 1, pp. 202–3.
66. Rix, "Indian Agriculture," p. 18.
67. Interview with K. Naidu et al., 20 November 1990. The survival of mixed farming depended on shared purchases of lorries. Controls meant that the small producer could not sell inferior quality produce on the local market and could not determine his own prices.
68. It is more "regular and reliable," according to Rix's technical study, "Indian Agriculture," p. 16.
69. Rix, "Indian Agriculture," p. 140. Vaughan, considering the alternatives to monocropping, reports that for African cane-growers today, so-called short crops are completely impractical to market.
70. *Ibid.*, p. 16; NICGA Annual Report, 1945.
71. Interview with K. Naidu et al., 20 November 1990; Maasdorp, "Survey of the Indian Community," pp. 164ff.; Greyling, "Indian Landownership," vol. 1, p. 56. In Greyling's massive survey of 2 700 farms, the median size in the late 1960s was 11,215 acres with only one-quarter of farms larger than 22 acres, vol. 1, p. 59. Less than 10 per cent of land was owned by women. "Indian Landownership," vol. 1, p. 114.
72. Greyling, "Indian Landownership," vol. 1, pp. 67–68. Although they are slightly less likely to be sugar farmers, Rix, "Indian Agriculture," p. 121. Greyling considered that Indian-owned farms of under 10 acres were unlikely to provide a minimally acceptable income. Median size of farms in 1969 was 11,215 acres and modal size 7,98 acres.
73. Davies and Greyling, *Indian Farming*, pp. 72ff.
74. Surprisingly few of the farmers in the Greyling survey shared ownership — 25,7 per cent. "Indian Landownership," vol. 1, p. 77.

75. I.G. Halliday, "The Indian Market Gardeners of the Durban Peri-urban Area," M.A. thesis, University of Natal, Durban, 1940. Current community leaders also feel constrained against fighting this practice, despite their awareness of its disastrous economic effects. Interview with K. Naidu et al., 20 November 1990.

76. D.M. Scotney and D.M. Rix, "Land Use Problems in Indian Agriculture," *Fiat Lux* 10, 1 (1975). For some figures from 1962–63, see Davies and Greyling, *Indian Farming*, p.144. In 1975, the Rand, which had been worth $US1.42 was devalued to $US1.15.

77. Davies and Greyling, *Indian Farming*, p.35. The authors also mention a poor ability to comprehend standard English.

78. Rix, "Indian Agriculture," p.61.

79. Davies and Greyling, *Indian Farming*, p.144.

80. Maasdorp, "Survey of the Indian Community," p.162; Rix, "Indian Agriculture," p.173; Greyling, "Indian Landownership," vol.1, p.65; Davies and Greyling, *Indian Farming*, p.144. The latter estimated that 58 per cent in their 1962/63 survey were dependent on non-farm income. Indians on the North Coast farms were largely living below the Poverty Datum Line in the 1960s, according to the latter. Rix suggests around 1970 this was true of the majority with only 9 per cent well above it, "Indian Agriculture," p.135.

81. B.A. Naidoo and J. Naidoo, "Economic Opportunities and Mode of Living of the Indian Community," in *The Indian as South African* (Johannesburg: Institute of Race Relations, 1956), pp.35–36.

82. Greyling, "Indian Landownership," vol.1, p.40; A government commission in 1921 pointed out that Indian growers "gradually get squeezed out as the sugar industry expands," Rix, "Indian Agriculture," p.15. See also UG4/1921, Asiatic Inquiry Commission, pp.41–42. For the generally steep grade of Indian-owned land, see Davies and Greyling, *Indian Farming*, who claim in their 1978 publication that 57 per cent of the total had a 15 per cent+ slope.

83. According to Greyling, "Indian Landownership," vol.1, p.266, the Indian peasantry of the 1960s listed their biggest problems as lack of water, lack of land, lack of capital, lack of labour (especially the bigger farmers), inadequate marketing arrangements and inadequate transport. This list was not in any particular order of importance.

84. Greyling, "Indian Landownership," vol.1, pp.250, 252.

85. Rix, "Indian Agriculture," p.74.

86. *Ibid.*, p.85.

87. *Ibid.*, p.180.

88. Davies and Greyling, *Indian Farming*, p.136.

89. Maasdorp, "Survey of the Indian Community," p.167; Greyling, "Indian Landownership," vol.1, p.236. The annual reports of the NICGA are replete with the problems of growers in dealing with millers.

90. NICGA Annual Report, 1963/64.

91. Maasdorp also points to the use of hired Indian child-labour. By contrast, Indian capitalist sugar farmers use Pondo migrant labour just as whites do. Interview with K. Naidu et al., 20 November 1990.

92. Of the few Indian wage labourers, most lived on the premises. By contrast, this was true of relatively few Africans and especially few African women workers. Greyling, "Indian Landownership," vol.1, p.244. According to Rix, "few Indian farmers keep permanent labourers" as of 1972, "Indian Agriculture," p.144.

93. Maasdorp, "Survey of the Indian Community," p.157. Farms of 53 acres and more represented in 1969 only 9,26 per cent of farms but covered 60,5 per cent of Indian-owned acreage on the North Coast. Greyling, "Indian Landownership," vol.1, p.60. The 200+ acre farms, however, occupied less than 10 per cent of the total.

94. Scotney and Rix, "Land Use Problems."

95. *The Leader*, 31 May 1941. To some extent NICGA served as the substitute for the co-operatives which played such an important role in white agriculture.

96. G.G. Maasdorp and P.N. Pillay, "Occupational Mobility among the Indian People of Natal," in H.J. van der Merwe and C.J. Groenewald, *Occupational and Social Change among*

Coloured People (Cape Town: Juta, 1976), p. 81; Davies and Greyling, *Indian Farming*, p. 28; Greyling, "Indian Landownership," vol. 1, pp. 32–34; Rix, "Indian Agriculture," p. 16. For an example of an Indian entrepreneur who lost substantial amounts of agricultural land in the wake of the application of Group Areas legislation, see the biography of moneylender and grain trader Mohangi in the *Daily News* supplement, 23 August 1983, p. 12. The president of NICGA claimed in the annual report for 1975 that 30 000 acres had been lost by Indian farmers under the Group Areas Act.

97. Halliday, "Market Gardeners of Durban," p. 109. Indians themselves consider this an absolutely key issue. Interview with K. Naidu et al., 20 November 1990.
98. NGG WCOM, p. 82.
99. Arkin, *Contribution of Indians*, p. 145.
100. Halliday, "Market Gardeners of Durban." A survey in 1949 found an average of only 1,4 acres; University of Natal, *Studies of Indian Employment*, p. 16.
101. Yet fruit production was in fact less time-consuming, University of Natal, *Studies of Indian Employment*, p. 25.
102. I. G. Halliday, "Durban's Food Supplies," D.Phil. thesis, University of South Africa, 1942. A Public Health Department survey from *c.* 1940 itemised the acreage by sub-district as follows:

640 acres	Clairwood Flats
220 "	Bay Head
130 "	Mayville
108 "	Umhlatuzana
337 "	Sea Cow Lake
117 "	Prospect Hill/Umgeni/Riverside
245 "	Springfield Flats (including some of the most fertile plots).

See also Halliday, "Market Gardeners of Durban."
103. Halliday, "Market Gardeners of Durban," p. 24.
104. University of Natal, *Studies of Indian Employment*, p. 17.
105. Halliday, "Market Gardeners of Durban," p. 50. Yet by this time, most Indians surveyed had actually lived in the same locale for a considerable period of time.
106. Neame, *Asiatic Danger*, p. 30.
107. For problems of marketing vegetables, see Rix, "Indian Agriculture," p. 98 and K. K. Naidoo, "Biography of Narayaddu," History III essay, University of Durban-Westville, n.d.. Yet few permanent stallholders in the market were also gardeners, Halliday, "Durban's Food Supplies," p. 72.
108. Halliday, "Market Gardeners of Durban," p. 30; University of Natal, *Studies in Indian Employment*, p. 28.
109. S. Govindsamy, "The History of the Indian Market Gardeners of Cliffdale," B.A. (Hons) thesis, University of Durban-Westville, 1987.
110. University of Natal, *Studies in Indian Employment*, p. 19.
111. *Ibid.*, p. 20.
112. Halliday, "Market Gardeners of Durban," p. 30. For living conditions, see also University of Natal, *Studies in Indian Employment*, p. 31.
113. Halliday, "Market Gardeners of Durban," p. 35.
114. Halliday, "Durban's Food Supplies," p. 94.
115. *Ibid.*, p. 55.
116. Davies and Greyling, *Indian Farming*, p. 93; Arkin, *Contribution of Indians*, p. 148.
117. M. A. Tatham, "A Study of the Urban Morphology of Durban," M.Sc. thesis, University of Natal, Durban, 1955; Maasdorp and Pillay, "Occupational Mobility," p. 245; Menaka Padayachee, "A Socio-economic Profile of Four Market Gardening Communities in Metropolitan Durban," Fact Paper no. 6, (Durban: University of Durban-Westville, Institute for Social and Economic Research, 1986). The latter is a fascinating study which focuses especially on Cliffdale, a community of Indian farmers in some respects combining the

characteristics of both North Coast sugar farmers and Durban market gardeners. It was more Tamil- and Telugu-speaking than the North Coast Greyling covered but more Hindi-speaking than the Durban periphery as well. Cliffdale is well above Durban-Pinetown off the national highway to Pietermaritzburg, but it is essentially a vegetable marketing zone. It was examined a generation earlier by the University of Natal Economics Department, in *Studies in Indian Employment*, pp.36ff. See also H.L. Watts, *The Indian Community of Wyebank: A Socio-economic Survey in the Borough of Kloof* (Durban: University of Natal, Institute for Social Research, 1971), on a community near the places that Padayachee later investigated.

118. *Indian Opinion*, 22 July 1905.

119. Rampersad, "Jaichoo Nanoo."

120. Halliday, "Market Gardeners of Durban," p.71.

121. Menaka Padayachee, "Four Market Gardening Communities," pp.4ff.

122. Figures from Maasdorp and Pillay, "Occupational Mobility."

123. *Fiat Lux* 8, 8 (1973).

124. Interview with K. Naidu et al., 20 November 1990.

125. NICGA Annual Reports, 1958, 1965.

126. Interview with K. Naidu et al., 20 November 1990. The possibility of leasing white land seems to have waxed and waned over time. Before the 1946 Land Bill, it was relatively common. *The Leader*, 25 May 1946.

127. *Fiat Lux* 8, 8 (December 1973). At this time, a division of agriculture was also created in the Department of Indian Affairs.

128. Rix, "Indian Agriculture," p.5.

129. They were admitted to the Natal Agricultural Union by 1980. *Fiat Lux* 15, 2 (March 1980). By the late 1980s, Pat Bodasing was on the executive committee of the South African Cane Growers' Association and the council of the South African Sugar Association, and officials of the Natal Indian Cane Growers' Association were regularly being co-opted for government boards, etc. dealing with agriculture. NICGA Annual Report, 1989.

130. At first, however, this provision was largely nominal. The first loan known to a set of prominent Indian farmers interviewed occurred in 1974. Interview with K. Naidu et al., 20 November 1990. Ownership of 200 acres was a minimum requirement for a loan in this period. The NICGA annual report for 1976 declared that "in the eyes of the Indian grower, the Land and Agricultural Bank has become a laughing stock." See also NICGA Annual Report, 1979/80. The appointment of Indian valuators was crucial in order to overcome the problem of land being overvalued due to the Group Areas Act making it artificially scarce for Indian purchasers. *Fiat Lux* 15, 2 (March 1980), pp.6–7.

131. NICGA Annual Report, 1983/84.

132. Some 117 Indian farmers got loans of Rl l74 250 from the Land Bank. NICGA Annual Report, 1982/83. Aid was also fairly widely available in the wake of the September 1987 floods. NICGA Annual Report, 1989. In a group interview the importance of this aid was stressed. A secondary reform was the recognition of the growers' ability to determine their own fire accident claims. The wounds of nature rank high amongst the credit concerns of those who live off the land. Interview with K. Naidu et al., 20 November 1990.

133. A grower described them as "toothless bulldogs" but admitted that even with only gums to hold on with, they were not useless. They became a channel to state officialdom of some value. Interview with K. Naidu et al., 20 November 1990.

134. *Ibid.*

135. NICGA Annual Report, 1986.

136. Interview with K. Naidu et al., 20 November 1990.

137. Menaka Padayachee, "Four Market Gardening Communities," p.54.

138. *Ibid.*, section 7; confirmed in interview with K. Naidu et al., 20 November 1990.

139. Menaka Padayachee, "Four Market Gardening Communities," p.10.

140. Interview with K. Naidu et al., 20 November 1990.

141. NICGA Annual Report, 1970/71.
142. A recent estimate suggests 23 000 African growers, ten times the number in 1961 (see NICGA Annual Report) and some thirteen times the number of Indian growers. They produce perhaps 8 per cent of South African sugar cane, or double the Indian farmers' quota share. *Financial Mail*, 23 December 1989. Vaughan, "Cane, Class and Credit," is the germ of a major study of sugar-cane producers in KwaZulu.

Chapter 3
The Edge of Town: Durban and the Indian Working Class, 1900 –1930

1. Lucille Heydenrych, "Port Natal Harbour *c*. 1850–1897," in Guest and Sellers, *Enterprise and Exploitation*, p. 41.
2. Heyn Heydenrych, "Railway Development in Natal to 1895," in Guest and Sellers, *Enterprise and Exploitation*.
3. May Katzen, *Industry in Greater Durban, Part I: Its Growth and Structure*, Report no. 3 (Pietermaritzburg: Natal Town and Regional Planning Commission, 1961), pp. 95–96.
4. *Ibid.*, p. 60.
5. *Ibid.*, p. 71; Bruce Young, "The Industrial Geography of the Durban Region," Ph.D. thesis, University of Natal, Durban, 1972, p. 355.
6. Katzen, *Industry in Durban*, p. 78.
7. Bill Freund, "The Social Character of Secondary Industry in South Africa 1915–45 (with Special Reference to the Witwatersrand)," in Alan Mabin, ed., *Organisation and Social Change* (Johannesburg: Ravan, 1989), p. 81.
8. Katzen, *Industry in Durban*, pp. 59–60.
9. Young, "Industrial Geography of Durban," chapter 4; Katzen, *Industry in Durban*, p. 60; *Hunt, Leuchars and Hepburn 1850–1950*.
10. Young, "Industrial Geography of Durban," pp. 71–72; Katzen, *Industry in Durban*, p. 33.
11. Katzen, *Industry in Durban*, p. 17.
12. *Ibid.*, p. 25.
13. *Ibid.*, p. 133.
14. *Ibid.*, p. 128.
15. Interview with I. M., 14 November 1989.
16. M. W. Swanson, "The Asiatic Menace: Creating Segregation in Durban 1870–1900," *International Journal of African Historical Studies* 16 (1983), p. 406.
17. *Ibid.*
18. Natal Archives, [hereafter NA] 3/DBN, 14/4/1/2, Durban Borough Boundaries Commission.
19. Despite the attempts of the municipality to regulate activities in the barracks, here too there were remunerative activities that could be practised the more easily because of the proximity to the centre of town. For instance, many women peddled. V. Sirkari Naidoo, "Survey of Income and Expenditure of Indian Employees of the Durban Corporation Living at the Magazine Barracks, Durban," *South African Journal of Economics* 14, 1 (1946), p. 48.
20. Interview with B. R., 13 January 1992.
21. There are interesting official discussions of this issue in NA, 3/DBN, 1/2/6/1/1, Durban Public Health (Slums) Committee and NA, 3/DBN, 1/3/3/1/2, Durban Special Committee *re* Housing.
22. Although it can be argued that many purchasers of tiny plots on hire purchase were little better than tenants. NA, 3/DBN, 1/2/6/1/1, Durban Public Health (Slums) Committee.
23. As mentioned for instance in Rampersad, "Jaichoo Nanoo" and N. A. Naidoo, History III essay, University of Durban-Westville, 1984.
24. Dhianaraj Chetty, "The Durban Riots and Popular Memory," unpublished seminar paper, Durban, 1989. See Halliday, " Market Gardeners of Durban," p. 30; A. Bridgraj, History III essay, University of Durban-Westville, n.d.

25. P. Moodley, "Life of Rangasamy Pillay," History III essay, University of Durban-Westville, n.d.
26. "The Indian Fishing Community," in University of Natal, *Studies in Indian Employment*, p. 78.
27. *Ibid*, p. 101.
28. ". . . a nice free life in Fynnlands"; Dianne Scott and Costas Criticos, "Hanging up the Nets: The History of the Durban Bay Fishing Community," videorecording, 37 mins, Media Resource Centre, University of Natal, Durban, 1991.
29. NGG WCOM, pp. 75–77, for the beginnings, and Scott and Criticos, "Hanging up the Nets" for the end.
30. Moodley, "Rangasamy Pillay."
31. *Ibid.*
32. *Ibid.*; Scott and Criticos ("Hanging up the Nets") also show social mobility out of fishing, which first tended to become *either* a part-time *or* a professionalised activity divorced from the old Bayhead community life before individuals abandoned any connection to the trade.
33. Paul la Hausse, "Drink and Cultural Innovation in Durban: The Origin of the Beerhall in South Africa 1902–16," in Charles Ambler and Jonathan Crush, eds., *Liquor and Labor in Southern Africa* (Pietermaritzburg: University of Natal Press; Athens, Ohio: Ohio University Press, 1993).
34. Interview with P. B., 30 November 1989.
35. In 1974, a survey claimed that 30 per cent of Indians showed an interest in soccer, 19 per cent in fishing, 15 per cent in swimming, 13 per cent in cricket and 10 per cent in athletics, *Fiat Lux* 9, 1 (February 1974).
36. Interview with P. B., 30 November 1989; Scott and Criticos, "Hanging up the Nets."
37. NBB, Census of 1904.
38. Thus a successful family is remembered to have been residing, by the middle 1930s, in such a house containing no less than fourteen rooms. Rampersad, "Jaichoo Nanoo."
39. Bernard S. Cohn, *India: The Social Anthropology of a Civilisation* (Englewood Cliffs, New Jersey: Prentice-Hall, 1971), pp. 118–21.
40. Sabitha Jithoo, "Complex Households and Joint Families amongst Indians in Durban," in John Argyle and Eleanor Preston-Whyte, eds., *Social System and Tradition in Southern Africa* (Cape Town: Oxford University Press, 1978). T. Scarlett Epstein refers to more egalitarian joint family structures that have arisen as "share families," *South India: Yesterday, Today and Tomorrow* (New York: Holmes and Meier, 1973), pp. 207–10.
41. Hilda Kuper, *Indian People in Natal* (Pietermaritzburg, University of Natal Press: 1960), p. 64.
42. C. B. Bissessor, History III essay, University of Durban-Westville, n.d.
43. Cohn, *India*, p. 113.
44. Gita Sen, "Subordination and Sexual Control: A Comparative View of the Control of Women," *Review of Radical Political Economics* 16, 1 (1984), p. 134.
45. Ronnie Govender, *At the Edge* (unpublished, cited from the viewing of a performance) and *The Lahnee's Pleasure* (Johannesburg: Ravan, 1981). The latter play ultimately revolves around the question of male control over women.
46. Bill Freund, "Indian Women and the Changing Character of the Working Class Indian Household in Natal 1860–1990," *Journal of Southern African Studies* 17, 3 (1991), pp. 414–29. The number of Indian women over the age of 15 described as "economically active" fell from 4 368 to 3 710 between 1921 and 1936, p. 418. The Scott and Criticos video brings out the range of distinct secondary but (added together) critical, unpaid jobs that women in the fishing community performed. In the interview with K. G., 19 January 1990, it emerged that the women in his extended-family laundry business played a crucial role. The mother and wife of the interviewee were key figures in running the accounts. Daughters-in-law provided paid meals for the staff.
47. Joanna Liddle and Rama Joshi, *Daughters of Independence: Gender, Caste and Class in India* (New Brunswick, New Jersey: Rutgers University Press; London: Zed Press, 1986), pp. 59, 90–91; Maria Mies, *The Lace Makers of Narsapur* (London: Zed Press, 1982), p. 33.
48. Mies, *Lace Makers of Narsapur*, p. 7.

49. *Ibid.*, pp. 66, 133.
50. *Ibid.*, pp. 3–4.
51. Speech by Sir J. L. Hulett recorded in *Indian Opinion*, 14 September 1903.
52. Else Skjønsberg, *A Special Caste? Tamil Women of Sri Lanka* (London: Zed, 1982), p. 121.
53. Govender, *At the Edge.*
54. Rampersad, "Jaichoo Nanoo"; University of Durban-Westville, Documentation Centre, D. V. Naidoo papers.
55. Patricia Jeffrey, Roger Jeffrey and Andrew Lyon, "Midwifery and Childbearing in Rural North India," in Haleh Afshar, ed., *Women, State and Ideology* (London: Macmillan, 1987), pp. 154ff.
56. KCAL, File 28, MS Mabel Palmer, Indo-European Council, Unemployment Questionnaires.
57. For its presence among low-caste Bengalis, see Kalpana Bardhan, *Of Women, Outcastes, Peasants and Rebels* (Berkeley: University of California Press, 1990), p. 272. Skjønsberg, *A Special Caste?* This practice has been confirmed for me as common in Natal.
58. Mies, *Lace Makers of Narsapur*, p. 156.
59. Interview with Clive Forster, November 1989.
60. Govender, *At the Edge.*
61. Govender, *The Lahnee's Pleasure*; Interview with P. B., 30 November 1989. The latter also spoke to me about *caromboard*, a variant of billiards and darts, as part of the ambience.
62. *Ibid.*
63. According to a Mrs Padayachee, *The Leader*, 5 June 1948. They would actually be more likely to have been drinking *gavini*, or cane spirit.
64. Govender, *At the Edge.*
65. Diesel and Maxwell, *Hinduism.*
66. *The Leader*, 14 October 1960.
67. Mesthrie, *Language in Indenture*, p. 18.
68. See for instance, Jay Naidoo, *Coolie Location* (London: South African Writers, 1990); Govender, *The Lahnee's Pleasure.*
69. Leo Kuper, Hilstan Watts and Ron Davies, *Durban: A Study in Racial Ecology* (London: Jonathan Cape, 1958).
70. G. H. Calpin, *A. I. Kajee: His Work for the South-African Indian Community* (Durban: Iqbal Study Group, *c.* 1950).
71. Uma Mesthrie, "From Rose Day Shows to Social Welfare: White and Indian Women in Joint Co-operation in the 1930s," Paper presented to the Conference on Women and Gender in Southern Africa, Durban, 1991.
72. Theo Gerdener, "Socio-economic Position of the Indian," South African Bureau of Racial Affairs, *c.* 1952, (typewritten) p. 16.
73. Ronnie Govender, *The Lahnee's Pleasure* and *At the Edge*; Chetty, "The Durban Riots."
74. Jay Naidoo, *Coolie Location.*
75. *Ibid.*, p. 58.
76. *Fiat Lux* 2, 3 (1967), p. 69.
77. Benny Singh, *My Champions were Dark* (Durban: Pennant, 1963).
78. M. M. John in *Fiat Lux* 9, 2 (March 1974).
79. University of Durban-Westville, Documentation Centre, J. S. Gabriel papers; See also Jay Naidoo's memoirs, *Coolie Location*, p. 103, on waiters and Christianity or Gina Buijs, "A Study of Indian Pentecostal Church Membership," Ph.D. thesis, University of Cape Town, 1985, p. 127.
80. Govender, *At the Edge.*
81. Singh, *My Champions*, captures this world.
82. *Ibid.*
83. Boxing declines notably as a subject of interest in the Indian press in the 1960s.
84. For the relative intensity of Coloured-Indian social networks, see Singh, *My Champions, passim* and University of Durban-Westville, Documentation Centre, J. S. Gabriel papers.

This is equally notable in Jay Naidoo, *Coolie Location*. Naidoo points out the contrast between his own upbringing and that of other Indians who lived as a small minority in Lady Selborne township amongst Africans. There is no real Durban equivalent, but the mix in Cato Manor would have always meant more contact with Africans than there would have been in some parts of peripheral Durban.

85. Ginwala, "Indian South Africans," p.303.
86. Jay Naidoo, *Coolie Location*, p.84.
87. For an Indian view, see the report of the annual meeting of the Durban Indian Benevolent Society which cited unemployment as the main source of family desertion and disease. *The Leader*, 12 August 1950; A.L. Müller, "The Position of the Asians in Africa," *South African Journal of Economics* 33, 2 (1965), p.125; University of Natal, *Studies in Indian Employment*, chapter 5.
88. Goonam, *Coolie Doctor*, p.60.
89. V.S. Naidoo, "Income and Expenditure," p.56.
90. Halliday, "Market Gardeners of Durban," p.94.
91. Arkin, *Contribution of Indians*, p.113.
92. Katzen, *Industry in Durban*, p.25.
93. Beall and North-Coombes, "The 1913 Disturbances"; Maureen Swan, "The 1913 Strike."
94. Evangelos Mantzaris, "The Indian Tobacco Workers Strike of 1920: A Socio-historical Investigation," *Journal of Natal and Zulu History* 6, p.121.
95. Mantzaris, "Tobacco Workers Strike," p.119. See also the account by a descendant of the owner, R.B. Chetty in V. Chetty, History III essay, University of Durban-Westville, n.d.
96. *The Leader*, 31 March 1945.
97. *Indian Views*, 16 July 1937.
98. NA, 3/DBN, 1/2/27/1/2/1, Durban Municipal Staff Board (non-European) meetings, *passim*.
99. Rooksana Omar, "The Relationship Between the Durban Corporation and the Magazine Barracks," B.A. (Hons) thesis, University of Durban-Westville, 1989, pp.40ff. Compare with the prevalence of diseases of deprivation in rural Natal amongst Indians twenty years later, notably tuberculosis and malnutrition. Malaria was prevalent until the 1930s and bilharzia remained endemic in the 1950s. Maasdorp, "Survey of the Indian Community," pp.198–99.
100. V. Padayachee collection, manuscript reporting on the 1942 meeting at Red Square at which it was claimed that 30 of 200 workers were children earning far under half the Wage Determination rate and employed for 12 hours a day or more.
101. NA, 3/DBN, 1/5/4/1/2, Durban Indian Joint Advisory Sub-committee; also see the Presidential Address of Maurice Webb to the South African Institute of Race Relations, 22 January 1945.
102. Omar, "Durban Corporation and the Magazine Barracks," p.40.
103. NA, 3/DBN, 1/5/4/1/2, Durban Indian Joint Advisory Sub-committee, 9 March–19 March 1945.
104. Omar, "Durban Corporation and the Magazine Barracks," pp.44–45.
105. *Ibid.*, pp.8ff.
106. *Ibid.*, p.45.
107. *Ibid.*, pp.17–18. See the investigation, partly union-sponsored, reported in *The Leader*, 7 June 1941. Inevitably the barracks were labelled Durban's Black Hole of Calcutta.
108. Omar, "Durban Corporation and the Magazine Barracks," p.29.
109. *Ibid.*, pp.28, 81.
110. *Ibid.*, p.28.
111. *Ibid.*, pp.85–86.
112. NA, 3/DBN, 1/5/4/1/2, Durban Indian Joint Advisory Sub-committee.
113. Cited in notes from *The Leader*, April issue, 1943, V. Padayachee collection, manuscript.
114. *The Leader*, editorial, 18 September 1943.
115. Interview with B.R., 13 January 1992; Interview with K.G., 19 January 1990.

116. NBB, 1887, Protector of Immigrants' Report, p. A16.
117. Neame, *Asiatic Danger*, p. 94.
118. Neame, *Asiatic Danger*, p. 94; Ginwala, "Indian South Africans," p. 315.
119. Testimonial letter from J. Grant, 18 February 1947, Baynesfield farm, manuscript collection.
120. NBB, 1887, Protector of Immigrants' Report, p. A16.
121. UG 4/1921, Asiatic Inquiry Commission, p. 44.
122. Lincoln, "Culture of the Sugarmill," pp. 232–33, 267.
123. *Ibid.*, p. 167.
124. *Fiat Lux* 9, 8 (November 1974).
125. Young, "Industrial Geography of Durban," p. 348.
126. Soap and match factories are mentioned. *Indian Opinion*, 11 April 1908.
127. See Maasdorp and Pillay, "Occupational Mobility."
128. Arkin, *Contribution of Indians*, p. 189.
129. UG 4/1921, Asiatic Inquiry Commission, especially citing the findings of the 1914 Economic Commission, p. 48; Maurice Evans, *Black and White in South East Africa* (London: Longmans, Green, 1911), p. 287.
130. Evans, *Black and White*, p. 288.
131. KCAL, File 28, MS Mabel Palmer, Indo-European Council, Unemployment Questionnaires.
132. Lincoln, "Culture of the Sugarmill," p. 216.
133. Evans, *Black and White*, p. 287.
134. See the discussion in UG 4/1921, Asiatic Inquiry Commission, p. 48.
135. Govender, *At the Edge*; Interview with B. R., 13 January 1992; Interview with I. M., 14 January 1989.
136. H.S. Ringrose, "A History and Description of Trade Unions in Natal," M.Com. thesis, University of Natal, Durban, 1948.
137. For the case of hotel and catering workers, see the letter from the Registrar of Trade Unions to A.I. Kajee, 9 July 1928 from V. Padayachee collection, Margaret Ballinger papers, University of the Witwatersrand. Also *Indian Opinion*, 12 July 1928. The Indian hotel and catering workers however resisted the idea of forming a racially defined union. N.G. Moodley in *The Graphic*, 30 December 1960. The Indian printers' union formed in 1917 was denied membership in the South African Typographical Union, *ibid.*
138. Interview with I.M., 14 November 1989.
139. Speech of Albert Christopher to the Trade Union Council of Indian Workers and the Natal Indian Congress, 1 December 1928 in V. Padayachee collection, MS Margaret Ballinger papers, University of the Witwatersrand.
140. NBB, Census of 1904.
141. Kailas Kilchu, "Memorandum on Indian Education in Natal" for the Indian Education Inquiry Commission, 1928, University of Durban-Westville Documentation Centre.
142. Ringrose, "Trade Unions in Natal," p. 35.
143. Mantzaris, "Tobacco Workers Strike," pp. 117, 121. Sigamoney represented the IWU at the International Socialist League in Johannesburg *c.*1918. V. Padayachee collection, *The International*, 11 January 1918.
144. Singh, *My Champions*. He was also a significant figure in Indian football organisation during the inter-war years.
145. *Ibid.*, p. 196.
146. Letter from Revd Sigamoney, 4 April 1946, V. Padayachee collection, Margaret Ballinger papers, University of the Witwatersrand.
147. Albert Christopher speech to the Trade Union Council of Indian Workers and the Natal Indian Congress, Durban, 1 December 1928 from V. Padayachee collection, Margaret Ballinger papers, University of the Witwatersrand.
148. Srinivasan Sastri, the High Commissioner, was an interested member of the audience to this speech. See N.G. Moodley in *The Graphic*, 6 January 1961 for the involvement of Christopher, other Christian notables such as B.K. Lazarus and Simon Paul as well as Natal Indian Congress stalwart A.I. Kajee in the organisation of Indian unions of the 1920s.

149. Ruth M. Imrie, *A Wealth of People* (Johannesburg: Trade Union Council of South Africa, 1979).
150. *Natal Mercury*, 4 May 1937.
151. Omar, "Durban Corporation and the Magazine Barracks," p. 30.
152. N. G. Moodley in *The Graphic*, 6 January 1961.
153. Mantzaris, "Tobacco Workers Strike," p. 118.
154. Katzen, *Industry in Durban*, p. 20. White wage earners were about equally numerous but Africans ranged between 40 and 50 per cent of the total.
155. For another community that tried to combine urban advantages with life on the periphery of town, the Afrikaners of the Rand, see Charles van Onselen, "The Main Reef Road into the Working Class: Proletarianisation, Unemployment and Class Consciousness amongst Johannesburg's Afrikaner Poor 1890–1914," in *New Nineveh*.
156. KCAL, File 28, MS Mabel Palmer, Indo-European Council, Unemployment Questionnaires.
157. *Indian Opinion*, 5 July 1935.

Chapter 4
"It is my Work": Labour Segmentation and Militancy, 1935 –1960

1. From a newspaper clipping of the 1913 general strike of Indian workers, KCAL, KCAL 32545, MS Marshall Campbell.
2. Iain Edwards, interview with Rowley Arenstein, 24 July 1985.
3. David Hemson, "Dock Workers, Labour Circulation and Class Struggles in Durban 1940–59," *Journal of Southern African Studies* 4 (1977); Tim Nuttall, "African Worker Militancy and Organisation in Durban 1937–49," Paper presented to the Twentieth Century Natal History Workshop, Pietermaritzburg, 1988. Nuttall does show a ferment amongst African workers in the early war period. In a forthcoming Ph.D. thesis, Peter Alexander will be recording in detail labour struggles and state reaction during the war years. He feels even white labour militancy has been underestimated for this period.
4. Maureen Swan, "Ideology in Organised Indian Politics, 1891–1948," in Shula Marks and Stanley Trapido, eds., *The Politics of Race, Class and Nationalism in Twentieth Century South Africa* (London and New York: Longmans, 1987), p. 202.
5. Ginwala, "Indian South Africans."
6. Vishnu Padayachee, Shahid Vawda and Paul Tichman, *Indian Workers and Trade Unions in Durban: 1930–50*, Report no. 20, (Durban: University of Durban-Westville, Institute for Social and Economic Research, 1985). This book also contains a very useful data base on the unions. See also a work of popularisation, Shamim Marie, *Divide and Profit: Indian Workers in Natal* (Durban: Worker Resistance and Culture Publications, University of Natal, Sociology Department, 1986).
7. Freund, "Social Character of Secondary Industry."
8. David Yudelman, *The Emergence of Modern South Africa: State, Capital and the Incorporation of Organized Labor on the South African Gold Fields, 1902–39* (Westport and London: Greenwood, 1983); Robert Davies, *Capital, State and White Labour in South Africa 1900–1960: An Historical Materialist Analysis of Class Formation and Class Relations* (Atlantic Highlands: Humanities Press, 1979). There are many other studies of the white working class and trade-unionism in South Africa during the first quarter of the twentieth century.
9. Yunus Carrim, "Trade Unionism in Natal: Shopfloor Relations between African and Indian Workers," *South African Labour Bulletin* 11, 4 (1986), portrays African worker views, which favour a conspiratorial explanation that goes with their acceptance of the moral order of non-racialism as the only correct and natural worker response.
10. Jeff Guy and Motlatsi Thabane, "Technology, Ethnicity and Ideology: Basotho Miners and Shaft Sinking on the South African Gold Mines," *Journal of Southern African Studies* 14, 2 (1988), pp. 257–78.

11. Gillian Burke and Peter Richardson, "The Profits of Death: A Comparative Study of Miners' Phthisis in Cornwall and South Africa 1876–1918," *Journal of Southern African Studies* 4, 2 (1978).
12. Atkins, "Origins of an African Work Ethic."
13. Nuttall, "African Worker Militancy"; Iain Edwards, "Mkhumbane, our Home: African Shantytown Society in Cato Manor Farm 1946–50," Ph.D. thesis, University of Natal, Durban, 1989.
14. Padayachee et al., *Indian Workers and Trade Unions*, pp. 83–136. Another major source on this issue is David Hemson, "Class Consciousness and Migrant Workers: The Dockers of Durban," Ph.D. thesis, University of Warwick, 1979.
15. See also Ginwala, "Indian South Africans," p. 396.
16. V. Padayachee collection, Durban committee, South African Trade and Labour Committee to General Secretary, 22 June 1937.
17. *Indian Views*, 11 June 1937.
18. Padayachee et al., *Indian Workers and Trade Unions*, p. 104; Calpin, *A. I. Kajee*, especially p. 71. Indian employers were often deeply hostile to trade-unionism amongst their own workers: *Daily News*, 8 October 1943 for the bakery trade; Kandosamy, "Glendale Sugar Mill," p. 17, for the Glendale sugar mill. Lincoln shows the intensity of the struggle at Glendale between an Indian capitalist and an Indian workforce, eventually terrorised into defeat, "Culture of the Sugarmill," pp. 351ff.
19. Calpin, *A. I. Kajee*, p. 66; *Daily News*, 1 June 1937.
20. Interview with I.M., 14 November 1989.
21. Calpin, *A. I. Kajee*, p. 91; *The Guardian*, 21 January 1943.
22. Jon Lewis, *Industrialisation and Trade Union Organisation in South Africa, 1924–55: The Rise and Fall of the South African Trades and Labour Council* (Cambridge: Cambridge University Press, 1984), pp. 123–24; University of Natal, *The African Factory Worker: A Sample Study of the Life and Labour of the Urban African Worker* Report no. 2, Natal Regional Survey, (Cape Town: Oxford University Press, 1950) 1946.
23. Padayachee et al., *Indian Workers and Trade Unions*, p. 128.
24. *The Graphic*, 6 January 1961.
25. *The Leader*, 12 January 1946; 19 January 1946.
26. Padayachee et al., *Indian Workers and Trade Unions*, p. 126.
27. *The Leader*, 19 March 1949.
28. *The Leader*, 18 September 1943.
29. Lincoln, "Culture of the Sugarmill," p. 349.
30. V. Padayachee collection, Letter to the South African Trades and Labour Council, National Executive, 5 June 1942.
31. Padayachee et al., *Indian Workers and Trade Unions*, p. 56.
32. Lincoln, "Culture of the Sugarmill," p. 352.
33. V. Padayachee collection, Sugar Mill Workers' Union, Durban and District Local Committee minutes, Quarterly meeting, 9 October 1947. This was equally true of the one Indian-owned sugar mill. *The Guardian*, 15 June 1944.
34. *The Guardian*, 2 September 1948 and see Lincoln, "Culture of the Sugarmill," p. 356. Also Mervyn David Lincoln, "Flies in the Sugar Bowl: The Natal Sugar Industry Employees' Union in its Heyday 1940–53," Paper presented to the World Plantation Conference, Lafayette, Indiana, 1989, p. 14.
35. Lincoln, "Culture of the Sugarmill," p. 356.
36. Lincoln, "Flies in the Sugar Bowl," p. 21.
37. V. Padayachee collection, Errol Shanley for the Sugar Industry Employees' Union to the Sugar Industrial Council, 18 December 1952.
38. Lincoln, "Culture of the Sugarmill," p. 359.
39. *Ibid.*, p. 363.
40. Alan Hirsch, "An Introduction to Textile Worker Organisation in Natal," *South African Labour Bulletin* 4, 8 (1979), pp. 27–28; see also Bettie du Toit, *Ukubamba Amadola* (London: Onyx, 1978), pp. 97–99.

41. Robert V. Lambert, "Political Unionism in South Africa: The South African Congress of Trade Unions 1955–65," Ph.D. thesis, University of the Witwatersrand, 1988, p. 317.
42. *Ibid.*, pp. 310ff.
43. Of 430 workers fired in August 1950, some 350 were Indian. *The Leader*, 8 July 1950; 5 August 1950.
44. S.A. Trade and Labour Council papers, Durban Indian Municipal Employees Union report, 1950.
45. *The Leader*, 8 July 1950; Durban Indian Municipal Employees Union report, 1950.
46. *Race Relations News*, 1953.
47. Iain Edwards and Tim Nuttall, "Seizing the Moment: The 1949 Riots, Proletarian Populism and the Structures of African Urban Life in Durban during the late 1940s," Paper presented to the History Workshop, Johannesburg, 1990.
48. Young, "Industrial Geography of Durban," p. 310; V. Padayachee collection, Memorandum from Durban Indian Municipal Employees Society to South African Trades and Labour Council, 26 June 1950.
49. Chetty, "The Durban Riots."
50. Edwards, "Mkhumbane, our Home," 1989.
51. Goonam, *Coolie Doctor*, p. 138.
52. Chetty, "The Durban Riots," p. 7.
53. David Hemson, "Dock Workers and Class Struggles," p. 112.
54. *The Leader*, passim.
55. *The Leader*, 20 July 1962.
56. Allan Wilkinson, "Manufacturing Industry in the Pinetown Magisterial District," M.A. thesis, University of Natal, Durban, 1963, pp. 101, 106.
57. By 1949/50, 74,3 per cent of private sector employment was in firms with more than 85 employees. Katzen, *Industry in Durban*, p. 21.
58. *Ibid*, p. 16.
59. Lewis, *Industrialisation and Trade Union Organisation*, chapter seven.
60. Padayachee et al., *Indian Workers and Trade Unions*, chapter three.
61. Calculated from Katzen, *Industry in Durban*, p. 25.
62. Baruch Hirson, "Trade Union Organizer in Durban: M.B. Yengwa 1943–44," *Journal of Natal and Zulu History* 11 (1988), p. 97.
63. *The Leader*, 4 March 1944.
64. See the analysis in Padayachee et al., *Indian Workers and Trade Unions*, pp. 157ff.
65. Iain Edwards interview with Rowley Arenstein, 24 July 1985.
66. Marie, *Divide and Profit*, p. 79; Interview with K.G., 19 January 1990.
67. N.G. Moodley in *The Graphic*, 6 January 1961.
68. Marie, *Divide and Profit*, p. 82.
69. *Ibid.*, p. 83.
70. See the description in Lambert, "Political Unionism."
71. V.S.M. Pillai papers, University of Durban-Westville, Documentation Centre.
72. See M.P. Naicker papers, University of Durban-Westville, Documentation Centre; interview with K.G., 19 January 1990.
73. Swan, "Ideology in Indian Politics," p. 203.
74. Lambert, "Political Unionism," p. 456.
75. Chetty, "The Durban Riots," p. 9.
76. Interview with K.G., 19 January 1990.
77. Ginwala, "Indian South Africans," p. 336.
78. Raymond Burrows, *Indian Life and Labour in Natal*, revised ed., (Johannesburg: South African Institute of Race Relations, 1952), p. 17.
79. Ginwala, "Indian South Africans," p. 392 but see also Ray Alexander and Jack Simons, *Job Reservation and the Trade Unions* (Woodstock: Enterprise, 1959), p. 32.
80. Interview with I.M., 14 November 1989.
81. Katzen, "Industry in Durban," p. 34.

Chapter 5
Destroying Communities: The Impact of Group Areas, 1950–1980

1. Alan Mabin, "Comprehensive Segregation: The Origins of the Group Areas Act and its Planning Apparatuses," *Journal of Southern African Studies* 18, 2 (1992).
2. Brij Maharaj, "The 'Spatial Impress' of the Central and Local States: The Group Areas Act in Durban," in David Smith, ed., *The Apartheid City and Beyond* (London and New York: Routledge and Johannesburg: Witwatersrand University Press, 1992), p. 81.
3. *The Leader*, 11 October 1963.
4. Alan Mabin looks critically at the extent to which South African urban planners thought of themselves as part of international practices current in this era in "The Witwatersrand Joint Town Planning Committee 1932–40: Of Rigour and Mortis," Paper presented to the Planning History Workshop, Johannesburg, 1992.
5. For a particularly relevant study, see C. M. Rogerson, "From Coffee-Cart to Industrial Canteen: Feeding Johannesburg's Black Workers, 1945–62," in Alan Mabin, ed., *Organisation and Economic Change*, (Johannesburg: Ravan, 1989).
6. For an early exception, see the speech of A. I. Kajee to the Indo-European Council in 1929 which does suggest the need both for urban amenities to be extended to the Durban periphery and for land to be released specifically to create public housing for Indians. KCAL, File 28, MS Mabel Palmer "Indian Housing in and around Durban."
7. John Western, *Outcast Cape Town* (Minneapolis: University of Minnesota Press, 1981). See also Shamil Jeppie and Crain Soudien, eds., *The Struggle for District Six, Past and Present* (Cape Town: Buchu Books, 1990).
8. Kuper et al., *Durban: Racial Ecology*.
9. Maharaj, "Group Areas Act in Durban," p. 76.
10. *Ibid.*, p. 74.
11. NA, 3/DBN, 14/4/1, Durban Borough Boundaries Commission.
12. *Ibid*.
13. NA, 3/DBN, 14/4/1–3; 14/5/1, Durban Borough Boundaries Commission.
14. Interview with K.G., 19 January 1990.
15. NA, 3/DBN, 14/4/2, Durban Borough Boundaries Commission, Evidence, Natal Indian Congress.
16. V. Padayachee collection, Natal Indian Congress, 5th Congress, 1951, Agenda Book.
17. NA, 3/DBN, 14/6/1, Durban Borough Extension Enquiry Committee, 1935.
18. Omar, "Durban Corporation and the Magazine Barracks," pp. 8ff.
19. NA, 3/DBN, 1/2/6/1/1, Durban Public Health (Slums) Committee, 5 August 1937.
20. Susan Parnell, "Racial Segregation in Johannesburg: The Slums Act 1934–39," *South African Geographical Journal* 70 (1988), p. 123.
21. See the evidence of the Town Clerk, who could not conceive of how to improve the quality of Indian housing unless Indians were prepared to give up opposition to housing segregation. NA, 3/DBN, 14/4/2, Durban Borough Boundaries Commission. Or look at the assumptions of white speakers in the records of the Special Committee *re* Housing, NA, 3/DBN, 1/3/3/1/2.
22. Bill Freund, "Forced Resettlement and the Political Economy of South Africa," *Review of African Political Economy* 29 (1984).
23. Martin Legassick, "Capital Accumulation and Violence in South Africa," *Economy and Society* 3, 3 (1974).
24. NA, 3/DBN, 14/6/1, Durban Borough Extension Enquiry Commission, 1935.
25. Louise Torr, "Lamontville—Durban's Model Village: The Realities of Township Life, 1934–60," *Journal of Natal and Zulu History* 10 (1987).
26. For a kinder view, see B. A. Naidoo and J. Naidoo, "Economic Opportunities," p. 44. In 1945, only 221 houses had been completed in Springfield Estate with 269 more under construction and 168 on tender. NA, 3/DBN, 1/3/3/1/3, Special Committee *re* Housing, 26 July 1945.

27. NA, 3/DBN, 1/3/3/1/2, Special Committee *re* Housing, 3 August 1939, 26 January 1940, 8 March 1940.
28. See the characteristic view in A. I. Kajee, P. R. Pather and A. Christopher, *Treatment of Indians in South Africa* (Cape Town and New York: South African Indian Congress, 1946). These, moreover, were relatively conservative men. Kuper et al., *Durban: Racial Ecology*, also express scepticism here. Perhaps for that reason, this crucial analysis seems to overestimate the possibilities for successful resistance to application of the Group Areas Act.
29. NA, 3/DBN, 1/2/6/1/1, Evidence of S. J. Smith, Councillor to Durban Public Health (Slums) Committee, 25 February 1938.
30. David Bailey, "The Origins of Phoenix 1957–76: The Durban City Council and the Indian Housing Question," M.A. thesis, University of Natal, Durban, 1987, p. 100.
31. The malevolence of white opinion in general is a constant theme in Kuper et al., *Durban: Racial Ecology*.
32. *The Leader*, 24 April 1948.
33. NA, 3/DBN, 1/2/6/1/2, Durban Public Health (Slums) Committee, 24 June 1947.
34. Kuper et al., *Durban: Racial Ecology*, give a clear exposition of the theory.
35. *The Leader*, 19 March 1949.
36. V. Padayachee collection, Natal Indian Congress, 1951 conference resolutions.
37. *The Leader*, 22 July 1960.
38. Clairwood and District Ratepayers and Residents Association to the Mayor of Durban, 5 October 1964, University of Durban-Westville, Documentation Centre.
39. *The Leader*, 20 March 1964.
40. Bailey, "Origins of Phoenix," pp. 100–1.
41. The Paruks alone, for instance, collected rent from no less than 900 tenants in Riverside slums in 1936. For this and other information on slum ownership, see Durban Public Health (Slums) Committee, 21 July 1936 and other correpondence, in NA, 3DBN 1/2/6/1/1. The file does show, however, that Indian slum dwellers were far more apt than "Natives" to own their own shacks, even where they lived together in the same neighbourhood.
42. *The Leader*, 7 October 1955.
43. For conditions there, see Gavin Maasdorp and Nesen Pillay, *Urban Relocation and Racial Segregation: The Case of Indian South Africans* (Durban: University of Natal, Department of Economics, 1977).
44. Goonam, *Coolie Doctor*, chapter 17, is a good example.
45. Interview with B.R., 13 January 1992, which stressed how pleased the family, which had waited in vain for a council house at Springfield, was to move to Chatsworth to their own house. There was as well resentment of the undemocratic and racist nature of the process but, as my informant said, "anger wouldn't help you."
46. Marie, *Indian Workers in Natal*, p. 94.
47. *The Leader*, 4 October 1963.
48. Halliday, "Market Gardeners of Durban," p. 94.
49. See the evidence of Councillor S. J. Smith, NA, 3/DBN, 1/2/6/1/1, Durban Public Health (Slums) Committee.
50. Halliday, "Market Gardeners of Durban," p. 30.
51. B. A. Naidoo and J. Naidoo, "Economic Opportunities," p. 42.
52. *The Leader*, 14 September 1962, 24 January 1964. This low rental figure was estimated to be only about 3 per cent of the monthly wage on average.
53. Maasdorp and Pillay, "Occupational Mobility," pp. 123ff. See also their *Urban Relocation and Racial Segregation*, where more negative reactions are also recorded.
54. Margo Russell, "A Study of a South African Interracial Neighbourhood," M.Soc.Sc. thesis, University of Natal, Durban, 1961.
55. For the early planning of Merebank in the late 1940s, see NA, 3/DBN, 1/3/3/1/3 and 1/3/3/1/6 Special Committee *re* Housing. For the survival of shacks into the 1960s, see *The Leader*, 15 December 1961.

56. *The Leader*, 2 September 1960.
57. *The Leader*, 26 August 1960.
58. Menaka Padayachee, "Four Market Gardening Communities," p.4; Maasdorp and Pillay, "Occupational Mobility," p.245.
59. According to Margaret Sugden, Chatsworth per capita income was R33 compared to the Durban Indian average of R42. *The Potential Indian Labour Force: Durban/Pietermaritzburg Region*, Report no.37, part 2 (Pietermaritzburg: Town and Regional Planning Commission, 1978), p.48.
60. G.C. Oosthuizen and J.H. Hofmeyr, *A Socio-economic Survey of Chatsworth*, Report no.7 (Durban: University of Durban-Westville, Institute for Social and Economic Research, 1979), p.17. The figure given for 1961 was 150 000. *The Leader*, 3 March 1960.
61. Bailey, "Origins of Phoenix," p.147.
62. *Ibid.*, pp.107–8.
63. Interview with S.M., 15 November 1989.
64. *The Leader*, 5 January 1962.
65. *The Leader*, 28 February 1964.
66. Such an indictment is made very forcefully in Maharaj, "Group Areas Act in Durban," Bailey's Masters' thesis is also insistent on the crucial shaping role of the Durban town bureaucracy.
67. See Sugden, *Indian Labour Force*.
68. Scott and Criticos, "Hanging up the Nets."
69. University of Durban-Westville, Documentation Centre, J.S. Gabriel papers.
70. Zubeida Kassim Seedat, "The Zanzibaris in Durban: A Social Anthropological Study of the Muslim Descendants of African Freed Slaves Living in the Indian Area of Chatsworth," M.A. thesis, University of Natal, Durban, 1973.
71. Omar, "Durban Corporation and the Magazine Barracks," p.16.
72. *Ibid.*, p.17.
73. *Ibid.*, pp.17–18.
74. *Ibid.*, p.22.
75. *Ibid.*, p.24.
76. *Ibid.*, p.79.
77. Interview with P.B., 30 November 1989.
78. Bailey, "Origins of Phoenix," pp.89–90, 120, 147; *Fiat Lux* 11, 1 (March/April 1976); *The Leader*, 24 April 1964; Interview with S.M., 15 November 1989.
79. Bailey, "Origins of Phoenix," pp.89–90.
80. Interview with P.B., 30 November 1989.
81. Maharaj, "Group Areas Act in Durban," pp.84–86.
82. See the account by Dianne Scott, "The Destruction of Clairwood: A Case Study on the Transformation of Communal Living Space," in Smith, *The Apartheid City*, pp.87–98.
83. See Jeppie and Soudien, *Struggle for District Six*. There is a section of the urban core of Durban, its old northern edge, Block AK containing a great cross-section of people, which was levelled but it is quite small and much of it has been replaced through commercial property use.
84. Scott and Criticos, "Hanging up the Nets."
85. For a famous parallel study in Britain, see Michael Young and Peter Willmott, *Family and Kinship in East London* (London: Routledge and Kegan Paul, 1957). For a similar perspective see also Kogila Moodley, "South African Indians: The Wavering Minority," in Leonard Thompson and Jeffrey Butler, eds., *Change in Contemporary South Africa* (Berkeley: University of California Press, 1975).
86. J.F. Butler-Adam and Win Venter, "Public Housing and the Pattern of Family Life: Indian Families in Metropolitan Durban," in *Aspects of Family Life in the South African Indian Community*, Occasional Paper no.20 (Durban: University of Durban-Westville, Institute for Social and Economic Research, 1987).
87. Interview with P.B., 30 November 1989.

88. Cassim Saloojee, Transvaal Indian Congress activist, in Manfred Hermer, *The Passing of Pageview* (Johannesburg: Ravan, 1978).

Chapter 6
Insiders and Outsiders: The Working Class of the Apartheid Era, 1960–1990

1. It was still measured as 22,7 per cent in the 1960 census and as 16 per cent in 1963 by the University of Natal Department of Economics, L. P. McCrystal and G. Maasdorp, "The Role of the Indian in Natal's Economy," 1966. D. T. van der Spuy's estimate for Durban-Pinetown is only 10,9 per cent of males in 1964, *Die Arbeidspatroon van Indiers in Natal* Navorsingsreeks nr. 62 (Pretoria: Department of Higher Education, National Bureau for Economic and Social Research, 1968), pp. 67ff. Unemployment has certainly again increased in the 1980s as the South African economy has faltered but the Indian share has not been inordinate.
2. *The Leader*, 1964 onward, *passim*.
3. *Ibid.*
4. R. T. Bell, *Growth and Structure of Manufacturing Employment in Natal*, Report no. 7 (Durban: University of Durban-Westville, Institute of Social and Economic Research, 1983), p. 50.
5. Maasdorp and Pillay, "Occupational Mobility."
6. Bell, *Manufacturing Employment*, pp. 2, 36.
7. Maasdorp and Pillay, "Occupational Mobility," p. 245.
8. For a survey of where Indian workers could be found, particularly in the 1960s, see Young, "Industrial Geography of Durban," p. 110. He notes that apart from textiles, clothing and footwear, the sugar mills, Baker's and Durban Confectionary Works, both biscuit manufacturers and Metal Box, were major employers in this category.
9. John Stanwix, "Capital Accumulation, Crisis and Spatial Restructuring: A Study of Spatial Shifts in South African Manufacturing with Particular Reference to Natal," M.Com. thesis, University of Natal, Durban, 1987, p. 205; p. 199.
10 Young, "Industrial Geography of Durban," pp. 277–81, Katzen, *Industry in Durban*, pp. 34ff.
11. Young, "Industrial Geography of Durban," p. 277; see Katzen, *Industry in Durban*, p. 33.
12. Hirsch, "Textile Worker Organisation," p. 19; Wilkinson, "Manufacturing in Pinetown," p. 97. This process is far better known for the Cape garment industry thanks to the work of Martin Nicol. See for instance his " 'Joh'burg Hotheads' and the 'Gullible Children of Cape Town': The Transvaal Garment Workers' Union's Assault on Low Wages in the Cape Town Clothing Industry, 1930–31," in Belinda Bozzoli, ed., *Class, Community and Conflict: South African Perspectives* (Johannesburg: Ravan, 1987) and "Riches from Rags: Bosses and Unions in the Cape Clothing Industry 1926–37," *Journal of Southern African Studies* 9, 2 (1983).
13. Katzen, *Industry in Durban*, p. 34.
14. University of Durban-Westville, Documentation Centre, GWIU papers, Garment Workers Industrial Union commemorative booklet, 1985.
15. Young, "Industrial Geography of Durban," p. 279.
16. See Katzen, *Industry in Durban*, p. 128. This was also true of the footwear industry, Wilkinson, "Manufacturing in Pinetown," p. 114.
17. Katzen, *Industry in Durban*, p. 36.
18. Katzen, *Industry in Durban*, pp. 8–9. By 1964, a survey revealed very favourable views of Indian workers by Natal Chamber of Industry and Durban Chamber of Commerce employers, a remarkable turnabout from views expressed during the militant era ten to twenty years earlier. Müller, "Position of the Asians," p. 125.
19. Wilkinson, "Manufacturing in Pinetown," p. 63.
20. Katzen, *Industry in Durban*, p. 36.
21. Bell, *Manufacturing Employment*, p. 50.

22. For Bata Shoes, see Young, "Industrial Geography of Durban," p. 230; for Ninian and Lester, a major clothing manufacturer which in particular did not want to bother with separate toilet and other amenities for different "race groups" and had moved to Durban by 1940, Young, "Industrial Geography of Durban," p. 313.
23. Wilkinson, "Manufacturing in Pinetown," p. 111.
24. *Ibid.*
25. Stanwix, "Spatial Shifts in Manufacturing," p. 205.
26. Hirsch, "Textile Worker Organisation," p. 6. One Durban firm, Frames, held a commanding position in the textile industry for forty years after World War II.
27. A. M. Moolla in *Fiat Lux* 3, 5 (1968), pp. 131ff. See Young, "Industrial Geography of Durban," p. 390, for Indian industrialists' expansion in the 1960s. Arkin reports that by 1976 there were 251 Indian-owned private limited liability companies employing 14 654 persons with output worth over R106 million, *Contribution of Indians*, p. 307.
28. Moolla in *Fiat Lux* 3, 5 (1968), p. 134.
29. Young, "Industrial Geography of Durban," p. 282.
30. *Ibid.*, p. 310.
31. *Fiat Lux* 5, 6 (1970).
32. Young, "Industrial Geography of Durban," p. 394.
33. While in general, movement to border areas signalled an interest in shifting to African workers, particularly African female workers, an exception lay in certain parts of rural Natal where a considerable pool of poor Indian workers could be found. See *Fiat Lux* 3, 3 (1968), pp. 95–96, with reference to the Tongaat area. For this trend towards deconcentration, see Bell, *Manufacturing Employment*, p. 84.
34. Fatima Meer et al., *Black-Woman-Worker* (Durban: Madiba Press for the Institute for Black Research, 1990), p. 34.
35. Ginwala, in "Indian South Africans," has estimated the figure at 20 per cent of Indian industrial workers in 1970.
36. J. Naidoo, *Coolie Location*, p. 128.
37. Talk, Pregs Govender, GAWU, Industrial Sociology Department, University of Natal, Durban, 1990; Carrim, "Trade Unionism in Natal."
38. Thus Siva Reddy, who employed 600 workers at Redbro in Chatsworth, had once been a factory machinist himself, *Natal Mercury*, 1982 supplement; *Daily News*, supplement, 23 August 1983, p. 10. Sylvia Singh, a machinist rendered redundant in 1977 was manufacturing luggage five years later. Sympathetic bosses lent her vinyl and made space available to her cheaply while former fellow-workers joined her. *Fiat Lux* 8, 5 (June–July 1982).
39. See Freund, "Indian Women," for an in-depth discussion of this issue.
40. See the references to the moral threat imposed by factory girls in *The Leader*, 16 October 1959, 20 October 1959, 5 March 1960, 1 April 1960. "Factory girls" are denounced as loose of morals, gangsters, and even "touts for abortionists."
41. As in Mies, *Lace Makers of Naraspur*, pp. 3–4.
42. Luz Gabriela Arango, "Femmes ouvrières, familles et politiques au sein de l'entreprise," *Pratiques sociales et travail en milieu urbain* 19 (1992), pp. 27–28. My translation.
43. Meer, pp. 151ff.
44. *Ibid.*, p. 111.
45. Interview with P.B., 30 November 1989.
46. Meer, *Black-Woman-Worker*, p. 97; interview with P.B., 30 November 1989.
47. *Ibid.*, p. 119; van der Spuy, *Arbeidspatroon van Indiers*.
48. Meer, *Black-Woman-Worker*, pp. 149–50.
49. T. D. Chetty, "Factory and Family: Indian Factory Workers in Durban," in *Aspects of Family Life in the South African Indian Community*, Occasional Paper, no. 20 (Durban: University of Durban-Westville, Institute for Social and Economic Research, 1987).
50. Fatima Meer, *Factory and Family: The Divided Lives of South Africa's Women Workers* (Durban: Institute for Black Research, 1984), p. 41.

51. Hemson, "Class Consciousness," p. 340.
52. N. G. Moodley in *The Graphic*, 6 January 1961; Imrie, *Wealth of People*, pp. 121–24; Young, "Industrial Geography of Durban," p. 279. See also Alexander and Simons, *Job Reservation*, p. 32; Hirsch, "Textile Worker Organisation," p. 17; du Toit, *Ukubamba Amadola*, p. 27; *The Leader*, 12 February 1960.
53. For this history more generally see Steven Friedman, *Building Tomorrow Today: African Workers in Trade Unions 1970–84* (Johannesburg: Ravan, 1987), chapters 1 and 3.
54. Imrie, *Wealth of People*, pp. 96–97.
55. M. [Vishnu] Padayachee, "Determinants of Wages and Wage Differentials among Indians in the Durban Municipal Area," *Journal of the University of Durban-Westville* 4, 2 (1983), p. 182.
56. *The Leader*, 20 July 1962.
57. Du Toit, *Ukubamba Amadola*, p. 18.
58. *Ibid.*
59. Speech by W. A. Maree, 4 November 1965, in the P. R. T. Nel papers, University of Durban-Westville, Documentation Centre.
60. Maasdorp, "Survey of the Indian Community," p. 34.
61. Speech by W. A. Maree in P. R. T. Nel papers, University of Durban-Westville, Documentation Centre.
62. *Fiat Lux* 8, 1 (1973).
63. P. R. T. Nel papers, University of Durban-Westville, Documentation Centre. See Maasdorp and Pillay, "Occupational Mobility" and Oosthuizen and Hofmeyr, *Survey of Chatsworth*.
64. *Fiat Lux* 8, 3 (1973).
65. Interview with I.M., 14 November 1989.
66. Interview with S.M., 15 November 1989; Interview with P.B., 30 November 1989.
67. Interview with P.B., 30 November 1989.
68. Phoenix resident in Steve Schmidt, "Phoenix New Town (Same Old Problems)," video-recording, 55 mins, University of Durban-Westville, *c.* 1989.
69. For the organisation of Residents Associations in Chatsworth, concerned to expedite the construction of schools, traffic signs, etc. and improve transport, see *The Leader*, 20 September 1963.
70. Buijs, "Pentecostal Church Membership," p. 160.
71. Interview with B.R., 13 January 1992.
72. *Fiat Lux* 18, 1 (January–February 1983).
73. Sugden, *Indian Labour Force*, p. 48. She reports other sources of income at only 10 per cent of the total in her survey published in 1978 by contrast to the older way of life of Indians on the Durban periphery.
74. Schmidt, "Phoenix New Town."
75. Interview with P.B., 30 November 1989.
76. Epstein, *South India*, pp. 203ff.
77. Interview with P.B., 30 November 1989.
78. *Fiat Lux* 18, 1 (January–February 1983). Of course, this also shows that a significant minority miss the extended or multiple family unit. Sugden reported in 1978 an average Indian household size of 1,2 basic families with 70 per cent of households consisting of 5 persons or less, *Indian Labour Force*, p. 29.
79. Meer, *Black-Woman-Worker*, p. 190.
80. *Fiat Lux* 5, 4 (1970). These estimates belong to a better-off than average sample. For similar or higher figures see J. J. A. Steenkamp, *Income and Expenditure Patterns of Urban Indian Households in Durban*, Research Report, no. 50/7 (Pretoria: University of South Africa, Bureau of Market Research, 1976). A market survey four years later reported automobile ownership at only about half that level, *Fiat Lux* 9, 1 (February 1974).
81. Butler-Adam and Venter survey as reported in *Fiat Lux* 18, 1 (January–February 1983).
82. Interview with P.B., 30 November 1989.

83. The importance of indebtedness for hire purchase was stressed by P.B. in my interview, 30 November 1989.

84. A research "snapshot" taken in the early 1960s on the North Coast revealed that some 45 per cent of school pupils were reporting English as their home language but all were by preference speaking it amongst themselves. Maasdorp, "Survey of the Indian Community," p. 52. By 1974, a national market survey of Indian urban dwellers reported that 48 per cent spoke English as home language. *Fiat Lux* 9, 1 (February 1974).

85. Sugden, *Indian Labour Force*, p. 35. As compared to only 55 per cent of those over fifty years of age.

86. Mesthrie, *Language in Indenture*, p. 16.

87. Buijs, "Pentecostal Church Membership."

88. *Ibid.*, p. 127.

89. *Ibid.*, p. 8.

90. *Ibid.*, pp. 113–16.

91. *Ibid.*, pp. 83, 117. It is possible that Buijs relies too much on the views of the white founder of the church, J. F. Rowlands and that a somewhat different picture would emerge if studied from "below."

92. Schmidt, "Phoenix New Town."

93. Buijs, "Pentecostal Church Membership," pp. 37, 154, 164, 207–11. Buijs refers to "village rituals" which could be performed without the sanction of a priestly Brahmin caste. She tends to suggest that neo-Hinduism had a much greater appeal to people of north-Indian origin (who also retain more of a sense of caste) whilst conversion to Christianity has instead appealed largely to those of Tamil and Telugu origin.

94. *The Leader*, 15 August 1969.

95. Buijs, "Pentecostal Church Membership," p. 147.

96. Meer, *Black-Woman-Worker*, pp. 102–3.

97. T. D. Chetty et al., "Election Survey: Preliminary Description of Data," in V. Padayachee collection.

98. Steve Schmidt, "Phoenix New Town"; Interview with S.M., 15 November 1989.

99. Thus Schmidt recorded workers whose pay covers barely twice the monthly rent, "Forgotten Workers," videorecording, 50 mins, University of Durban-Westville, c. 1989.

100. Meer, *Black-Woman-Worker*, p. 105, for a survey of women working in factories. More than half of the Indian women surveyed were in owner-occupant households and few tenants were either lodgers or sub-tenants. See also Community Research Unit and Michael Sutcliffe, "Socio-economic Conditions and Household Subsistence Levels in Four Durban Communities: Chatsworth, Newlands East, Phoenix and Wentworth," report for the Durban Housing Action Committee, 1986.

101. See Jeremy Seekings, "The United Democratic Front and the Changing Nature of Opposition in Natal, 1983–85," Paper presented to the Conference on Ethnicity, Society and Conflict in Natal, Pietermaritzburg, 14–16 September 1992.

102. T. D. Chetty et al., "Election Survey."

103. Interview with S.M., 15 November 1989.

104. Durban Housing Action Committee, *Rents We Can Afford* (Durban: Durban Housing Action Committee, 1989).

105. *The Daily News*, 13–14 September 1991, 21 September 1991.

106. Interview with P.B., 30 November 1989.

107. *The Daily News*, 19 July 1992.

108. Meer, *Black-Woman-Worker*, p. 264.

109. I have understood this submerged tenth much better since viewing the videos made by Steve Schmidt, "Forgotten Workers" and "Phoenix New Town." These deal with the lot of very poorly paid contract service workers, all Indian, often in debt to Indian management within the firm.

110. Talk, P.G., GAWU, 1990. Interview with P.H., 4 January 1990: "People's whole way of relating together does change" in the union but this organiser made clear how very carefully and thoughtfully her union had moved in integrating Indian workers effectively. She herself envisioned that the longer-term future would be one where Indians form a diminishing share in the working class due to their effective social mobility.
111. Interview with P.H., 4 January 1990. Indians need to be found as well on representative committees thereafter.
112. This distinction is made in Schmidt, "Forgotten Workers." Interview with P.H., 4 January 1990. There is an excellent contrast between African and Indian worker culture in the workplace drawn by Carrim, "Trade Unionism in Natal." Carrim points to Indian workers as being more individualistic and less supportive of the idea of unity, relatively timid and psychologically disturbed by emotional displays of militancy, highly interested in existing benefits that they are reluctant to sacrifice and generally averse to strikes. They are very vulnerable to pressure because they have been drawn into indebtedness through hiring practices as well as hire-purchase agreements for consumer durables. He contrasts the good reputation of individual militant Indian shop stewards with the bad reputation for lack of militancy Indian workers have amongst Africans. Carrim finally points as well to the considerable racist attitude Indians do display towards Africans, an attitude he hopes is on the wane.
113. Interview with F.D., 21 November 1989. She reports much fear of Africans as a reason for union membership and active willingness to scab against striking African workers but contrasts these phenomena with the greater solidarity that Indian women in garment factories achieve with African co-workers.
114. *South African Labour Bulletin* 14, 6 (1990).
115. Jeremy Baskin, *Striking Back: A History of COSATU* (Johannesburg: Ravan Press, 1991), p. 394.
116. South African Chamber of Business, *Economic Options for South Africa* (Johannesburg: South African Chamber of Business, 1990), table 1.
117. Arkin, *Contribution of Indians*, p. 283.
118. I have been stimulated to think a little about the need for a new post-apartheid "critical politics of identity" by Dhianaraj Chetty, "Identity and 'Indianness': Reading and Writing Ethnic Discourses," Paper presented at the Conference on Ethnicity, Society and Conflict in Natal, Pietermaritzburg, 14–16 September 1992.

BIBLIOGRAPHY

BIBLIOGRAPHICAL GUIDES

Chetty, K., compiler. *A Bibliography on Indians in South Africa: A Guide to Materials at the Documentation Centre*. Documentation Centre Series, no. 1. Durban: University of Durban-Westville, 1990.

Naicker, Jayarani. "A Selective, Annotated Bibliography of the History of Economic Activities of Indians in Natal from 1910 to the 1980s." B.A. honours dissertation, Department of Economic History, University of Natal, Durban, 1986.

ARCHIVAL SOURCES

Baynesfield Farm
Manuscript collection

Documentation Centre, University of Durban–Westville
Assorted individual collections of private papers.
Clairwood and District Ratepayers' and Residents' Association.
Department of History, History III essays
    C.B. Bissessor
    S.J. Bodasing, biography of Babu Bodasing, 1983.
    A. Bridgraj
    V. Chetty, biography of R. B. Chetty.
    N. R. Kandosamy, "A Brief History of the Glendale Sugar Mill," 1985.
    S. Maharaj, biography of Jesudossen Lazarus.
    P. Moodley, biography of Rangasamy Pillay.
    Ranjanitheni Moodley, biography of Pungavanam Moodley.
    B. A. Naidoo
    K. K. Naidoo, biography of Narayadu.
    N. A. Naidoo, 1984.
    P. Naidoo
    S. Rampersad, biography of Jaichoo Nanoo.
Durban Indian Municipal Employees' Society papers.
Gabriel, J.S. papers.
Garment Workers' Industrial Union papers.
Nel, P. R. T., Director of Indian Education, papers.

Killie Campbell Africana Library, University of Natal, Durban
KCM 32545. Marshall Campbell papers.
File 7. Mabel Palmer papers. Durban Indian Child Welfare Association.
File 28. Indo-European Council, unemployment questionnaires.

Natal Archives, Pietermaritzburg
MSC/137 Supreme Court.
3/DBN (Durban Town Clerk) 1/2/6/1/1, Public Health (Slums) Committee.
3/DBN 1/2/27/1/2/1, Durban Municipal Staff Board (non-European) meetings.
3/DBN 1/3/3/1/1–6, Durban Special Committee *re* Housing.
3/DBN 1/5/4/1/2, Durban Indian Joint Advisory Sub-committee.
3/DBN 14/4/1–3; 14/5/1, Durban Borough Boundaries Commission.
3/DBN 14/6/1, Durban Borough Extension Enquiry Commission.
UG 4/1921. South Africa. Asiatic Inquiry Commission.

Natal Indian Cane Growers' Association,* Stanger
Annual Reports.

V. Padayachee, private collection, Durban
This collection includes archival material from elsewhere collected for research purposes.

INTERVIEWS AND ORAL SOURCES

Arenstein, R.J. 24 July 1985. I am grateful to Iain Edwards for letting me see his interview notes.

P. B. 30 November 1989. Resident in Phoenix, a professional employee, male, in his thirties, from a working-class background in Clairwood.

F. D. 21 November 1989. A white trade-unionist in her twenties organising in the distribution and service sector.

K. G. 19 January 1990. A small businessman, son of indentured workers, from a working-class family with a history of political activism, born 1909.

Govender, P. GAWU organiser. Talk delivered in the Industrial Sociology Department, University of Natal, Durban, 1990.

P. H. 4 January 1990. A trade union organiser in the chemicals sector, aged 40.

I. M. 14 November 1989. Born 1926. A retired metal worker who never acquired full skill prerogatives. His family background included a mix of Indian, white and Coloured.

S. M. 15 November 1989. Phoenix community activist in his thirties. Expert on the material conditions of working-class people in the township.

Krish Naidu and friends from the Natal Indian Cane Growers' Association, interviewed at the Glendale Sugar Mill, 20 November 1990.

B. R. 13 January, 1992. Son of an indentured worker, born 1913. Retired semi-skilled worker living in Chatsworth.

SOUTH AFRICAN PERIODICALS

Daily News.
Daily News. Supplements, 20 March 1973; 23 August 1983.
Fiat Lux.
Graphic.
Guardian.

*   After 1989 – Natal Cane Growers' Association

Indian Opinion.
Indian Views.
The Leader.
Natal Mercury.
Natal Mercury. Supplement, 1982; Review, 1982.
NUMSA News.
Post. Supplement, 16 November 1983.
Race Relations News.

PUBLISHED PRIMARY SOURCES

Kajee, A. I.; Pather, P. R.; and Christopher, A. *Treatment of Indians in South Africa.* Cape Town and New York: South African Indian Congress, 1946.
Kilchu, Kailas. *Memorandum on Indian Education in Natal.* For Indian Education Inquiry Commission, 1928.
Natal Blue Books. Annual District Reports.
Natal Blue Books. Protector of (Indian) Immigrants' Annual Reports.
Natal Government Gazette. Wragg Commission Report, supplement 20 September 1887.
Census of the Colony of Natal 17th April, 1904. Separate publication, 1904.

BOOKS, ARTICLES AND CHAPTERS IN BOOKS

Alexander, R., and Simons, H. J. *Job Reservation and the Trade Unions.* Woodstock: Enterprise, 1959.
Arango, L. G. "Femmes ouvrières, familles et politiques au sein de l'entreprise." *Pratiques sociales et travail en milieu urbain,* 19 (1992).
Arkin, A. J. *Contribution of the Indians to the South African Economy, 1860–1970.* Occasional Publication, no. 14. Durban: University of Durban-Westville, Institute for Social and Economic Research, 1981.
———. "Indian Business Enterprise in South Africa, 1860–1980." *Journal of the University of Durban-Westville* 3 (1986): 125–48.
Bardhan, K. *Of Women, Outcastes, Peasants and Rebels.* Berkeley: University of California Press, 1990.
Baskin, J. *Striking Back: A History of COSATU.* Johannesburg: Ravan Press, 1991.
Beall, J. "Women under Indentured Labour in Colonial Natal, 1860–1911." In *Women and Gender in Southern Africa to 1945.* Edited by C. Walker. Cape Town: David Philip, 1990.
Beall, J., and North-Coombes, M. D. "The 1913 Disturbances in Natal: The Social and Economic Background to 'Passive Resistance.'" *Journal of Natal and Zulu History* 6 (1983).
Beinart, W.; Delius, P.; and Trapido, S. *Putting a Plough to the Ground: Accumulation and Dispossession in Rural South Africa, 1850–1930.* Johannesburg: Ravan Press, 1986.
Bell, R. T. *Growth and Structure of Manufacturing Employment in Natal.* Report no. 7. Durban: University of Durban-Westville, Institute for Social and Economic Research, 1983.
Bendheim, P. M., with Padayachee, M. *Clairwood: The South Coast Road Trading Area.* Report no. 19. Durban: University of Durban-Westville, Institute for Social and Economic Research, 1985.
Bhana, S. ed. *Essays on Indentured Indians in Natal.* Leeds: Peepal Tree Press, 1990.
Bhana, S., and Brain, J. *Setting Down Roots: Indian Migrants in South Africa, 1860–1900.* Johannesburg: Witwatersrand University Press, 1990.
Blackburn, R. *The Overthrow of Colonial Slavery, 1776–1848.* London: Verso, 1988.
Boeyens, J. "'Zwart Ivoor': Inboekelinge in Zoutpansberg, 1848–69." *South African Historical Journal* 24 (1991): 31–66.

Bryce, J. *Impressions of South Africa*. London: Macmillan, 1897.

Buijs, G. "Divide and Rule: The Mechanisms of Control on a Natal Sugar Estate." In *The Struggle for Social and Economic Space: Urbanization in Twentieth Century South Africa*. Edited by R. Haines and G. Buijs. Special Publication, no. 3. Durban: University of Durban-Westville, Institute for Social and Economic Research, 1985.

Bundy, C. *The Rise and Fall of the South African Peasantry*. Berkeley and Los Angeles: University of California Press, 1979.

Burke, G., and Richardson, P. "The Profits of Death: A Comparative Study of Miners' Phthisis in Cornwall and South Africa, 1876–1918." *Journal of Southern African Studies* 4, 2 (1978).

Burrows, H. *Studies of Indian Employment in Natal*. Natal Regional Survey, vol. 11. Cape Town: Oxford University Press, 1961.

Burrows, R. "Durban's Growing Pains." *Race Relations Journal* 7 (1940).

—————. *Indian Life and Labour in Natal*. New Africa Pamphlet, no. 23; revised ed. Johannesburg: South African Institute of Race Relations, 1952.

Butler-Adam, J. F., and Venter, W. "Public Housing and Patterns of Family Life: Indian Families in Metropolitan Durban." In *Aspects of Family Life in the South African Indian Community*. Occasional Paper, no. 20. Durban: University of Durban-Westville, Institute for Social and Economic Research, 1987.

Calpin, G. H. *A. I. Kajee: His Work for the South African Indian Community*. Durban: Iqbal Study Group, *c.* 1950.

Carrim, Y. "Trade Unionism in Natal: Shopfloor Relations between African and Indian Workers." *South African Labour Bulletin* 11, 4 (1986).

Chetty, T. D. "Factory and Family: Indian Factory Workers in Durban." In *Aspects of Family Life in the South African Indian Community*. Edited by J. Butler-Adam and W. Venter. Occasional Paper, no.20. Durban: University of Durban-Westville, Institute for Social and Economic Research, 1987.

Cohn, B. S. *India: The Social Anthropology of a Civilisation*. Englewood Cliffs, New Jersey: Prentice-Hall, 1971.

Coulson, J. C. *Richmond: Its People and History*. Richmond, Natal: Women's League Institute, 1986.

Crush, J. "Uneven Labour Migration in Southern Africa." *South African Geographical Journal* 66, 2 (1984).

Davies, R. *Capital, State and White Labour in South Africa, 1900–1960: An Historical Materialist Analysis of Class Formation and Class Relations*. Atlantic Highlands: Humanities Press, 1979.

Davies, R.J., and Greyling, J.J.C. *Indian Farming on the Natal North Coast*. Natal Town and Regional Planning Reports, no.39. Pietermaritzburg: Natal Town and Regional Planning Commission, 1978.

Davis, D. B. *The Problem of Slavery in the Age of Revolution 1770–1823*. Ithaca: Cornell University Press, 1975.

Diesel, A., and Maxwell, P. *Hinduism in Natal: A Brief Guide*. Pietermaritzburg: University of Natal Press, 1993.

Du Toit, B. *Ukubamba Amadola*. London: Onyx Press, 1978.

Duminy, A., and Guest, B. *Natal and Zululand from Earliest Times to 1910: A New History*. Pietermaritzburg: University of Natal Press and Shuter & Shooter, 1989.

Durban Housing Action Committee. *Rents We Can Afford*. Durban: Durban Housing Action Committee, 1989.

Epstein, T. S. *South India: Yesterday, Today and Tomorrow*. New York: Holmes and Meier, 1973.

Evans, M. *Black and White in South East Africa*. London: Longmans, Green, 1911.

Foner, E. *Free Soil, Free Labor, Free Men: The Ideology of the Republican Party Before the Civil War*. London: Oxford University Press, 1970.

Freund, B. [W.M.] "Forced Settlement and the Political Economy of South Africa." *Review of African Political Economy* 29 (1984).

————. "The Cape under the Transitional Governments, 1795–1814." In *The Shaping of South African Society, 1652–1840*, pp. 324–58. 2nd ed. Edited by R. Elphick and H. Giliomee. Cape Town: Maskew Miller Longman, 1989.

————. "The Social Character of Secondary Industry in South Africa, 1915–45 (with Special Reference to the Witwatersrand)." In *Organisation and Social Change*. Edited by A. Mabin. Southern African Studies, no. 5. Johannesburg: Ravan Press, 1989.

————. "Indian Women and the Changing Character of the Working Class Indian Household in Natal, 1860–1990." *Journal of Southern African Studies* 17, 3 (1991).

————. "The Rise and Decline of an Indian Peasantry in Natal." *Journal of Peasant Studies* 18, 2 (1991).

Friedman, S. *Building Tomorrow Today: African workers in Trade Unions, 1970–84*. Johannesburg: Ravan Press, 1987.

Ginwala, F. *Indian South Africans*. Report no. 34. London: Minority Rights Group, n.d.

Goonam, Dr [Gonarathnam]. *Coolie Doctor*. Durban: Madiba Press, 1992.

Govender, R. *The Lahnee's Pleasure*. Johannesburg: Ravan Press, 1981.

Guest, B., and Sellers, J. eds. *Enterprise and Exploitation in a Victorian Colony: Aspects of the Economic and Social History of Colonial Natal*. Pietermaritzburg: University of Natal Press, 1985.

Guy, J., and Thabane, M. "Technology, Ethnicity and Ideology: Basotho Miners and Shaft Sinking on the South African Gold Mines." *Journal of Southern African Studies* 4, 2 (1978).

Gwala, N. "Poltical Violence and the Struggle for Control in Pietermaritzburg." *Journal of Southern African Studies* 15, 3 (1989).

Hemson, D. "Dock Workers, Labour Circulation and Class Struggles in Durban, 1940–59." *Journal of Southern African Studies* 4 (1977).

Hermer, M. *The Passing of Pageview*. Johannesburg: Ravan Press, 1978.

Hey, P. D. *The Rise of the Natal Indian Elite*. Pietermaritzburg: Natal Witness, 1961.

Hirsch, A. "An Introduction to Textile Worker Organisation in Natal." *South African Labour Bulletin* 4, 8 (1979): 3–42.

Hirson, B. "Trade Union Organizer in Durban: M. B. Yengwa, 1943–44." *Journal of Natal and Zulu History* 11 (1988): 93–113.

Horwood, O. P. F. "Some Aspects of Urban African Employment in the Durban Area." *Race Relations Journal* 25 (1958).

Houghton, D. H., and Dagut, J. *Source Material on the South African Economy, 1860–1970*. 3 vols. Cape Town: Oxford University Press, 1972–1973.

Hughes, R. *The Fatal Shore: A History of the Transportation of Convicts to Australia, 1787–1868*. London: Collins Harvill, 1987.

Hunt, Leuchars and Hepburn, 1850–1950. Durban: Hunt, Lechars and Hepburn, *c.* 1950.

Imrie, R. M. *A Wealth of People*. Johannesburg: Trade Union Council of South Africa, 1979.

Jeffrey, P.; Lyon, J.; and Lyon, A. "Midwifery and Childbearing in Rural North India." In *Women, State and Ideology*. Edited by H. Afshar. London: Macmillan, 1987.

Jeppie, S., and Soudien, C. eds. *The Struggle for District Six, Past and Present*. Cape Town: Buchu Books, 1990.

Jithoo, S. "Complex Households and Joint Families amongst Indians in Durban." In *Social System and Tradition in Southern Africa*. Edited by J. Argyle and E. Preston-Whyte. Cape Town: Oxford University Press, 1978.

Kajee, A. I.; Pather, P. R.; and Christopher, A. *Treatment of Indians in South Africa*. Cape Town and New York: South African Indian Congress, 1946.

Katzen, M. *Industry in Greater Durban, Part I: Its Growth and Structure*. Natal Town and Regional Planning Reports, no. 3. Pietermaritzburg: Natal Town and Regional Planning Commission, 1961.

Kuper, H. *Indian People in Natal*. Pietermaritzburg: University of Natal Press, 1960.

Kuper, L.; Watts, H.; and Davies, R. *Durban: A Study in Racial Ecology*. London: Jonathan Cape, 1958.

La Hausse, P. "Drink and Cultural Innovation in Durban: The Origin of the Beerhall in South Africa, 1902–16." In *Liquor and Labor in Southern Africa*. Edited by J. Crush and C. Ambler. Pietermaritzburg: University of Natal Press; Athens, Ohio: Ohio University Press, 1993.

Legassick, M. "Capital Accumulation and Violence in South Africa." *Economy and Society* 3, 3 (1974).

Lewis, J. "*The Rise and Fall of the South African Peasantry*: A Critique and Reassessment." *Journal of Southern African Studies* 11, 1 (1984): 1–24.

Lewis, J. *Industrialisation and Trade Union Organisation in South Africa, 1924–55: The Rise and Fall of the South African Trades and Labour Council*. African Studies Series, no. 42. Cambridge: Cambridge University Press, 1984.

Liddle, J., and Joshi, R. *Daughters of Independence: Gender, Caste and Class in India*. New Brunswick, New Jersey: Rutgers University Press; London: Zed Press, 1986.

Maasdorp, G. G. *A Natal Indian Community: A Socio-economic Study in the Tongaat-Verulam Area*. Natal Regional Survey, Additional Report no. 5. Durban: University of Natal, Department of Economics, 1968.

Maasdorp, G. G., and Pillay, N. *Urban Relocation and Racial Segregation: The Case of Indian South Africans*. Durban: University of Natal Department of Economics, 1977.

Maasdorp, G. G., and Pillay, P. N. "Occupational Mobility among the Indian People of Natal." In *Occupational and Social Change among Coloured People*. Edited by H. W. van der Merwe and C. J. Groenewald. Cape Town: Juta, 1976.

Mabin, A. "Comprehensive Segregation: The Origins of the Group Areas Act and its Planning Apparatuses." *Journal of Southern African Studies* 18, 2 (1992).

Malcolmson, R. *Popular Recreations in English Society, 1700–1850*. Cambridge: Cambridge University Press, 1973.

Mantzaris, E. "The Indian Tobacco Workers Strike of 1920: A Socio-Historical Investigation." *Journal of Natal and Zulu History* 6 (1983): 115–25.

Marie, S. *Divide and Profit: Indian Workers in Natal*. Worker Resistance and Culture Publications. Durban: University of Natal, Department of Sociology, 1986.

Mason, J. E. "The Slaves and their Protectors: Reforming Resistance in a Slave Society, the Cape Colony 1826–34." *Journal of Southern African Studies* 17, 1 (1991): 104–28.

McCarthy, J. "Planning Issues and the Political Economy of the Local State: An Historical Case Study of Durban." *Urban Forum* 2, 2 (1991).

Meer, F. *Portrait of Indian South Africans*. Durban: Avon House, 1969.

——— . *Factory and Family: The Divided Lives of South Africa's Women Workers*. Durban: Institute for Black Research, 1984.

Meer, F., with Skweyiyua, S.; Jolobe, S.; Westmore, J.; and Meer, S. *Black-Woman-Worker*. 1st ed. Durban: Madiba Press for the Institute of Black Research, 1990.

Mesthrie, R. *Language in Indenture: A Sociolinguistic History of Bhojpuri-Hindi in South Africa*. Johannesburg: Witwatersrand University Press, 1991.

——— . *A Lexicon of South African Indian English*. Leeds: Peepal Tree Press, 1992.

Mies, M. *The Lace Makers of Narsapur*. London: Zed Press, 1982.

Mies, M., with Lalita, K.; and Kumari, K. *Indian Women in Subsistence and Agricultural Labour*. Women, Work and Development, no. 12. Geneva: International Labour Organisation, 1986.

Miles, R. *Capitalism and Unfree Labour: Anomaly or Necessity*. London: Tavistock, 1987.

Moodley, K. "South African Indians: The Wavering Minority." In *Change in Contemporary South Africa*. Edited by L. Thompson and J. Butler. Berkeley: University of California Press, 1975.

Morris, M. L. "The Development of Capitalism in South African Agriculture: Class Struggles in the Countryside." *Economy and Society* 5 (1976).

Müller, A. L. "Some Non-economic Determinants of the Economic Status of Asians in Africa." *South African Journal of Economics* 33, 1 (1965): 72–79.

——— . "The Position of the Asians in Africa." *South African Journal of Econonmics* 33, 2 (1965): 114–30.

Naidoo, B. A., and Naidoo, J. "Economic Opportunities and Mode of Living of the Indian Community." In *The Indian as South African*. Johannesburg: Institute of Race Relations, 1956.

Naidoo, J. *Coolie Location*. London: South African Writers, 1990.

Naidoo, K. "The Politics of Youth Resistance in the 1980s: The Dilemmas of a Differentiated Durban." *Journal of Southern African Studies* 18, 1 (1992): 143–65.

Naidoo, V. S. "Survey of Income and Expenditure of Indian Employees of the Durban Corporation Living at the Magazine Barracks, Durban." *South African Journal of Economics* 14, 1 (1946): 40–62.

Neame, L. E. *The Asiatic Danger in the Colonies*. London: George Routledge and Sons, 1907.

Neumark, S. D. *Economic Influences on the South African Frontier, 1652–1836*. Stanford: Stanford University Press, 1957.

Nicol, M. "Riches from Rags: Bosses and Unions in the Cape Clothing Industry, 1926–37." *Journal of Southern African Studies* 9, 2 (1983).

——— . " 'Joh'burg Hotheads' and the 'Gullible Children of Cape Town': The Transvaal Garment Workers' Union's Assault on Low Wages in the Cape Town Clothing Industry, 1930–31." In *Class, Community and Conflict: South African Perspectives* pp. 209–34. Edited by B. Bozzoli. Johannesburg: Ravan Press, 1987.

Oosthuizen, G. C., and Hofmeyr, J. H. *A Socio-economic Survey of Chatsworth*. Report no. 7. Durban: University of Durban-Westville, Institute for Social and Economic Research, 1979.

Padayachee, M. [Vishnu]. "Determinants of Wages and Wage Differentials among Indians in the Durban Municipal Area." *Journal of the University of Durban-Westville* 4, 2 (1983): 176–90.

——— . "A Socio-economic Profile of Four Market Gardening Communities in Metropolitan Durban." Fact Paper, no. 6. Durban: University of Durban-Westville, Institute for Social and Economic Research, 1986.

Padayachee, V.; Vawda, S.; and Tichmann, P. *Indian Workers and Trade Unions in Durban: 1930–50*. Report no. 20. Durban: University of Durban-Westville, Institute for Social and Economic Research, 1985.

Padayachee, V., and Morrell, R. "Indian Merchants and *Dukawallahs* in the Natal Economy, c. 1875–1914." *Journal of Southern African Studies* 17, 1 (1991): 71–101.

Parnell, S. "Racial Segregation in Johannesburg: The Slums Act, 1934–39." *South African Geographical Journal* 70 (1988).

Pillay, P. N., and Ellison, P. A. *The Indian Domestic Budget: A Socio-economic Study of Incomes and Expenditures of Durban Indian Households*. Natal Regional Survey, Additional Report no. 6. Durban: University of Natal, Department of Economics, 1969.

Richardson, P. "The Natal Sugar Industry, 1849–1905: An Interpretative Essay." *Journal of African History* 23 (1982): 515–27.

Robinson, Sir J. *A Life-Time in South Africa*. London: Smith, Elder and Co., 1900.

Rogerson, C. M. "From Coffee-Cart to Industrial Canteen: Feeding Johannesburg's Black Workers, 1945–62." In *Organisation and Economic Change*. African Studies, no. 5. Edited by A. Mabin. Johannesburg: Ravan Press, 1989.

Russell, M. "Unemployment among Indians in Durban, 1962." Durban: University of Natal, Institute for Social Research, 1962.

Scotney, D. M., and Rix, D. M. "Land Use Problems in Indian Agriculture." *Fiat Lux* 10, 1 (February 1975).

Sen, G. "Subordination and Sexual Control: A Comparative View of the Control of Women." *Review of Radical Political Economics* 16, 1 (1984).

Singh, B. *My Champions were Dark*. Durban: Pennant, 1963.

Skjønsberg, E. *A Special Caste? Tamil Women of Sri Lanka*. London: Zed Press, 1982.

Slater, H. "The Changing Pattern of Economic Relations in Rural Natal, 1838–1914." In *Economy and Society in Pre-industrial South Africa*. Edited by S. Marks and A. Atmore. London: Longmans, 1980.

Smith, D., ed. *The Apartheid City and Beyond*. London and New York: Routledge; Johannesburg: Witwatersrand University Press, 1992.

South African Chamber of Business. *Economic Options for South Africa*. Johannesburg: South African Chamber of Business, 1990.

Steenkamp, J. J. A. *Income and Expenditure Patterns of Urban Indian Households in Durban*. Research Report no. 50/7. Pretoria: University of South Africa, Bureau of Market Research, 1976.

Storper, M., and Walker, R. *The Capitalist Imperative: Territory, Technology and Industrial Growth*. New York and Oxford: Basil Blackwell, 1989.

Sugden, M. *The Potential Indian Labour Force: Pietermaritzburg/Durban Region*. Town and Regional Planning Reports, no. 37, part 2. Pietermaritzburg: Town and Regional Planning Commission, 1978.

Swan, M. "The 1913 Natal Indian Strike." *Journal of Southern African Studies* 10, 2 (1984): 240–58.

———. "Ideology in Organised Indian Politics, 1891–1948." In *The Politics of Race, Class and Nationalism in Twentieth Century South Africa*. Edited by S. Marks and S. Trapido. London and New York: Longmans, 1987.

———. *Gandhi: The South African Experience*. Johannesburg: Ravan Press, 1985.

Swanson, M. W. "The Sanitation Syndrome: Bubonic Plague and Urban Native Policy in the Cape Colony, 1900–09." *Journal of African History* 18, 3 (1977): 387–410.

———. "The Asiatic Menace: Creating Segregation in Durban, 1870–1900." *International Journal of African Historical Studies* 16 (1983): 401–22.

Thompson, L. M. "Indian Immigration into Natal (1860–72)." *Archives Yearbook for South African History* 15, 2 (1952): 1–77.

Tinker, H. *A New System of Slavery: The Export of Indian Labour Overseas, 1830–1920*. London: Oxford University Press, 1974.

———. "Indian Servitude: Indian Labour in the Sugar Industry, 1833–1970." In *International Labour Migration*. Edited by S. Marks and P. Richardson. London: Maurice Temple Smith, 1984.

Torr, L. "Lamontville—Durban's Model Village: The Realities of Township Life, 1934–60." *Journal of Natal and Zulu History* 10 (1987).

University of Natal, Department of Economics. *The African Factory Worker: A Sample Study of the Life and Labour of the Urban African Worker*. Natal Regional Survey, Report no. 2. Cape Town: Oxford University Press, 1950.

———. *Studies in Indian Employment in Natal*. Natal Regional Survey, vol. 11. Cape Town: Oxford University Press, 1961.

Van der Merwe, P. J. *Trek: Studies oor die Mobiliteit van die Pioniersbevolking aan die Kaap*. Cape Town: Nasionale Pers, 1945.

Van der Spuy, D. T. *Die Arbeidspatroon van Indiers in Natal*. Navorsingsreeks, nr. 62. Pretoria: Department of Higher Education, National Bureau for Educational and Social Research, 1968.

Van Onselen, C. *Studies in the Social and Economic History of the Witwatersrand, 1886–1914: New Babylon, New Nineveh*. London: Longmans, 1982.

Waiz, S. A. *Indians Abroad Directory*. Bombay, 1934.

Watson, R. G. T. *Tongaati: An African Experiment*. London: Hutchinson, 1960.

Watts, H. L. *The Indian Community of Wyebank: A Socio-economic Survey in the Borough of Kloof*. Durban: University of Natal, Institute for Social Research, 1971.

Western, J. *Outcast Cape Town*. Minneapolis: University of Minnesota Press, 1981.

Yudelman, D. *The Emergence of Modern South Africa: State, Capital and the Incorporation of Organized Labor on the South African Gold Fields, 1902–39*. Westport and London: Greenwood Press, 1983.

PAPERS, THESES AND UNPUBLISHED MANUSCRIPTS

Atkins, K. "The Cultural Origins of an African Work Ethic and Practices: Natal, South Africa 1843–75." Ph.D. thesis, University of Wisconsin, 1986.

Bailey, D. "The Origins of Phoenix, 1957–76: The Durban City Council and the Indian Housing Question." M.A. thesis, University of Natal, Durban, 1987.

Beinart, W. "Transkeian Migrant Workers and Youth Labour on the Sugar Fields, 1918–40." Seminar Paper for the History Workshop, University of the Witwatersrand, Johannesburg, 1990.

Bridglal, P. "The Economic Structure of the Durban-Inanda-Pinetown Region with Special Reference to the Tourist Industry." M.A. thesis, University of Durban-Westville, 1980.

Buijs, G. "A Study of Indian Pentecostal Church Membership." Ph.D. thesis, University of Cape Town, 1985.

Chetty, D. "The Durban Riots and Popular Memory." Seminar Paper for the History Workshop, University of Witwatersrand, Johannesburg, 1990.

—————. "Identity and Indianness: Reading and Writing Ethnic Discourse." Paper presented to the Conference on Ethnicity, Society and Conflict in Natal, Pietermaritzburg, 14–16 September 1992.

Community Research Unit and M. Sutcliffe. "Socio-economic Conditions and Household Subsistence Levels in Four Durban Communities: Chatsworth, Newlands East, Phoenix, and Wentworth." Report for the Durban Housing Action Committee, 1986.

Edwards, I.L. "Mkhumbane, Our Home: African Shantytown Society in Cato Manor Farm, 1946–60." Ph.D. thesis, University of Natal, Durban, 1989.

Edwards, I., and Nuttall, T. "Seizing the Moment: The 1949 Riots, Proletarian Populism and the Structures of African Urban Life in Durban during the late 1940s." Seminar Paper for the History Workshop, University of the Witwatersrand, Johannesburg, 1990.

Freund, B. "It is My Work: Labour Segmentation, Militancy and the Indian Working Class of Durban." Seminar Paper, Centre for African Studies, University of Cape Town, 1992.

Gerdener, T. "Socio-Economic Position of the Indian." South African Bureau of Racial Affairs, *c.*1952. (Typewritten)

Ginwala, F. "Class, Consciousness and Control: Indian South Africans, 1860–1946." D.Phil. thesis, Oxford University, 1974.

Govindasamy, S. "The History of the Indian Market Gardeners of Cliffdale." B.A. Hons. dissertation, Department of History, University of Durban-Westville, 1987.

Greyling, J.J.C. "Problems of Indian Landownership and Land-occupation on the Natal North Coast: A Socio-geographic Investigation." 3 vols. Ph.D. thesis, University of Natal, Durban, 1969.

Halliday, I.G. "The Indian Market Gardeners of the Peri-urban Area." M.A. thesis, University of Natal, Department of Economics, 1940.

—————. "Durban's Food Supplies." D.Phil. thesis, University of South Africa, 1942.

Hemson, D. "Class Consciousness and Migrant Workers: Dock Workers of Durban." Ph.D. thesis, University of Warwick, 1979.

Kahn, R. "The Changing Character of the Traditional Role of Working Class Women in Durban: A Study of the Experiences of some Indian Working Class Women Employed in Clairwood." B.A. Hons. dissertation, Department of Economic History, University of Natal, Durban, 1991.

Lambert, R.V. "Political Unionism in South Africa: The South African Congress of Trade Unions, 1955–65." Ph.D. thesis, University of the Witwatersrand, Johannesburg, 1988.

Leverton, B.J.T. Joseph Baynes, biography, 1978. (Baynesfield, manuscript collection)

Lincoln, M.D. "A Sociological Perspective on South African Sugarmill Workers' Wages." Paper written for the Association of Southern Africa, 1984.

—————. "The Culture of the South African Sugarmill: The Impress of the Sugarocracy." Ph.D. thesis, University of Cape Town, 1985.

————— . "Flies in the Sugar Bowl: The Natal Sugar Industry Employees' Union in its Heyday, 1940–54." Paper presented to the World Planatation Conference, Lafayette, Indiana, 1989.

Maasdorp, G.G. "A Socio-economic Survey of the Indian Community in the Tongaat-Verulam Region." M.Com. thesis, University of Natal, Durban, 1966.

Mabin, A. "The Witwatersrand Joint Town Planning Committee, 1932–40: Of Rigour and Mortis." Paper presented to the Planning History Workshop, Department of Town and Regional Planning, University of the Witwatersrand, Johannesburg, 1992.

Maharaj, B. "Ethnicity, Class and Conflict: The Indian Question in Natal." Paper presented to the Conference on Ethnicity, Society and Conflict in Natal, Pietermaritzburg, 14–16 September 1992.

McCrystal, L.P., and Maasdorp, G. "Role of the Indian in Natal's Economy." Department of Economics, University of Natal, Durban, 1966.

Mesthrie, R. "The Linguistic Reflex of Social Change: Caste and Kinship Terms among People of Indian Descent in Natal, South Africa." Paper revised for *Anthropological Linguistics*.

Mesthrie, U. "From Rose Day Shows to Social Welfare: White and Indian Women in Joint Co-operation in the 1930s." Paper presented to the Conference on Women and Gender in Southern Africa, University of Natal, Durban, 1991.

Nuttall, T. "African Organisation and Militancy in Durban, 1937–49." Paper presented to the Workshop on Twentieth Century Natal History, University of Natal, Pietermaritzburg, 1989.

Omar, R.H. "The Relationship between the Durban Corporation and the Magazine Barracks." B.A. Hons. dissertation, Department of History, University of Durban-Westville, 1989.

Pahad, E. "Indian Opposition Movements in South Africa, 1927–46." D.Phil. thesis, University of Sussex, 1972.

Patel, S. "Indian Businessmen in the Durban Area." B.A. Hons. dissertation, Department of History, University of Natal, Durban, 1984.

Ringrose, H.G. "A History and Description of Trade Unions in Natal." M.Com. thesis, University of Natal, Durban, 1948 (also published as a volume in the Natal Regional Survey).

Rix, D.M. "Indian Agriculture on the North Coast of Natal: Technical Aspects." M.Agric. thesis, University of Pretoria, 1972.

Russell, M. "A Study of a South African Interracial Neighbourhood." M.Soc.Sc. thesis, University of Natal, Durban, 1961.

Seedat, Z.K. "The Zanzibaris in Durban: A Social Anthropological Study of the Muslim Descendants of African Freed Slaves Living in the Indian Area of Chatsworth." M.A. thesis, University of Natal, Durban, 1973.

Seekings, J. "The United Democratic Front and the Changing Nature of Opposition in Natal, 1983–85." Conference on Ethnicity, Society and Conflict in Natal, Pietermaritzburg, 14–16 September 1992.

Stanwix, J. "Capital Accumulation, Crisis and Spatial Restructuring: A Study of Spatial Shifts in South African Manufacturing with Particular Reference to Natal." M.Com. thesis, University of Natal, Durban, 1987.

Sugden, M. "The Bantu of the Durban Metropolitan Area: A Case Study in Population Analysis." M.Sc. thesis, University of Natal, Durban, 1965.

Tatham, M.A. "A Study of the Urban Morphology of Durban." M.Sc. thesis, University of Natal, Durban, 1955.

Vaughan, A. "Cane, Class and Credit." Department of Economic History, University of Natal, 1990. (Typewritten)

Wilkinson, A. "Manufacturing Industry in the Pinetown Magisterial District." M.A. thesis, University of Natal, Durban, 1963.

Young, B. "The Industrial Geography of the Durban Region." Ph.D. thesis, University of Natal, Durban, 1972.

OTHER SOURCES

Govender, R. "At the Edge." Play. Performance viewed by the author.
Schmidt, S. "Forgotten Workers." Videorecording. 50 mins. University of Durban-Westville, *c.*1989.
———. "Phoenix New Town (Same Old Problems)." Videorecording. 55 mins. University of Durban-Westville, *c.*1989.
Scott, D. and Criticos, C. "Hanging Up the Nets: The History of the Durban Bay Fishing Community." Videorecording. 37 mins. Media Resource Centre, University of Natal, Durban, 1991.

INDEX